DEAD SHARP

SCOTTISH CRIME WRITERS ON COUNTRY AND CRAFT

LEN WANNER

TWO RAVENS PRESS

Published by Two Ravens Press Ltd.
Taigh nam Fitheach
26 Breanish, Uig
Isle of Lewis HS2 9HB
United Kingdom

www.tworavenspress.com

ISBN: 978-1-906120-58-0

British Library Cataloguing in Publication Data: a CIP record for this book can be obtained from the British Library.

Designed and typeset in Sabon by Two Ravens Press.
Cover design by Two Ravens Press.

Cover image: Brendan MacNeill / Alamy

Printed in Poland
on Forest Stewardship Council-accredited paper.

'Len Wanner is a gift to any serious writer, but especially contemporary crime writers, who see their genre not as some ghettoized backwater of the entertainment industry but the legitimate heir of the social and political novels that seem to have lost their cache in literary circles. The interviews are insightful gems, full of invention, wit and cleverness as well as the honesty and perceptiveness one expects from men and women whose job is to craft well-told tales. Wanner captures these writers at their best, lures them into unconventional terrain and obliges improvisation, with bracing results.'
– David Corbett, author of *Do They Know I'm Running?*

'These include some of the best crime writers around anywhere, and in response to Len Wanner's intelligent, probing and sometimes cheeky questions, they all interview superbly. If James Ellroy's off-the-cuff term "Tartan Noir" gets short shrift from several as a collective tag, it at least helps to focus minds on the vivid mix of the dark and the colourful concentrated in Scottish crime writing just now.'
– Martin Priestman, University of Roehampton

'Len Wanner's interviews with crime writers represent the gold standard for literary conversation. As interviewer, Wanner is erudite and smart, but also subtle and sharp. Each writer's personality comes off the page and each exchange is brimming with revelations. Indeed, these exchanges with Wanner may well represent the authors' career-defining interviews.'
– Craig McDonald, author of *Art in the Blood and Rogue Males*

'Wanner has compiled a must-read anthology of the witty, the wise, the weird and the wonderful. Highly recommended, not only as a fascinating peek behind the Oz curtain, but also as a journal of achievement from some of our brightest and best.'
– R.J. Ellory, author of *A Quiet Belief in Angels*

'You've heard the rumors, now here's the proof that Tartan Noir is not only one of the most important literary movements in crime fiction of the past twenty years, but one of the most important movements in all of literature. Wanner asks the tough questions and gets the tougher answers from this stellar cast of crime writers. Entertaining, insightful, heartbreaking, and hard to put down.' – Jason Starr, author of *The Pack*

'In this milestone work, Len Wanner serves as interlocutor for a number of Scotland's most eloquent crime writers. His thoughtful probing has resulted in a book that will fascinate fans, serve as

a guideline to emerging writers and be devoured by established authors. If crime writing in Scotland is a subject that interests you, Wanner's book is a "must-read".'
– Leighton Gage, author of *Every Bitter Thing*

'If you want to gain an insight into the current origins and direction of Scottish crime fiction, you couldn't do better than read this book by Len Wanner. Wanner doesn't simply get answers; he gets explanations ... about writing, about thinking, about reason; about where Scottish writers are coming from and where they are going, collectively and individually.'
– Adrian Magson, author of *Red Station*

'I thought Tartan Noir was what Scottish Goths made their kilts from until I read this book. Len Wanner's fascinating interviews are not just a compelling introduction to crime writing north of the border, they are also as good an insight as you are ever likely to get into what it is actually like to be a crime writer: the craft, the hard graft, the pleasure and the pain of our profession.'
– Tom Cain, author of *Dictator*

'In nine probing interviews Wanner provides an almost definitive overview of the movement known as Tartan Noir. Allan Guthrie's and Stuart MacBride's are my favourites, although they're mates of mine, and I got stuff from both that I didn't know, so that's a hell of a job.' **– Ray Banks, author of *Beast of Burden***

'In interviews as whiplash-smart as they are meticulous, these nine authors reveal the kind of insight about craft that makes you want to take a copy and start bludgeoning creative writing students out into streets. There's no gang of folks you could better spend an evening with, and no guide better suited to give you a tour of their world-weary and shrunken hearts than the immensely knowledgeable Len Wanner.'
– Benjamin Whitmer, author of *Pike*

'Interviews as thorough as any you'd get in an interrogation room, as one by one Scotland's finest crime writers reveal where the bodies are buried. The only way you'll learn more about the art of murder is to commit one yourself.'
– Stephen Leather, author of *Rough Justice*

'Len Wanner knows where the bodies are buried. In this incisive series of interviews, he cuts straight to the heart of what makes "Tartan Noir" a unique and wondrous genre of its own.'
– Wallace Stroby, author of *Cold Shot to the Heart*

About the Author

Len Wanner was born in the alpine republic of Bavaria. Reluctant to criticise the acts of an all-wise providence, he quickly forgave the demise of the monarchy for ruling out his promised career as a court jester, and left the country. A masters degree later, Ireland was rethinking its sense of humour so he moved to the United Kingdom. He currently lives with his lady friend in Edinburgh where he is patiently finishing a PhD on Crime Fiction, and not so patiently awaiting the Queen's call. In the meantime, he works as a freelance translator and the editor of the fiction review http://thecrimeofitall.com.

For more information about the author see
www.tworavenspress.com

Acknowledgements

I wish to thank all those who have given their time and support to this book. If you don't know who I mean, I hope it is nonetheless gratifying to know that I do.

My deepest gratitude is to my family for making it possible for me to write, and to the nine writers who have made this book possible by treating me as one of their own. Thanks to Aaron Kelly and Louise Welsh for adding your names and thoughts to these pages, and to the good people at Two Ravens Press for publishing them.

Thanks to Ken Bruen for giving me a grip on writing and the title for this book, Terry Dolan for giving me an education and the will to use it, and Conor Tannam for giving me my first crime novel and the wisdom to read it.

Finally, thanks to Chrissie Goddard for more than I can thank you for.

For Chrissie

'Let's talk about it over a few pints!'
– Ian Rankin, The Oxford Bar

Contents

Foreword
Why Read This Book?

These days, what we are told about the crime novel of the moment amounts to a cover summary: 'Awesome!' Criticism is blurbage. Hyperbole sells. So abundant is the literary world and so little time do we want to waste on any one book that the critics have finally signalled defeat. Instead of helpful access to art we get their fitful stamps of approval, and the sneaking suspicion that such value judgments are just about as facile as they are final. Art is either right or shite. But what happens when the language of intelligent analysis regresses to such inchoate advertising lingo? The problem remains – art does not disseminate itself unaided – yet as soon as lavish praise becomes commonplace it loses its intensity, and objects of consideration are treated as articles of consumption. What follows is an attrition of feeling. Soon enough no one will care that we are not supposed to think for ourselves, bestseller lists might as well be called shopping lists, and the majority of less successful writers can copy the monopolies or find other jobs. After all, we have a star system that celebrates every kilt with a publishing contract as 'the next King of Tartan Noir'.

But sooner or later we remember that 'these days' always seem bad, that bargaining by outrage is an old game, and that what this culture of criticism cannot hide is its spectacular failure to deal with new challenges. For instance, was it not our new way of sustaining art that first turned the artist into an entrepreneur, an advertiser-dealer-manager of his or her own artistry? And now the need for individuals to singularise themselves in the growing market of the talented is met with a demand for sensation and sedation. Nevertheless, art still is and always will be for contemplation and conversation. Those are the only significant sequels to the reading experience, no matter how many awesome must-reads await. What this aesthetic attitude calls for is the interview. Besides, posterity alone cannot settle or redeem merit, and anyone who has thought about a book long enough to write a blurb will agree that it is essential to read with something more than prejudice. In other words and in opposition to neo-classic absolutism – thumbs-up versus thumbs-down – the wide-angled view offered in the following pages makes it a pleasure to handle the products of culture. After all, when is it not best to let writers speak for themselves?

Introduction
by Dr. Aaron Kelly

Tartan Noir, the phrase most associated with recent Scottish crime writing and which results from a transatlantic exchange of ideas between Ian Rankin and James Ellroy, is perceptively apt rather than blandly (I'm tempted to say 'brandly' given its commercial branding of innumerable book covers) stereotypical. Rather than simply slapping two ready-made labels together, the moniker Tartan Noir can be slyly evocative. A noir tartan, if such a thing were possible, encourages us to consider that patterns exist beneath an absolute, inscrutable darkness. This premise goes right to the heart of crime fiction. The genre has always sought to uncover the hidden connections, meanings or designs of the everyday. The genius of detection (which in the crime genre is not of course the sole preserve of the professional detective or police officer) resides in probing deeper into webs of anterior causes and effects, intimate intricacies or submerged devices and desires which those of us who take the world at face value will always miss.

At least, that's my pseudo-philosophical alibi for the commercial category Tartan Noir. But all good crime readers know when they are being spun a spurious story. Tartan of course always carries with it – rightly or wrongly – the historical baggage of a once organic, even seditious, expression of tradition transmuted into kitsch. And the term 'Noir' itself is not immune from the requirements of commodity branding. 'Noir' as a label was applied retrospectively by French critics in the late 1960s and 1970s to fiction and film stretching back to the 1920s. Although 'Noir' remains an enabling critical or creative orientation, it also became a ready means by which a diverse array of crime stories and films were repackaged and newly remarketed. In addition, that rebranding further facilitated new markets of generic pastiche, parody, appropriation and reuse through the 1970s to the present day.

Mentioning commerce in relation to crime writing seems axiomatic. Genre fiction is particularly pressurised by the marketing needs of publishers. Nonetheless, to reduce crime fiction to mere market imperative is to visit upon it a massive injustice. It is also to labour under the delusion that there are other areas of culture untouched by capitalism. Since the inception of crime fiction a range of critics and writers from both left- and right-wing positions (for example, Theodor Adorno on the left, T.S. Eliot on the right) have wanted to dismiss it and other forms of popular culture as sheer trash, as pulp for the half-educated. This kind of prevailing attitude really gained sway in the early decades of the twentieth century with the emergence of High Modernism, with its supposedly more worthy response to modernity. Attendant to High Modernism was the putative widening of a gap between elite and mass cultures. And this dichotomy again rests on the notion that there was some arena of culture untainted by the debasements of modernity.

But if you take a look at the membership of the High Modernist canon then you can find more than a few figures who got their hands dirty in the grubbiest crimes of modern life – all the way from colonialism to fascism. However, the usual argument maintains that, for all the moments when Modernism's formal experimentations bemoaned the loss of feudal hierarchies or mourned the collapse of empires, as a wider assemblage of works High Modernism still provides a much more complex, considered and challenging set of responses to the convulsive social change and chaos of modernity. By contrast, according to this logic, crime fiction and the whole emergence of popular or mass culture can be remaindered as, at best, a reduction of the moral complexities of modernity to simple, easily and generically resolved issues of right and wrong, and, at worst, as pure escapism.

Walter Benjamin stands apart from his colleagues such as Adorno in suggesting the origins of crime fiction emerge as a response to modernity – and not in the manner of the aforementioned dismissal of the genre as the pulp expression of capitalism's ugliness and philistinism. Instead Benjamin finds in the nineteenth-century Paris of Baudelaire (but also, by extension, of Edgar Allan Poe and the genesis of the detective story) key examples of the disruption of identity, consciousness and belonging in modernity: the obliteration of the individual's traces in the anonymity of the urban throng. The mystery of the big city is also for Benjamin the riddle of the self. To him the dislocations of the modern city – a place too vast to be comprehended in its entirety by any one local experience; a space where the self can disappear, mutate, lose itself or make itself anew – necessitate the instigation of new bearings and orientations, new cognitive means by which we can chart or respond to this new dispensation in which traditional placements have dissolved. And for Benjamin the crime genre is one of these responses, not just an inferior or miscarried one. It is notable that from the very origins of the crime story it is not only the murderer who is trying to appear to be someone else.

Despite the crude disparagement of many critics who argue that the crime narrative has a basic, end-directed formal structure in which everything is resolved and the bad criminal element is removed so that society can return to normal, even the most formulaic examples of the genre often open up more questions than they can answer. Which is to say, in the course of the investigation in which the murderer is exposed, everyone is a potential suspect, everyone is engaged in subterfuges, has something to hide, has been someone or somewhere else, wants to be someone or somewhere else. However, this leads us to another means by which criticism has indicted crime fiction. The genre is habitually considered to be a reactionary genre. In other words, so this argument goes, it regulates society in the interests of the status quo. It criminalises and punishes anyone who would disrupt the social order. In this guise, the all-knowing perspective of the detective serves the interests of power and polices any threat to that power (whether in terms of race, social class, gender or sexuality).

For a critic like Franco Moretti, using the work of Michel Foucault on the interrelations between power and knowledge, the omniscience of the detective embodies the Panopticon prison model of Jeremy Bentham, the prison with an all-seeing eye which subjects its prisoners to total, constant scrutiny. By extension, the crime genre seeks to reassure vested interests that all criminals will be caught and punished. Under this interpretation, crime fiction is once again a kind of depleted version of mainstream modernity as a whole. In this case, Enlightenment reason – the avowed capacity of modern science and rationality to explain, systematise and collate all things – is offered a basic, crudely low cultural articulation in the form of the all-knowing detective, the omniscient narrative which can regulate everything to its own end of revealing the truth in its totality. This proposition is itself a rather totalising narrative which would make crime fiction a monolithic thing. Let's face it, yes, there will always be the likes of a Mickey Spillane who fits this template and who makes criminals of anyone who is Other (especially in terms of race and gender in his work) and must be punished to protect the way of the world.

Nevertheless, crime narrative is not reducible solely to this model. If everyone has something to hide, then everyone includes not only those criminalised by the more conservative model of the genre because of their class, gender or ethnicity, but also those in power. It is not simply guilty Golden Age villagers or those who walk the mean streets of Los Angeles that may be scrutinized though the lens of the crime narrative, but those in corridors of power, financial boardrooms and global institutions. Much crime fiction directs the genre's suspicion of hidden things towards the uncovering, indictment and indeed the criminalisation of the covert workings of apparently open or representative societies whose democratic credentials are thereby undermined by the ulterior, unrepresentative operation of their power. In this mode, the crime narrative is a formal method by which our knowledge of contemporary society is reclaimed for the purposes of evaluation and critique.

Moreover, the notion that the genre always arrives at total, singular knowledge – again as a sort of lower-class servant to a more proper Enlightenment rationality – doesn't really bear analysis. This kind of view would establish a literary history in which crime writing supplants mystery, horror or the gothic, where everything can now be explained rationally and scientifically, where there is no longer any mystery. But even the apparent exemplar of the omniscient detective, Arthur Conan Doyle's Sherlock Holmes, is so all-knowing that his prowess effaces itself or tilts itself off-kilter. For Holmes' reason attains a supernatural quality; it becomes, ironically, an enigma in works which professedly banish mystery. Investigative reason turns into magic, so even a set of works which promise to vanquish the unexplained are governed by a mystery. And crime writing is replete with writers who self-consciously examine precisely the limits of reason, science, information and knowledge.

While this is something that can be traced internationally, there is also a specific (but by no means peculiar) Scottish genealogy to this history of ideas. By way of the influence of Robert Louis Stevenson (who informs not only Ian Rankin but also the wider field of Scottish letters) there is a highly energised tradition of Scottish crime writing, which is itself indivisible from a broader tradition of Scottish writing in which realism or 'the truth' as some objective fixity is always undermined or at least in a dialogue with other modes and forms. This dialogue extends not only to genres like gothic, horror or the fantastic but also to the whole practice of assembling fictions and narratives. Hence, much Scottish crime fiction, like much other Scottish fiction, connects to key works like James Hogg's *Confessions* in which no singular, superintending knowledge is possible, and in which, as the tables are turned, the attempt to judge or police the supposed mystery or crime of others is itself exposed as an imposition both fictional and coercive. Rather than unfolding the one narrative leading to the one truth, so much crime fiction layers competing perspectives, multiple temporalities and contesting generic narratives which refuse to consent to the capacity of each to explain the other.

At an artistic level, again as a rebuttal of the dim view of crime writers as lowly, formulaic, join-the-dots merchants who lack the skill to be real 'literary' writers, crime fiction is of necessity a highly self-conscious process. The best of crime fiction must deliberate most concertedly on what is told, how it is told and when it is told. Crime fiction knows that something has happened, but also that the whole experience of the work depends upon how the narrative or narratives may tell the reader this, or indeed, mislead the reader, and unsettle expectations or confound lazy assumptions. And in all this, despite the pejorative account of the genre, readers of crime fiction are not passive consumers. Crime fiction forces you to be an active reader, a detective if you like, to be suspicious of every detail, to try to guess when you are being led astray. Hence, crime writers have a communion with criminals. The criminal acts and then tries to cover his or her tracks. So too the writer knows what has happened but tries to keep us guessing or to take us to places we had not expected. As with

James Hogg's *Confessions*, the exemplary tradition of Scottish crime writing proves that not only does the Devil have the best tunes, but he or she also has the best stories. Crime fiction at its best confronts the paradox of a narrative fiction trying to get to the truth. Often it's the fiction rather than the truth that grabs us in our detective work as readers.

The insightful collection of interviews gathered in this book provides an indispensable and illuminating casebook for anyone interested in contemporary Scottish crime writing. Good cop/bad cop interviews tease out the personal, artistic, social and cultural drives of the best writers of the current generation. The discussions shed light on a comprehensive selection of major writers which expresses the full range of Scottish crime fiction today. The capacity of Ian Rankin or Christopher Brookmyre to deploy crime narrative as a means of mapping the state of the nation comes across most fully. And Ian Rankin's sense of place and Brookmyre's dark comedy coalesce in the work of Aberdonian Stuart MacBride whose interview details the key concerns of his police procedurals. The discussion with Karen Campbell indicates that her work has as much to do with her literary education prior to joining the police force in Glasgow as with her subsequent career. Of course, her work also grants insight into the position of a female protagonist in the world of the procedural.

On the subject of moving into professional writing from a career elsewhere, Neil Forsyth's sway from journalism to creative writing is instructive, and his work shows as shrewd a capacity to process information analytically as his interview demonstrates how useful it is to have a nose for a good story. Allan Guthrie's interview indicates that his turn to writing was impelled in part by not finding enough good stories to read while working in a bookshop. His own take on Noir is avowedly existential rather than social or political, and his focus takes crime beyond the concerns of the detective and into a darkly metaphysical terrain. Aspects of the existential also imbue Alice Thompson's work, and the following conversation reveals the impulses that impel her to take the genre into Kafka-esque realms.

What the writers interviewed in this collection have in common is that each of them disrupts an attempt to construct a dichotomy between literary and genre fiction. Accordingly, Louise Welsh's conversation consummately articulates the range and depth of her imagination across times and spaces while Paul Johnston's futuristic Edinburgh crime novels and his imaginative (and literal) migration to Greece evince a comparable creative expansion. Indeed, this collection of conversations as a whole proffers a revealing series of snapshots that are both individually evocative and more widely indicative of the vibrant, demographic diversity of contemporary Scottish crime writing.

Dr Aaron Kelly
University of Edinburgh

Ian Rankin
Rough Justice in Tartan Noir

Ian Rankin was born in the Kingdom of Fife in 1960. Today he is known in thirty-six languages as 'the King of Tartan Noir'. Yet when a man holds a publishing record of thirty bestsellers, eighteen of which have established John Rebus as Scotland's most celebrated Detective Inspector; when every other promising crime writer in the country has been anointed 'the next Ian Rankin', chances are he is well known without being known well, and a certain impatience is likely to arise at the mere mention of his name. In short, a writer of his rank is hard to know, because his public image, once enough critics have dressed him in the emperor's new clothes, is at best a friendly caricature. At worst it obscures his writing.

In spite of the commercial and critical success he is today, Ian is the first to correct any romantic notions about the Scottish literary heritage. He never set out to be a crime writer. Long before the genre allowed him to become the UK's bestselling male writer, crime fiction was not a tempting choice for a Scottish debut author, nor was Ian interested in it. After writing comics as a child, poems as a teenager, and short stories as a student, it was during his postgraduate time at the University of Edinburgh that he started writing novels in the gothic vein of Robert Louis Stevenson. Much to Ian's dismay, when *Knots and Crosses* was published in 1987 his debut novel was labelled crime fiction.

Yet with the approval of then writer-in-residence Allan Massie, Ian decided he could wait for that of the professors of literature. Sales and sensibility alike have proved him right.

1

His patience paid off when his publishers paid for seventeen novels featuring Inspector John Rebus, ten of which have been televised by ITV with John Hannah and later Ken Stott in the leading role. Ian has since received four honorary doctorates from the Universities of Edinburgh, St Andrews, Abertay, and Hull, and in June 2002 he was made an Officer of the Order of the British Empire for his services to literature.

What is more, his list of honours includes a Palle Rosenkrantz Prize, a Grand Prix du Roman Noir, a Deutscher Krimipreis, a Chandler-Fulbright Award and a Hawthornden Fellowship. He has been awarded two CWA Daggers for his short stories and a CWA Macallan Gold Dagger for *Black and Blue* (1997). Having previously made the shortlist for the MWA Edgar Award for best novel, he came back to take the award with *Resurrection Men* in 2004. In 2005 he received the CWA Cartier Diamond Dagger to mark a lifetime's achievement in crime writing, and in 2008 Ian was honoured with the ITV3 Crime Thriller Award for Author of the Year in celebration of his final Rebus novel, *Exit Music*.

In other words there is no need to forget the legends of his literary apprenticeship as a swineherd, taxman, grape-picker, alcohol researcher, hi-fi reviewer, college secretary and punk musician. Yet you might just find it rewarding to move them aside a little to appreciate the man behind the name and fame, since the Ian Rankin you are about to meet is a writer who combines traits which the admirer from afar is unlikely to recognise as literary merits: the sharp wit that can be self-assertive while remaining detached, the quiet intent of a subversive mind, and the artist's sense of isolation that can never be exclusive to fiction.

Following Ian's invitation to his Edinburgh home, where he lives with his wife, two sons and 'Big Ger Cafferty', I wanted to ask him a simple question: What does a man do once he has set his country a literary monument? The obvious answer would seem to be: he takes time out from his writing life to answer that question. If the obvious is not what you were hoping to find within the following pages, welcome to the pleasures of Ian Rankin's mind. But do remember: you're entering a Kingdom of Noir.

~

Let's find out who started it all: 'Tartan Noir' ... I hear that was your idea.

Ha! 'Tartan Noir' is a term that I'm confident I invented, but I gave it to James Ellroy. I met him at a crime fiction convention in Nottingham many years ago and I wanted to get him to sign a book for me. I was explaining to him that I was a crime writer as well, and wrote about Edinburgh and the darker side of Scottish life. I said, 'You could call it Tartan Noir.' He laughed and signed the book to 'the King of Tartan Noir'. So then I pretended that he'd invented it. But in fact, I told him and then he wrote it down. Chris Brookmyre nicked it after that and started using it.

Didn't he call it 'chromatically impossible'?

Yeah! Well, it is. It's an oxymoron. Tartan can't just be black otherwise it's not a tartan. But anyway, I've still got my James Ellroy book upstairs so I can prove that he wrote that on the book. Or somebody wrote it on the book ... I can't prove it was him.

Can you say what it means to you?

Tartan Noir ... well, there's no tradition of crime fiction in Scotland but there is a great tradition of quite dark, psychological, Gothic horror stories. Specifically in the 70s, I think in Glasgow, there was a move towards a kind of realistic school of writing about working-class life, writing about hard men, writing about hard lives, and writing about urban experience. So it was a move away from the 'kaleyard', which was this romanticised view of Scotland. I think crime fiction tapped into that very nicely, and because there was no

3

tradition of crime fiction in Scotland it meant a completely
level playing field. Nobody had to be worried about writing
in a certain tradition, and most of us weren't influenced by
the English.

I'd better speak for myself and not for anybody else: I
certainly wasn't influenced by the English crime novel because
I'd never read any. I'd never read any Agatha Christie, Margery
Allingham, Dorothy L. Sayers – but I'd read a lot of Muriel
Spark, which is very dark, and I'd read William McIlvanney,
James Kelman, Alasdair Gray, some John Buchan, Alistair
MacLean, a Scottish thriller writer, very famous in the 60s
and 70s. But because there was no Agatha Christie figure you
didn't feel you were looking over your shoulder and you had
to write a certain kind of book.

So, in fact, there's a huge catholicism to Scottish crime
fiction. If you look at the stuff that Alexander McCall Smith
writes, if you look at the stuff that Kate Atkinson writes, if
you look at some of the historical crime novels that Alanna
Knight and others are writing and then if you look at the
really, really dark stuff like Stuart MacBride, it seems to me
there's somebody writing in every kind of crime fiction. I mean,
when Paul Johnston started he was writing crime novels set
in the twenty-first century. He was writing about a futuristic
Edinburgh, so you have sci-fi crime fiction, historical crime
fiction, you have comic crime fiction like Chris Brookmyre
influenced by Carl Hiaasen, you have psychological crime
fiction like Denise Mina, cop novels like I was writing... Other
people are writing about private eyes. Allan Guthrie came
along and seemed to enjoy writing about criminals rather
than cops.

It just seemed there was room for all of that because
we weren't expected to write any particular kind of crime
novel. But the balance has swung towards noir, quite dark
fiction, and I think that comes out of the fact that the current
generation of crime writers has grown up with things like

4

Hannibal Lecter and slasher movies and Hollywood serial killers who are exaggerated in their means and motives. We've grown up with American cop shows on the television; we find that crime fiction is a very good way of writing about urban experience and society, about current affairs and politics ...so we're doing a lot more than just trying to tell a good story that will keep you engaged on a train journey so that at the end you'll go, 'Ach, *that's* who the killer was.' I think quite a lot of writers in Scotland aren't that interested in the traditional notion of the English detective story, the structured novel that's full of red herrings and in the penultimate chapter the detective gets all the possible suspects together in a room and explains who did it and who didn't do it.

There don't seem to be many novels like that coming out of Scotland. They seem to be quite dark. They seem to be close to the Scandinavian model of crime fiction. When I read Per Wahlöö and Maj Sjöwall writing in Sweden and about Swedish society in the 60s, it seems very modern, and it seems to me very much like a lot of the stuff that's coming out of Scotland at the moment. It's not a school because there are other writers who don't fit that, but they're still writing crime fiction whether they like it or not.

You mentioned the similarities between Scandinavian and Scottish crime fiction. Is your shared popularity the product of Anglo-Saxon coolness and Northern innocence?

Well, what I find about a lot of Scandinavian crime fiction is that it's quite politically engaged. I mean, Per Wahlöö and Maj Sjöwall were Marxists who were trying to write about what they felt was a decline in standards and civilisation in their country. I think there are several crime writers out there who are trying to do something similar to that; writers who are saying, 'Look at the terrible mess we're in. How the hell did we get here?'

But also, these are quite introspective countries. The people are quite inward-looking. If you watch Kenneth Branagh doing Wallander on television you get a sense of that. This guy is just angsty. We do like a good angsty detective and we think of Scandinavia as a place where you can do angst quite well. By the same token I think you can do it very well in Scotland because the Scots also have this Jekyll and Hyde thing going on. We can be lovely one minute but give us some alcohol and suddenly we turn into monsters. We do hide our feelings a lot of the time. It's weird, isn't it? We're all supposed to be Celts but you look at Ireland and everybody's so chatty and friendly. Glaswegians are, but you go elsewhere in Scotland and everybody's very reserved. They'd rather say nothing than say the wrong thing.

Si tacuisses, philosophus mansisses?

It's hilarious! I used to see it in tutorials all the time. All the students who'd come from Scottish working class comprehensive school backgrounds would sit there and say nothing for the whole course of a tutorial, and there'd be all these really chatty English folk sitting there who were very, very self-confident and self-aware, and even if they didn't know the answer they would say something. And then all the wee working class Scots would be sitting there writing everything down that they said. It was about two and a half years before I spoke in a tutorial. But once I started you couldn't shut me up.

It didn't take you quite as long to find your narrative voice, though, did it?

No. I mean, I was writing from a very young age. I was trying to do comics and strip cartoons and song lyrics from before I was a teenager. And then in my mid-teens I was writing song lyrics and poetry, and when I came to Edinburgh University I was a poet. I'd had one poem published. I'd won second prize in a competition so I'd been published in a magazine. So that was me. I thought, 'This is what I'm doing.' But the poems were telling stories. The poems were not emotion recollected in tranquillity. They were narratives.

So when a short story competition was announced I went in for it and got second prize and then the next year I won a short story competition and I thought, 'Oh, I can do this!' So I moved away from poetry into short stories and then that smoothed the way for a transition to the novel.

And then, after a couple of novels, one of which was never published, I came up with Rebus without having really read any crime fiction at all – with the possible exception of William McIlvanney and some film tie-ins. You know, things like *Shaft* and maybe *The French Connection* and *The Godfather*. I'd read those because they were films. But McIlvanney was quite important because of *Laidlaw*, which came along just as I was getting an inkling of writing a dark, contemporary take on *Jekyll and Hyde*, which was *Knots and Crosses*, where all the way through you're supposed to think that Rebus, the detective, is potentially the killer – he just doesn't know it.

Hard to fool people with that these days when they know that there are seventeen Rebus novels. He's probably not the bad guy in the first book. But it was never meant to be a series and I was kind of reluctant to see it even as crime fiction because at that time crime fiction was very much the poor relation. You'd go into a bookshop and you'd struggle to find a crime section. It was tucked away at the back of the shop somewhere.

Is it true that when Knots and Crosses *was first published you moved a copy from the crime section to where you thought it should be shelved?*

Yeah, I wanted it to be in Scottish literature at the front of the shop beside Spark and Stevenson and McIlvanney. I went back the next day and they'd moved it back to the crime section ... This is going back to 1987, so it's going back quite some time.

After all those years, are you tired of being seen as the guy who writes Rebus?

Well, I'm not the guy who writes Rebus any more. I wrote

the last Rebus novel about three years ago. Of course I still get asked. Every time I do a gig I get asked if I'm going to bring back Rebus: 'When are we going to see him again?' I get emails from people saying, 'I like your books post-Rebus but when are we going to get another Rebus book?'

I mean, he was and he remains a useful character. He's a useful means of looking at society. He's a useful prism through which you can show all the different aspects of human life because a detective, unlike almost any character in fiction, has access to every area, every layer of society. So if you want to write about politicians and big business and backhanders and corruption but you also want to write about the dispossessed, the disenfranchised folk living on the edge, folk living on housing benefit, folk with drug problems, you can do all of that with this one character because he can explore all of that and everybody's got to open their door to him.

So I do think a detective is a very, very good tool for opening up the world and exploring it. That's what I think I try to do in the books. It's like putting together a jigsaw puzzle of modern Scotland, whether it's local politics, national politics, the economy, the country's history and possible future, racism, religious bigotry … all these things can be tackled in crime fiction very easily. The slightly frustrating thing is that you can't show that the world is also a very nice place because your detective tends not to be dealing with happy, shiny people. Your detective is dealing with suspects, grieving relatives and all that, which is frustrating when you live in Edinburgh. I mean, look at how nice it is.

You've managed to show that in a couple of successful short story collections. Would you write more of them if there was a bigger market?

Probably. The short story is a nice form. It's like a little jewel. You can hold the shape of it in your head – you can't with a novel – and they're really good to read. I enjoy reading short stories or listening to them in the car, and I enjoy writing them, but whether I could ever get enough ideas to be a full-time short story writer... You'd want to get a story published every single week. You'd have to have fifty-two good ideas, whereas writing a novel you only have to have one good idea a year – maybe two: plot and subplot.

And then, at the end of two or three days' work, you've got something. You've got something there that you've physically made that nobody's made before. That's one of the wonderful things about writing. There are twenty-six letters in the alphabet. There are only so many words in the language, and yet everybody can write a sentence that's never been written before. Think how incredible that is. You can sit and write a sentence that nobody in the entire history of human existence has written before. That's the great challenge as well: trying to write something different – do something that's not been done before.

Doing English at university you're told there are seven basic plots and you go, 'Well, I'm fucked then. I can do seven books and that'll be it.' But then you learn that these seven plots are actually completely malleable and interchangeable. There might only be seven basic *plots* but the well of *stories* is inexhaustible.

When I was younger plots were flying at me because I was very receptive to them. I'd walk down the street and I'd get an idea for a story because I would hear or see something. In the end I tried to switch off because I was getting more ideas than I could possibly use. And then how do you sort them out and decide which ones to write and which ones not to write?

You mentioned James Ellroy a little while ago. Early in his career he noticed that he could execute anything he could envisage. Can you?

Hmm ... yes. But he hit a wall. Well, did he hit a wall? He told me once that when he wrote *White Jazz*, the linguistic experimentation in that book was so extreme that he actually lost readers. People weren't buying it because it was too hard to read so he back-pedalled a wee bit after that. The narrative became more fluid and the language became slightly less opaque. But yeah, there's no doubt that he gets big ideas and is able to execute them. I've got storylines upstairs that I've not used yet because I can't think how the hell to do it.

Like what?

Things like, you want to write from an eight-year-old boy's point of view and I'm going, 'Well, can I? Would it be realistic? Could I make it realistic? That's awfully hard, I'll try something else.'

Is there a risk to such professionalism?

I think you can fall into a trap. If you've got a very successful career in one genre with one character it's very easy just to keep on writing stories that are slightly different from previous stories but just different enough so they don't put off your publisher or your reader. I'm sure every crime fan in the world can name writers who probably should have stopped by now or tried something new.

Then again, Stuart MacBride said one of your greatest regrets was making Rebus too old to begin with.

Ha! I know. Limiting the life span of the series... Well, he had to be forty in the first book because he had to have had a previous life that he'd managed to block out. Time had to have passed. Young man, training for the SAS, something terrible happens, and he's able to sort of push it to the back of his mind or stick it into a compartment and not think about it again. So I thought, 'Well, how long would have passed? Probably the best part of fifteen or twenty years.' I totalled that up and thought, 'That makes him about forty.'

Thinking it was only going to be one book that decision didn't matter. But then about three or four books into the series, I decided, 'He's actually going to age in real time. He's not going to be preserved in aspic the way a lot of detectives are in fiction.' And that was fine because realistically I could show the changing nature of Edinburgh. Some time has passed from his first adventure set in 1987. So we get the parliament, we get the G8 coming to town, and you can show the changes that are taking place in Edinburgh and in Scottish society, but then you come up against that eventual problem, 'When does he have to retire?'

I thought he'd probably have to retire at sixty-five. It was a cop who told me, 'No, it's sixty for detectives: mandatory retirement.' So I totalled it up and thought, 'Hang on, '87 he's forty. That means 2007 he's sixty. So 2007's book has to be his retirement book.' It was as straightforward as that. I'd given myself a problem but the answer to the problem was for him to retire. Doesn't mean to say he'd stop being a cop. I know what he's doing. He's working in the cold case unit at Fettes Police Head Quarters in a team of four: one serving police officer and three retired detectives who look at old unsolved murders. Perfect for Rebus.

After seventeen novels and twenty years with Rebus, what's it like not to be writing about him every day?

Terrific! It was a great sense of freedom. I went off and did lots of different things. I did a libretto for an opera. I did a comic book. I did some lyrics for a band in Edinburgh, Saint Jude's Infirmary. I also wrote the lyrics of one song on an album called *Ballads of the Book* which paired Scottish writers with Scottish musicians. I got paired up with Aidan Moffat and did a song, 'The Sixth Stone', about the sixth member of The Rolling Stones, Ian Stewart, who was born in Pittenweem in Fife. I did a serial for The New York Times, and I did a little novella, *A Cool Head*, for a literacy project. It was all great, and none of it was Rebus. Then *Doors Open*, which was the serial for *The New York Times*, got turned into a novel and now looks like it might be made into a television series.

That was all brilliant but then it became time to write a new novel and I sat down and thought, 'What do I want to write about? What do I want to explore this time round?' and of course all the financial problems were underway by then and Edinburgh was looking a bit wobbly – so many jobs in the city depending on the financial sector – so I thought, 'This will make an interesting theme for a book.' Then somebody told me about the Complaints Department. I did some research and before I knew it I was hooked on the idea of writing about these cops who investigate other cops. I think what interested me was that Rebus is the kind of cop these people would investigate. They're not rule-breakers. They're not natural chance-takers. They play things very safe. They've got to be abiding by the law at all times. They've got to be whiter than white, very careful and very canny. They're like spies.

Whereas Rebus is –

– like a private eye. He would go off and do his own thing and not listen to his superiors. So it's a very different mindset for the main character, Malcolm Fox, and I thought that'd be good fun. And it was good fun but it's given me a problem now because I don't know if I want to write another book about the Complaints Department. Do I want to bring Rebus back working cold cases? I could write about Siobhan, his sidekick, his colleague. *Doors Open*, which is a heist novel, sold remarkably well. It actually outsold the Rebus novels.

So my publishers are going, 'Well, do you want to write something in a similar vein to that, which is lighter and show-ing a different side of Edinburgh, a different side of Scotland?' I've got at least three and maybe four things that I could do next and my publisher is coming up to Edinburgh next week to talk about it because I don't know. I don't have any strong feelings one way or another.

Are you considering parallel series along the lines of Michael Connelly's Bosch and Haller novels with the occasional tie-in?

Yeah! But there's a slight problem with Rebus. If I've got the Complaints investigating Rebus it becomes a Rebus novel. As far as I know Scottish Television have still got the rights to film Rebus, which would mean I couldn't sell it to anybody else. *The Complaints* has been bought for television by the BBC. If I write about the Complaints Department but don't have Rebus in it then the BBC get it, but if suddenly the Complaints and Rebus are in the same book then we've got an almighty fucking lawyer's fee trying to work out who's got the rights to film the book. So I need to get legal advice before I can bring Rebus back, bizarrely.

Are you still in touch or has Rebus left the building?

I did actually write a Rebus short story not that long ago and it was great fun. I wrote a story that was based just after his retirement for a charity night down at the brewery, and it was published in *The Scotsman*. They raised a lot of money for charity, and it was good fun. It was Rebus and Siobhan back together again, and it was amazing to me that, not having written about either of them for three years, the voices just jumped straight back into my head. The wisecracks were still there, the relationship between them was still there ... They hadn't got rusty in the interim. So, you know, he's sitting there. All these compartments inside my head: one of them has Rebus sitting crouched in it just waiting to be sprung free. He hasn't left the building.

That said, do you remember when you learned most about Rebus and writing?

Well, the first Rebus book is not very good. I say that in the introduction. It's over-written. It's a bit up itself. It's obviously written by a literature student. 'The manumission of dreams' – no idea what that means. It took me a while to learn what you can and can't do with crime fiction, and to learn what I could and couldn't do with Rebus. In the first novel he's just a means of pushing the plot along. He's the guy who's going to be explaining to you what's going on here, and I don't think he becomes a fully rounded, three-dimensional character until probably book four. The first books sold very poorly and didn't even get very good reviews, so I was just lucky that my publisher hung onto me.

I remember delivering *Black and Blue*, which was Rebus number eight, and I'd written about four other novels by then, and my publishers were getting ready to chuck me because I was midlist. I was ticking over. I was selling enough copies to go into profit but just barely, and they were running out of options. They'd toured me. They'd done promotional tea towels and mugs. They'd tried to get the booksellers on side and spent some money on advertising, and the books kept selling a few thousand and a few thousand and a few thousand. I knew *Black and Blue* was a much better book than previous books, a much more complex book and a much more successful book.

What happened to trigger that transition?

Oh, I think lots of things happened. I mean, the books before that had been my apprenticeship and I suddenly realised you could do a lot more than I'd been doing. You could make it quite convoluted. You could take your character out of his comfort zone – take him out of Edinburgh altogether. The book could be darker. I could introduce real elements like a real-life serial killer, Bible John, who was never caught. I'd learnt a lot from James Ellroy about using real characters and real crimes in your books, and putting in some historical perspective. So I had Rebus going into libraries and reading newspapers from the 60s and actually getting a sense of how Scotland had changed from the 60s to what was then the late 80s and early 90s.

And, you know, my youngest son had been born. He was disabled, and I was shaking my fist at God: 'Why me, why me?' So I was channelling quite a lot of anger and frustration and questions about the universe into that book, and giving it all to Rebus to deal with – so it was quite cathartic. I think I'd learnt how to write, so the book was going to be better anyway, and I'd a much stronger sense of plot and theme and how to shape the book. There was a lot of personal stuff in it as well, all of which seemed to tick the right boxes and it went

14

on to win the Gold Dagger. I remember it well. That was when my publisher suddenly thought, 'Oh, right, Ian has delivered a better book.' Up till then I'd never even been shortlisted for a prize for my novels, so to get shortlisted for the first time and then win… Never won it since, mind.

Which one do you personally consider the best in the series?

I've got a lot of time for *The Naming of the Dead*, the one about the G8. *Dead Souls* I thought I liked and then I reread it and thought, 'No, I don't like this at all and I don't understand what's going on. Who are these people? What's happening?' It was way too complicated. Some of the early ones, the wee short ones! The jump from *Knots and Crosses* to *Hide and Seek* I think is as big as the jump from *Let it Bleed* to *Black and Blue* in terms of confidence.

Would you rewrite any of them?

No. You could spend your whole life rewriting. I can see things that I wish I had said differently but I'm not going to go back and change them. For the twentieth anniversary of *Knots and Crosses* we put out a special edition which had a whole chunk in the middle that my agent had asked me to take out.

The back story about the SAS?

Yeah! I was really sad to lose it because I'd done a lot of research into it but I think she and the editor agreed that it would take us away from the story for too long so I cut it back from about twenty pages to six. It's nice to put that back and let folk look at it if they want to. But I don't get that heavily edited these days. Partly because I have more power than I used to have so I can say, 'No.' But I think partly because I know what I'm doing now. But there's still stuff that gets changed at the last minute. In *The Complaints* one of the major characters could have turned out to be a baddy or a goody.

I was wondering why you delayed the revelation of Jamie Breck's hidden agenda.

Well, in the first draft he turns out to be a bit of a baddy,

15

and I think I showed it to my wife who liked him and said, 'If he's the baddy, you can't use him again in future books. He'd be very helpful to Malcolm Fox in the future to get that buddy-movie thing going.' And I think I showed it to my editor who said, 'I'd prefer it if he turned out not to be the bad guy.' So I changed that.

How do you feel about being edited?

Depends on who's editing me. I've had the same editor for donkey's years.

Caroline Oakley?

Yeah! She left publishing years ago but she asked to keep me on in a freelance capacity. I have a day-to-day editor who works down in London for the publishing house and who looks after stuff, but when it actually comes to asking for changes and checking things, Caroline does most of it.

Do you have an ideal reader?

Caroline is pretty close to it because she does pick up on a lot of stuff, but she's always looking for more. My American proofreader asks funny things. Malcolm Fox wears braces, right? Well, the word 'braces' doesn't exist in the States. It's 'suspenders'. So she said to me, 'Malcolm Fox comes into the office wearing his suspenders.' And I said, 'Look, Peggy, that's just put such a bad image in my head! You've taken me to a very dark place.' She said, 'I know, but for American readers we need to do it.' One of the biggest problems is translation from English into English like changing *Fleshmarket Close* to *Fleshmarket Alley* because nobody in America would know a 'close'. And then American readers get pissed off. They say, 'I came to Edinburgh and there's no 'Fleshmarket Alley' – it's called 'Fleshmarket Close'. Why did you change your title?' – I despair.

Speaking of despair, why are both Rebus and Fox divorced?

Oh, because it's a lot easier not to give your characters any baggage. Otherwise they can't be on the job 24/7. They're suddenly going off to a party, or collecting the kids from school, or taking the kids to the dentist, or going out for a meal with their partner, or having to go away for the weekend, or remembering somebody's birthday, and it just gets in the way. I much prefer my main characters to be loners, to have almost no family baggage at all.

I imagine that would have been a challenge while your own family situation was changing.

Yeah! When I invented Rebus I wasn't married and I didn't have any kids, and he was divorced with a daughter. I decided that Fox wasn't going to have any kids but he's more of a family man than Rebus ever was. But I just felt Rebus was this guy who pushes friends and family away. He was just very self-reliant. Yeah, he's got a good conceit of himself, as the Scots would say. I think Malcolm's got the potential for romance. I can envisage him in a relationship in a way that I can't with Rebus. I mean, I tried it with Rebus and he didn't want to be in a relationship.

Did he tell you?

Yeah! He just didn't get on with any of these women I introduced him to. My wife would say, 'Patience Aitken, she's boring.' And somebody else I tried to fix him up with, 'Oh no, she's boring as well!' So he ended up with nobody. But Malcolm, he's much more open to this sort of stuff, and he can show us a different side of Edinburgh. For him Edinburgh isn't just a series of crime scenes, which is what it is for Rebus. He says it himself and other people are trying to show Rebus, 'Look at the view! Look how amazing it is at night! It's all lit up.' And he's going, 'Yeah, yeah.' But he can't really see it, whereas Malcolm can. He's a much warmer character.

So if I do continue to write about him I can see him getting into a relationship and being more settled. But who knows? Maybe when I start to write it it'll all go a bit icky and I won't be able to do it because it'll get in the way of the plot. That's one complaint that's made about crime fiction in literary circles – if such things exist – it's plot-driven.

17

Isn't character plot?

I think that's been changing. This idea of your fairly two-dimensional characters who are only there as victims or suspects – that's kind of disappeared. Crime fiction has grown up. It's not just an entertainment to be read on the train any more. Serious writers are attracted to it and, I think, young writers who twenty or thirty years ago would have wanted to be 'literary' novelists now see no shame in writing popular or populist fiction because they can say what they want to say in that form. I mean, if I couldn't say what I wanted to say and explore the themes I wanted to explore in crime fiction I would find another way of doing it.

Do you feel partially responsible for that change?

Not really. Are you trying to say, 'Have I influenced all these younger writers?'

What I'm trying to understand is why so many of them are heralded as 'the new Ian Rankin'.

Oh yeah, I know. That's just lazy marketing.

Isn't there an implication that you personify a generational shift in Scottish literature?

There was a whole bunch of us who came along at much the same time and who felt different from the previous generation of English crime writers. 'Fresh Blood' I think we were called. It was Mark Timlin, Michael Dibdin, Philip Kerr, Denise Danks, Mike Ripley and me. We were all living near London at that time and used to get together and plot the overthrow of the traditional English crime novel – in pubs – and then wouldn't do anything about it.

There was a notion that crime fiction was a wee bit stuffy; upper-middle-class detectives investigating upper-middle-class crimes. We weren't interested in that. We wanted to get down and dirty. We were reading a lot of pulp fiction and American crime novels. The stuff I really liked was James Ellroy and Lawrence Block and the early George Pelecanos novels. They were gritty, they were urban, and I thought, 'There's a lot of urban plight in the UK. The Americans shouldn't have the monopoly.'

It was quite exciting. I mean, we were young and we were snotty. Philip Kerr was selling pretty well and I suppose Michael Dibdin was, but the rest of us were struggling so we thought we'd get together and struggle together. So no, it wasn't just me. I can't take the blame.

When your debut was labelled 'crime fiction', whose work gave you a sense of perspective?

McIlvanney was very important to me personally because he was a literary novelist. He'd won the Whitbread Prize for fuck's sake, and then suddenly he's writing gritty urban crime novels set in Glasgow. He said afterwards he only did it because he was skint and he thought it was a quick way to make some money, but it was important to me that a serious writer was writing crime fiction. I thought it obviously is no different from writing literature, so although I was doing my PhD on Muriel Spark it was okay to write popular fiction.

And Allan Massie, who was writer-in-residence at Edinburgh University at that time, was another huge help to me when I was a young writer. When I said, 'Oh my God, I seem to have written a crime novel by mistake while trying to write the great Scottish urban updating of *Dr Jekyll and Mr Hyde*,' he said, 'Well, you might never get the kudos but you'll get the cash.' He was wrong to start with but he was right eventually.

What makes this literature of social mobility and flexible morality so popular?

Throughout history we've always been drawn towards what we fear. Folk tales are lessons in how to avoid the big bad wolf, and crime fiction is all about the big bad wolf. At the same time it's an extension of myth and legend. Chandler was very clear on this. He was educated at a posh English school and he knew his classics. He knew that what he was dealing with were knights errant. Right at the end of *The Big*

Sleep there's a big description of California and it harks back to the Grail Myth. He was originally going to call his main character Mallory after *Morte D'Arthur* so he knew what he was doing. It fascinates me that throughout history we've had heroes who've gone on quests. What they're doing is they're trying to find the answers to questions.

We go through our entire lives trying to find out, 'Why is the world the way it is? How does it work? Is there an afterlife?' There are all these huge questions, and the nice thing about crime fiction is it doesn't just pose the questions – it gives you some answers, and that gives you a really good feeling as a reader.

In other words, if there's a more visceral feeling that goes with curiosity satisfied, is it the love of making order out of confusion?

Yeah! Humans are of necessity puzzle-solvers. We're confronted by problems and we find a way to deal with them. I think crime fiction is becoming less of a closed universe. We allow for some moral ambiguity that wasn't there in early crime fiction, and that's good because I think the world is much more like that. Rebus is an Old Testament sort of guy. He sees the world in terms of white and black, good and evil, and my job in the books is often to try and have an argument with him and say, 'Well, actually, there are shades of grey in the middle, pal,' which is what Siobhan does. Siobhan's sort of my spokesperson.

Is she saying that shades of grey are the new black?

Ha! I don't know. What a horrible phrase that is. It's like something you'd read in the fashion pages of the *Times*. But I think we do allow for ambiguity. I knew that we were onto something when I read a P.D. James novel – I think it was *A Certain Justice* and the clue is in the title – and at the end, for the first time in her entire body of work, her detective knows who the killer is but can't do anything about it because he can't prove it. It's a very loose ending. That's a writer saying,

'It doesn't always have to be cleared up at the end.'

Could that moral ambiguity explain the pop culture come-back of the 'noble savage'?

'Noble savage' – fucking hell! I was reading about that shit when I was nineteen. Thirty years later we're still talking about it. It's desperate. Still, you've done well. We've managed not to mention hermeneutics or deconstruction. There was an academic at the University of St Andrews who wrote a book about *Black and Blue* –

– *Gill Plain?*

Yeah! I said to her, 'If you mention semiotics or deconstruction I'm going to come up to St Andrews and hit you around the face.' Ha! She mentions that in the introduction. I wasted three years of my life reading all that shit. I quite liked Roland Barthes but deconstruction was just nonsense, and everybody got sucked into it. Suddenly you couldn't write an essay that didn't have it there. It was scientism. It was people saying, 'We need to look more scientific. We need to look like we know what we're doing.'

And yet you're a big fan of Thomas Pynchon?

Well, I'm a big fan of some of Thomas Pynchon. Maybe he does put all that stuff in on purpose to trick academics but it's a bit like James Joyce having a laugh: 'I'll write this *Finnegans Wake* and then folk will do nothing their whole lives except trying to explain *Finnegans Wake*.' He knew what he was doing. All he demanded of academics was that they spend their entire lives working on his book.

So how do you feel about your own work becoming compulsory academic reading?

It's funny, isn't it? Well, I think it's good news, and I'll tell you why it's good news. I want crime fiction to be taken seriously, and the way literature becomes literature is being studied in high schools and in universities. The imprimatur says that this is not just a pastime for the masses by the swimming pool. It says that these books are actually saying something that's worth investigating. So I'm for that.

As long as you get to draw the line at deconstruction?

Ha! You can't draw the line. I mean, if somebody wants to read stuff into your books, they'll read it into your books whether it's there or not. A lot of the time it's not there.

All right, let's assume that critics actually put more into books than writers, and that what you're after is simply to entertain your readers. Surely the interesting question then is: How do you define 'entertainment'?

Well, what crime fiction does is take the reader on a roller-coaster ride. It's that kind of funfair exhibit and you're going to be scared and thrilled but you're going to do it all from the comfort of your armchair. So it's a vicarious thrill that you're getting and you're entering quite dangerous territory, you're walking down mean streets side by side with your hero or your villain – but you can put the book down and walk away. It's that kind of trick that the reader always goes along with, because at some point you've got to put your main character in jeopardy.

I used to try and get Rebus into situations near the end of the book where he was going to be killed. My agent said I used to do it just to wind him up because he'd never know if this was going to be the final Rebus book or not. I'd have Rebus digging his own grave and somebody standing over him with a pistol, and then he'd get out of it. Hurray! I mean, it was good fun but in real life it doesn't happen that often that the case comes back to bite you. If you're a good enough writer you can get them to suddenly forget that they're reading book number twelve of a seventeen-book series, and make them think, 'Oh no, he's going to die!' I think it myself when I reread some of the early Rebus books.

It doesn't sound like you're a fan of plotting ahead of writing.

No. I start a book with a vague theme and usually a murder.

Do you write to surprise yourself?

Yeah. Recently I have been surprising myself. My publisher at the publication party for *Doors Open* said, 'Ian, you've written a very unusual crime novel here. Nobody dies.' I hadn't thought about it. There's plenty of jeopardy but nobody actually dies in that book. And in *The Complaints* in the opening chapter nothing happens. There's no murder. A case is being wound up, Malcolm Fox goes and visits his dad, and then he goes home.

Was that not a conscious inversion of your usual dynamic?

Yeah, that was conscious. I wanted a quiet opening to the book.

Like the end of a Rebus novel?

Ha! That's right. Everything's being wound up and I'm going home to have a cup of tea. And yet everything happens in that first chapter. We're getting to know him.

Were you writing that first chapter with his backstory in mind?

No.

So the personal information you reveal during Fox's interrogations –

– was just made up as I went along. If you saw my notes... I start with about three pages of A4 and by about page 10 or 15 of the book that's the end of the notes and everything after that I'm making up as I go along. I never know how it's going to end. If I knew how it ended I wouldn't bother writing it.

Does that mean you've written your own ten commandments, much like Elmore Leonard?

Ha! No. I met Elmore Leonard a few years ago. It was hilarious. He was talking about taking out all your adverbs and adjectives. Bollocks to that! There shouldn't be any rules. You write the way you want to write and write what you want to write. That's why I'm surprised that Allan Guthrie's doing a creative writing degree. I mean, he's published so many books. He should know how to do it, and this is only going to give him rules. Then he might feel he's got to follow these rules, and I think that will change his writing. I never did any creative writing classes.

Can writing be taught?

No. I've tried teaching it a couple of times. I did the Arvon Foundation once up at Loch Ness and I've done the occasional couple of hours with a bunch of students. I mean, if somebody's got talent then you can – A – spot it and – B – help them move it along, but you can't make somebody talented. You can't teach writing to that extent, I don't think. It amazes me that all these *How to be a Writer* books are all written by folk I've never heard of. Surely the people you're going to read should be the ones who've made it. *How to be a Writer* by John Grisham – I'll read that.

How about Stephen King's On Writing?

That was a funny book because bits of it were about his life and bits of it were wee essays on writing. It was a very good book but a lot of it was just written for himself when he was in that hospital bed. But yeah, that's the one book I would recommend to people. I wouldn't recommend *How to write a Bestseller* by Joe Blow.

Are you going to write your own book on writing?

No. I've written as much nonfiction as I'm ever going to write with *Rebus's Scotland*. That was it.

No chance of a sequel, perhaps Fox's Scotland?

Ha! I don't think so. I cannae see Malcolm go beyond three books.

Why is that?

Because I'll be fifty-five or sixty by then.

Do you see yourself ever retiring from writing?

I kind of wish I was retired from writing already. This year I'm supposed to be taking a year off, and I'm getting a bit antsy. How can I be so busy when I'm not writing anything? It's because writing is a terrific excuse for not doing anything else. You know, you turn down interviews, you turn down tours, you turn down charity events, you turn down everything and you say, 'I'm writing a book.' Folk just go, 'Oh, I'm sorry I've bothered you.' But when they know you're not writing a fucking book then they just keep pestering you.

Oh, I'm sorry I've bothered you.

Ha! I know. I somehow got suckered into doing this film script, *Justified Sinner*, and I thought that would all be done and dusted by the middle of last year. It's ongoing. The producer is in Cannes as we speak talking to directors. And then there's a TV thing of *The Complaints* that I'm involved in and a TV thing of *Doors Open* that I'm slightly involved in as an executive producer.

Has that behind-the-scenes work changed how you feel about adapting your own work?

Well, with Rebus I wasn't at all involved and in retrospect I wish I had been. So this time I've said I want to be involved. That's a bit time consuming because it's all fucking meetings, which I'm not used to as a novelist. I don't do meetings. I'll have lunch with my publisher, but that's about it. But sitting in a room with six other people who are saying to you, 'Well, can you just make this guy a woman and make this comedy a tragedy and set it in Siberia rather than Zimbabwe and make it the eighteenth century, not the future?' Scriptwriters are used to just going, 'Yeah, fine, I'll do that.' I'm sitting there thinking, 'Fucking hell.'

It's really easy being a novelist because you've got no boss except yourself. You don't have to take other people's stuff on board. We've got complete control over our characters and their destinies and everything else, and we don't have to satisfy anybody but ourselves. A novelist gets to play God.

Ezekiel 25:17? The path of the righteous man is beset on all sides by the inequities of the selfish and the tyranny of evil men. Blessed is he who, in the name of charity and good will, shepherds the weak through the valley of darkness –

– Yeah, except sometimes they do weird things that I'm not expecting them to do ... like die. *Set in Darkness* is quite a late book in the series and there I was writing away and then suddenly the politician was dead and I thought, 'Why is he dead?' Because the narrative had decided it didn't need him. I thought this person was absolutely intrinsic to my theme of the coming of the Scottish Parliament and how it was going to change Scotland, if at all. The narrative said, 'No, actually, this guy isn't that useful. You've invented him and now we need to get rid of him.' So he was just dead, and that was that. Characters are always surprising me.

In *Doors Open* I was being continuously surprised by what the characters were doing but that's because it was written as a serial. It had to be 2,500 words each chapter, and it was weekly installments so it couldn't be too convoluted. It couldn't have too many characters in it. These amateur heist merchants would get access to guns, and I would go, 'Jesus, how does it feel to be a self-made millionaire software businessman who's suddenly got a gun in his pocket?' It was great fun writing that. I don't know how it's going to work on television.

Having written lyrics as well as poetry and prose, what do you enjoy most?

I would say that the thing I enjoy doing most is writing a novel but my wife will tell you that when I'm writing a novel I'm insufferable and it's almost like I'm in pain. At times I get worried that I don't know where the plot's going and I don't know if it's actually going to work, and are these characters actually realistic? She says usually I'm fine for the first hundred pages and then I start to get really worried and think, 'It's all gone to shit.'

I've spoken to a lot of novelists and a lot of them feel the same way, and yet we keep on writing. I think partly it's because the payoff is that you get to play God. I mean, we're just kids who refuse to grow up. We're playing imaginary games with our invisible friends but instead of role-playing we're doing it on the page. It's great fun controlling these people's lives and giving them exciting things to do and putting them in jeopardy.

Which begs a question spanning twenty years: Why do you torture Rebus time and time again?

He asks for it. Partly. He gets himself into situations that demand that he then be a tortured soul. But also, it's cathartic. If I'm angry about something I can't go and punch somebody in real life. I'll get arrested. But I can put Rebus through the mangle and that's fine. It's a way of dealing with stuff – dealing with stress.

If Rebus is an 'Old Testament sort of guy', what kind of God are you?

I'm a much more forgiving God than Rebus would accept. If we ever met he wouldn't like me, I don't think. I understand him but I don't think he would understand me. He would see me as being too liberal and too wishy-washy and made soft by circumstance. Suckled by the state all my life: free health, free education, I never had to do a hard day's manual work in my life – he just can't comprehend that as an existence.

Is that the survivor guilt talking?

I don't know. There's a lot of that Presbyterian stuff going on. I think Chris Brookmyre talks about this and probably Stuart MacBride as well. There's quite a lot of that Old Testament, fire-and-brimstone 'We're all sinners. We're all going to be punished!' And I think to myself, 'I've got all this success. Where the fuck did that come from? Did it just come as a kind of accident?' You know, in some ways it was an accident. I was in the right place at the right time. Have I earned it? – I've met a lot of successful creative people, and I think they've got the same thing. Especially if they're Scottish they're thinking, 'I've not really earned this. I'm going to pay for it.'

Any chance I could see that painting in your attic? I'll give you a good price.

Ha! At some point I'm going to pay for it. There will be

payback.

Does that make Rebus's suffering your atonement?

Maybe it does. He's certainly grown. He became much bigger than I ever intended him to be to the extent that he seems more real to people than I am. People go on Rebus walking tours. People get worried about his smoking and his drinking, female fans would like him to settle down … and they're the very woman to help him. I hate to say it but he's just ink on paper, which they always find absolutely shocking. He doesn't actually exist. Of course he does for them because they've lived with him for twenty years and seventeen books, and when you read about him he is real. It's a funny thing.

The other thing they always say is, 'Oh, I expected you to be more like him.' It's like you can't write about this stuff unless you are Rebus. So in the early days it was, 'I thought you'd be a lot older.' There was one Canadian woman who came into the Oxford Bar and refused to believe that I was the author of the Rebus novels. She thought that they were winding her up and I had to produce my driving license to try and prove to her that I was Ian Rankin. I just didn't look like she imagined the author of these books.

How do you feel about such expectations?

This thing that you're supposed to look like your character is a bit weird. I don't know many crime writers who've lived the life that they write about. Not many of them have been cops and certainly not many of them have been criminals.

So where does Rebus come from?

I don't know where he comes from. Maybe there is that Rebus way of looking at the world somewhere inside my head, but mostly they're his opinions, not my opinions. I just think, 'He's a guy from a certain class, a certain background. He's got a chip on his shoulder. He's a certain age. He's got certain politics. Okay, what is his worldview? What's he like?' I think he's structurally very different from me. We were born in the same place, went to the same school, and that's about it.

At the age of about fourteen or fifteen our lives went in very different directions. I got very interested in literature, and he got very interested in leaving school and getting a job in the army. We've gone off in hugely different directions.

Folk say, 'He must be the Mr Hyde part of your personality or the man of action that you wish you had been.' No, he's just his own person. He's very separate from me, very different from me, and he's not like anybody that I know. I didn't know any cops when I started writing the books and none of my friends are like him.

Have you got a file on him to make sure you don't rewrite his past?

A guy did one for me once because somebody asked me a question about one of the books and I said, 'I can't remember that scene, I don't remember why I wrote that, and I can't answer your question.' Afterwards this guy said, 'What you need is a database of your characters.' And he did one for me. It was great, because I'd never done it. I've cocked up Rebus's background, or was it Cafferty's? I've got Cafferty going to two different schools in two different cities when he was a kid depending on which book you read. He grew up in Glasgow in one book. In the other book he grew up in Edinburgh.

And he lives here?

Oh, he lives in this house, yeah. This is Cafferty's living room and Rebus comes in and looks at all the art on the walls, yeah.

Does he share your taste?

Pretty much. I think his taste is a bit more abstract than mine but yeah, this is essentially his house. That's another weird thing: the hero lives across the road from the flat I lived in when I was a student. I live in the house that the villain lives in. Maybe that's this thing about getting success without having earned it. I feel a bit criminal about it all. One woman came up to me in the supermarket and said, 'I don't like it that Cafferty lives in my street.' Fucking funny. He's just ink.

He doesn't exist!

Let's talk about the part of your work that is actually 'just ink'. How do you write?

Ha! Well, it doesn't matter how fat the book is, the first draft tends to take me about eight weeks to write and that's substantially it. They come out about 350 pages. Five-day weeks, eight pages a day – that's nothing! I don't do the word count thing. Good day fifteen pages, bad day four pages. It's between six and eight weeks for a first draft.

Do you then let it sit for a while?

Yeah, I let it sit because the thing about making it up as you go along is you then need to go back and change stuff. That's why nobody sees the first draft. It's almost unreadable because of these big chunks that are just notes to me for the second draft which cleans all that up and makes sure that the prose actually works. That's where Miranda will say things like, 'Well, I think he should be the good guy.' The third draft would probably be what goes to my editor and my agent.

How does your narrative timeframe take shape?

When I'm writing the first draft of a book I don't keep any account of how much time is passing. In the second draft I break it up into days. Rebus always seemed to wrap up a case in about eight or ten days. You've got to be conscious that days are passing. Eventually you're going to hit a Sunday and your cop is probably not working on a Sunday. But I do that after the fact. I quite like this linear chronology and things to be wrapped up fairly quickly. It doesn't work like that in real life, of course. A case can take months if not years, but it's hard to keep a reader interested. It's much better just to have it happen in a short time even if that isn't very realistic.

Speaking of time management, what do you do between writing and hearing from your editors?

Walk away. Forget about it. Once it's down on paper that's it. It's gone. Then it comes back and you go, 'What? You want me to make him a woman?' The nice thing about putting it out of your head for a few weeks is that when you go back you're seeing it through a reader's eyes. You start to see the mistakes. But I don't like the mechanistic thing. That's partly why I don't like writing for television and film. They've all been to writing classes and they know about the arc of the narrative and this and that. 'The main character must go on a journey and must change.' Okay, that may be what happens in all my books but I don't want to think about it like that. I want to write something that I would enjoy reading and that nobody's written yet.

Talking about crossing literary barriers, Lee Child recently said that Ian McEwan would write crime novels if only he could. Do you agree?

Oh, yeah! I accused Ian McEwan of that. I gave him the James Tait Black Memorial Prize a few years ago and I accused him on stage of being a thriller writer manqué. Ian McEwan was thrilled at the idea. But then Martin Amis had a go as well. He wrote a crime novel about a female detective. Wasn't his best book. And Julian Barnes used to write private eye novels under a pseudonym. It does seem to me that the barriers are breaking down between literature and genre fiction. It's taken a wee while but it is happening.

What do you make of the divisive claim that 'hell will freeze over before a crime novel makes it onto the Booker shortlist?'

Miss Smilla's Feeling for Snow got on a lot of literature shortlists although it's very much a crime story. Everybody said, 'It's transcended the genre.' Well, how does that work? What does it mean to transcend a genre? I have no idea what that means but that's what they say when Thomas Pynchon and Martin Amis do it: 'They're bringing a literary sensibility to it.'

They also seem to avoid series. What attracted you to writing seventeen novels about one character?

The attraction of doing a series for me was that notion that you get the span of the central character's life. Rebus's perceptions of life have been altered by the job. No doubt about it and I quite like that. I like the fact that he's organic. You can't do that job and not be changed by it.

Is John Rebus the Scottish Harry Bosch?

They've got similarities. They've both been in the army before they became detectives. They are both always on the verge of getting kicked out of the police. They tend to be on their own a lot of the time. Yeah, there definitely are similarities, but not consciously. I never sat down and swapped notes with Michael Connelly. I mean, Rebus isn't alone in the annals of crime fiction. There are a lot of characters who are a bit like him.

Would you say he's realistic?

A previous Chief Constable said that he wished he had one cop like Rebus in real life because he's driven. Give him a job to do and that's him. He's focused on nothing except solving that problem, answering the questions, finding the answers. So although he is temperamental, doesn't obey the rules, is anti-authoritarian and all the rest of it, the Chief Constable was wanting somebody like that. He's realistic to the extent that the police would allow that kind of person to have a little bit of leeway but there's only room for one like that on any police force: one maverick.

But he really works much more like an American private eye than like a real-life British police officer. Taking stuff home with him, spreading it out over the dining room table – cops don't tend to do that in real life. Their home life is their sanctuary. But everywhere I go in the world somebody will come to get a book signed and say, 'I'm a cop and there's a guy like him in our police station.' Obviously these mavericks do exist. It's just that I didn't know any of them when I started writing the series.

What makes that perseverance of his so admirable?

On a very basic level we want the cops to be the good guys and we want them to be good at what they do: to be thorough.

Doesn't often happen. There are loads of police investigations that fuck up because of laziness or incompetence or stupidity. Rebus screws up occasionally but he's always got the best of intentions. He always wants to get to the truth.

Do good intentions justify a breach of procedure?

Not always. He's a professional voyeur and investigating other people's lives is a way of him deferring investigating his own life. He gets to ask other people questions and look at other people's lives for a short space of time – very much like the novelist. The detective and the novelist are very similar creatures. Rebus does all of that as a way of not looking at his own life and seeing what a fuck-up it's been: bad father, bad husband, antisocial human being. 'Maverick' is a kind way of putting it. He's fucked up in his head. That makes him a terrible human being, maybe, but a good detective. 24/7 he's thinking about the case and doing something about it.

You said earlier that the detective is a 'prism through which you can show all the different aspects of human life.' How important are Edinburgh and its society to your writing?

Edinburgh seems to me to be this incredibly stratified city, which is absolutely fascinating and why I enjoy writing about it. Edinburgh is still a place of gentlemen's clubs and club ties and people who read the *Daily Telegraph* and huge wealth, the headquarters of the Royal Bank of Scotland, institutions like the Law and the Church... There's not another city in Scotland with so many private schools. Edinburgh's got that sense that there are two cities here: the city of the haves and the city of the have-nots. This notion that Stevenson had that each human being has the potential to do good and the potential to do evil, which is what crime fiction is mostly about, that's there structurally in the city, which makes it a great place to set crime fiction in.

I think Glasgow, per capita, has got seven times the murder rate of Edinburgh. You'd think Glasgow should be a much more interesting place for crime writers to work in, but apparently not. Most of them seem to be bloody living here and writing about Edinburgh. I wish they'd all go away and write about somewhere else.

Like you did by taking Rebus from Fife to Edinburgh?

Yeah! It means we can look at the place with a dispassionate outsider's eye. I still don't know what makes Edinburgh tick. That's why I keep writing about the place. And partly I keep writing about it because it keeps changing.

Does it only seem that way in hindsight or did you set yourself the historian's task of writing the chronicles of Edinburgh?

Probably halfway through the series I got the notion that each book is a piece of the jigsaw and at the end of the series what you'll have is a complete jigsaw of the way Edinburgh was at the end of the twentieth and the beginning of the twenty-first century. It's a useful microcosm for shit that's happening. I write a book about asylum seekers in Edinburgh and then I go on tour in Australia and they say, 'We've got the same problem.' Turns out that something you thought was intrinsic to Edinburgh is actually more universal, but I didn't think, 'What's going to help me sell books in Australia or Canada or South Africa? Maybe I'll write about this subject.' I don't think like that.

How do you think?

I just find a question I want to answer – a theme I want to explore – and I say, 'What kind of book will allow me to do that?' Up till now it's been the crime novel. You shouldn't think about the market. A lot of writers do, but I don't allow myself to think, 'Will my Dutch translator know how to translate this joke? Is this cultural reference going to mean anything to people?'

I'm writing for myself and for a Scottish audience first of all, and if everybody else gets it – fine. If they don't get it – tough. Even when I was living in France I was kind of living in Edinburgh in my head and the city was the main character of the books because the city drove everything. It drove the plot and it drove Rebus's impressions. The city made the crime happen. And then that changes Rebus's impression of the place he lives in.

I was afraid I was going to scare people off. In fact, that was my secret plan: stop people from coming to Edinburgh. It didn't seem to work that way. People would say, 'Oh my God, you paint such a terrible portrait of Edinburgh. You just make it all crime.' Well, that does happen. There is crime here but the body count in the books is fairly low because there really aren't that many murders in Edinburgh in any one year.

Is it fair to describe your work as more than entertainment – as an archaeological dig into the present?

Yeah. I think the books become more political as they go on because I became more political. I think part of that was having kids and thinking, 'What kind of world are you leaving behind for your kids? Who changes the world?' Politicians change the world. They're the ones who can change the law and make the world a better place. Writers can't do it, but what writers can do is point the way: 'This is what you should be looking at.' So yeah, I became more political, the books became more political but I don't think Rebus became more political. I get the sense that he's an anarchist. He's the kind of guy who's more likely to give a small-time crook an even break than a financier who's bent the law or taken a bribe. These people have got a choice. Sometimes if you're a small-time crook you've not got much choice in your life.

Does that also account for the dark humour and drink issues in your books?

Well, cops have got a very dark sense of humour. I know that. I've met lots of them. It's a defence mechanism. It's a way of dealing with the job. I mean, I've been told very funny stories about Lockerbie, which wouldn't be funny to ninety-nine percent of the people you told them to. In context they're funny, and cops laugh about it because otherwise they'd be screaming about it. It's like humour in Shakespeare. You've got something like *Hamlet* and then suddenly you've got the grave-digger scene. You need that bit of release of tension just before the end – maybe just to remind you that the world is not as dark as it seems.

As for the drinking, a lot of cops I met early in my writing career had drink problems. Like the sense of humour, they drank as a way of dealing with the job. This is one of the problems of being a cop. You can't really take the job home with you. You can't sit at the dinner table and let off steam by saying, 'Oh, the horrible rape case today,' while your kids are sitting there eating their dinner. The only people you can talk to about it are other cops –

– in the pub confessional?

Yeah! You let off some steam in the pub. The only people you talk to are other cops. By extension they become your family. They're the people you're confiding in, and you get more distanced from your real family because there's stuff you can't say to them. Then you end up with a relationship breakdown. It's a cliché because it's true. Maybe not so much these days but the officers who were at Lockerbie didn't get any counselling when they came back. They just got back to doing the job having picked up body parts from fields all over southwest Scotland. I think that explains some of the drink issues and also why there's some humour in the books.

Cut to the present and teetotal Fox.

Yeah, Fox is a non-drinker. But that was partly me just trying to make sure that there was enough distance between him and Rebus so that folk couldn't see him as just 'Rebus-light'. He couldn't go to the Oxford Bar. He couldn't be a drinker. He couldn't listen to rock music …

It sounds like you're not particularly delighted with that.

Yeah! I was pissed off at that. In fact, somebody said to me when they read the book, 'Well, you should have made him a musician.' I thought, 'Fuck! I should have gone exactly the other way so I could still have talked about music in the books.' – The things you have to think about when you're writing a series.

Is there anything else you wish you'd known when you started your writing career?

That it was all going to turn out all right. So many days and nights of fretting and panicking and fearing I was about to be consigned to the publishing dustbin...

Stuart MacBride
Laughing in the Dark

Stuart MacBride was born in Dumbarton. At age nine Stuart took the only way out for a man. He ran away and joined the circus, soon to become a bear-wrestler representing Great Britain at the Atlanta Olympics. After retiring from the life athletic, he won the Nobel Peace Prize in 1975 for his revolutionary work on Irn-Bru, but upon recruitment to the secret intelligence service in 1989 he was invalided out after sustaining a back injury while performing a reverse-over-head-pile-driver on a grizzly, which has left him confined to his pyjamas and writing crime novels set in Aberdeen ... or so he would have you believe.

Stuart enjoys lying to journalists. That is to say, he is a born storyteller, which may or may not have a great deal to do with being born in Dumbarton, raised in Aberdeen, and schooled at Heriot Watt University in Edinburgh. If you ask him, it has everything to do with the lying. Having studied enough architecture to deem the discipline unfit to construct his life's design, Stuart embarked on a vocational journey from scrubbing toilets offshore to scraping the barrel, metaphorically speaking. The graphic designer became a web designer, a programmer, a professional actor, and, at his arguably lowest point, a project manager for a sizeable IT conglomerate.

His recovery is a matter of record. Stuart wrote his debut crime novel *Cold Granite*, introducing an international audience to a darker side of Aberdeen and DS Logan MacRae. Not only did this first outing in a bestselling series secure him a publishing contract in 2006, but Stuart also won the Barry Award for Best First Novel along with a CWA Dagger in the Library Award in 2007. The following year he received the ITV3 Crime Thriller Award for Breakthrough Author of the Year for *Broken Skin*. After considerable commercial and critical success, the initial three-book deal was first extended to six, and in 2009 Stuart signed on for at least another two instalments in the Logan MacRae series.

Peer reviews now seem to be vying with one another for the highest praise of Stuart's work. According to Reginald Hill, 'If you're looking for taut narrative, gut-churning incident, strong characterisation, all shot through with savagely dark humour, then look no further.' Adding his personal note to a long list of unreserved endorsements, Simon Kernick tells the worst-kept secret in contemporary crime fiction: 'Hard-hitting prose with a bone-dry humour and characters you can genuinely believe in, Stuart MacBride's Logan McRae series of novels are a real treat.'

Such a man of many reputations, some based in fiction, the rest based in bestselling fiction, might be forgiven for the odd eccentricity – like pretending to be a passionate potato-grower, making his wife Fiona live in Aberdeen, and calling his cat Grendel. And yet in spite of rumours and the discomfort of meeting in an Edinburgh café for the following interview, Stuart was not wearing pyjamas. He wasn't even wearing an attitude, and so hours would go by before the obvious became just that: no one has told Stuart of his success ... or so he would have you believe.

~

Having been heralded as 'the next Ian Rankin', can you explain why most reviewers prefer hyperbolic rants to reading recommendations?

It's because they're going through exactly the same process

as writers are. It's all about selling the review to a paper, so you can't write a review that says, 'This is actually quite a good book. It's maybe not as good as the last one but, on balance, it's very well constructed, the dialogue is good, so, yeah, give it a go.' Newspapers don't want those reviews. They want, 'This is the best thing since sliced monkeys!' or 'This is a steaming sack of shit!' If a reviewer wants to sell a review, *that's* the kind of review they have to write. So a book either doesn't get reviewed, it's trashed or it's lauded. Possibly slightly controversial? I don't know. Also, there are some fairly awful books out there.

Which seem to stain more than the offending author's reputation, but does general popularity warrant critical attention?

I come from a slightly different point of view. I'm becoming more convinced, the older I get, that there shouldn't be such a thing as genre separation in any way, shape or form. The only difference between a romance novel and a crime novel is the structure. All good novels are about people and their infractions and relationships, and crime is a very good way to explore that kind of stuff. The books I really like are the books where it's the people that come through. I don't want to read about a bank heist – I don't give a toss about a bank heist. I want to read about the people doing the bank heist. The whole idea that because it's crime the people involved are somehow less worthy to read about … well, it's not a very intelligent argument, is it?

John Banville / Benjamin Black … Enough said, or do you want me to go on?

Ha! No, no, no. Go on. I want to hear the whole question.

John Banville was doing a reading to several hundred crime fiction readers when he said that he only writes about two hundred words a day, while he knocks out an easy two thousand as Benjamin Black. Unfortunately, the impression the audience got was that he's slumming it in their favourite genre.

40

'How to judge your audience' 101.

Well, the point would seem to be that there is a difference between artistry and artisanship. What are your thoughts on that?

To be honest, I've never read his crime writing, or his non-crime writing. I find it quite difficult to separate the person from the work. And the whole 'I'm slumming it in crime fiction' attitude doesn't incline me to try his books. So I haven't read anything he's written and don't intend to – there are too many good books out there to waste time on this kind of stuff.

What I'm wondering is whether one can afford the attitude when the sales start picking up?

I don't know if you can ever afford to be arrogant about your books or your readers, because it's far too easy for people to say, 'No, I think you're a prick and I'm not going to read or buy any of your books.' Your publishers are not going to be very happy with that at all. But a bigger question for me would be: why does he feel that you can't bring poetry to crime fiction?

Surely the whole exercise is exactly the same. You're trying to put the best story and the best experience for the reader on paper. How much of a dick would you have to be to say, 'Well, I'm not going to bother, I can't be arsed, I don't care enough about my craft – or the people who're going to read the book – to bother putting in the effort, on the assumption that crime fiction is just a load of shit anyway.'

Not to disagree with you, but I'd rather –

– be diplomatic?

– bring this round to you. So my answer would have to be: perhaps John Banville is not so much concerned with the limitations of the genre as with the preconceptions of his audience, much like James Patterson and his writing firm. How different is your attitude to writing?

A lot of people seem to think that literature is a five-star restaurant and crime fiction is a burger van – that there's a difference in quality and the value of A versus B. But let's run with the analogy: if you're running a burger van, don't you want to make the best burgers you possibly can? And people that come expecting a burger will go away thinking, 'Fuck me! That was the best burger I have ever had in my *life*.' Or you can go down to Costco and buy a box of frozen mechanically recovered filth, slap it on the griddle and chuck it out. And that's what he's is doing. He's putting no effort at all into his crime fiction because he doesn't think he has to. I don't think that has anything to do with the preconceptions of the reader but his preconceptions of the reader.

So you're criticising his reinforcement of low expectations?

Yeah. He says he doesn't have to put the work in so he's not bothered. Or he could pull his socks up and actually do some work and write a decent crime novel. If he looks at crime novels and thinks, 'These are all shit.' – Fine, step up to the bloody mark.

But since marketability trumps quality and reviews are mostly ignored, aren't you tempted to churn out less accomplished work when many readers aren't deterred by dropping standards?

Well, it's back to the burger van analogy. I'm never happy with anything I write. And most of the writers that I like – both as people and as writers – are never happy with what they write, are always trying to do better, are always trying to improve because they really care about the work that they produce.

How much do you edit your writing?

I only go through two drafts because of the way my first book was contracted under HarperCollins. I'd just finished my first draft of *Cold Granite* when they saw it and said, 'Yeah, we really like this.' Then we had some editorial discussions, I delivered the second draft, we did the copy edit, the line edit and went through it. But the second draft was a vast rewrite.

I've heard that if you draw a single, unbroken straight line with a red biro, it'll stretch for one mile. I go through two of those every single time I do an edit: Two miles worth of changes. I don't just fiddle about with a couple of bits in the book; it's every single sentence, every single word, everything. I spend a phenomenal amount of time agonising over how everything hangs together, because I really believe it matters. And even when we get up to the point where the proofs come back from the typesetters, when traditionally – from what I've been told by various editors – many authors don't like to even look at it and just say, 'Ah yeah, that's fine,' I go through it and make changes to sentence structure, metaphors ... all the way through the process right up to the very last minute when they say, 'Right, that's it. That has to go to the printer now. Stop fucking about.'

What's it like to read your own work?

I've read the last two books for the audio editions unabridged and I found it an absolutely cringe-worthy experience. It's a very different process to going through a novel. You've got somebody on the other side of a pane of glass going, 'No, you're to be word-perfect on this,' and I'm going through it thinking, 'That is the most awful sentence I have read in my life.' I mark up the page as I'm reading through it, so I can change it for the paperback. I am that obsessive. I don't want any of the books to be a struggle for anyone to read.

I can't abide sentences that I have to read two or three times to figure out what the hell is being said. There has to be a balance of imagery, motion and clarity. If you have all this beautiful poetry in your prose and no-one can understand what the fuck is going on it's a badly written sentence and it has to be rewritten.

Shouldn't that clarity be guaranteed in good crime fiction?

I think it has to be to be successful. This is a realisation from the last two months. When I was up in Orkney doing some events with Allan Guthrie we were having a talk about the obvious difference between people who put a lot of effort into their fiction and people who just appear to have a loose grasp of what makes a sentence work and who, in some cases, write things that would make me want to gouge my eyes out if I'd written them. And it does seem to be the 'big idea' that makes bestsellers. It's not necessarily the technical quality of the prose that does it.

Take *The Da Vinci Code* as an example. I know it's very fashionable to knock Dan Brown, but the fact is: it was a worldwide bestseller. And it was a worldwide bestseller because people loved the story. The writing itself could have done with a serious edit and it could have been a much better book because of it. But I don't think you can say that Dan Brown is a dreadful writer because he's written a book that millions and millions of people around the world have loved. It's because it has that 'big idea' that people have hooked onto it and have really felt attached.

Yes, we can go through it and say the opening sequence is meant to be this breakneck dash across Paris, and, instead of getting a sense of speed and pace and pressure and anxiety, what we get is a lecture on how far it is, and how many panes of glass there are in the pyramid outside the Louvre, and who commissioned the pyramid, and who designed it, and the controversy, and how many miles of corridor there are, and all these bits and bobs, and that's not a breakneck rush – that's a history lesson. So I can wholeheartedly support that it could have been a great book – with a decent edit – because it obviously has the 'big idea' that has connected with people.

Does that mean technical finesse isn't appreciated enough to make it worth the effort?

One of the great things about books is that they can never have an objective value. You can never say that book A is good and book B is bad because to different people it might be the other way round. It has no intrinsic value until it's read by a reader. And yes, if you do your job well, no one's going to notice the technical stuff, they're just going to be swept along in the story. I think you've just got to write the best book that you can. Don't settle for crap: make the three-Michelin-star burger, even if it offends some people.

Does that extend to your use of dialect?

I like some dialect: as long as it's understandable, as long as you can pick up the meaning from the context. Have you ever tried to read *Trainspotting*?

'Tried' is the right word.

It's not easy, is it? Probably even for people who grew up in Leith. It's actually really difficult. It's that balance again – can someone understand that sentence or are they going to go, 'What the bastarding hell am I reading about?'

But aren't there readers who get their kicks from what frustrates most others – Joycean scholars, for instance?

I can only speak from personal experience. Those aren't the books I read. I don't want to write for academia. I want to write for people. I want to tell stories that will grab people – a story that will wrap them, and cocoon them, and absorb them all the way through to the very last word. I know that sounds really, really simple but it's not a very intellectual process for me. I do a lot of work when I write the books but I don't sit and think, 'Will this appeal to this or that demographic?' Most of the time, nowadays, I sit down and think, 'What haven't I done yet?'

I always wanted to make the books as realistic as possible. Well, obviously there are huge chunks that are incredibly fantastical for what's possible in real life, but there would always be this pressure on the police that there wouldn't just be one case for them to concentrate on – there would be lots and *lots* of cases. So I'm actually getting to the point now, in book seven, that I'm thinking, 'What crimes haven't we done yet?', and that's the big driver for me now. It's about, 'What the hell am I going to do next? How do I avoid repeating myself?'

Are you ever tempted to have Logan act contrary to readers' expectations?

I hope Logan never acts out of character. As I said: I'm trying to be as realistic as I can within the kind of story that I'm writing. So Logan has been getting progressively worse over the books because you can't go through the kind of stuff that he's gone through and still come out at the end of it exactly the same person as you were when you went in. So I'm now in the situation where I have to try and fix him otherwise the series will have to end because he'll end up either killing himself or someone else, or he's going to end up in a mental institution.

Your debut was unusual in that sense. Does it indicate your way of dealing with trauma?

When I started the first novel I didn't want it to read like the first novel of a series. I wanted it to read as if it had appeared in the middle of a series. I loathe backstory in all its myriad forms. Come on, there's nothing worse than getting to page six of a novel where you get three pages recapping what has just happened, usually in dialogue: 'Oh, John, do you remember the time when your brother became a serial killer?' – 'Hmm, I do remember that, indeed.' – 'And your wife, she was having an affair with him, wasn't she?' Hate that. I absolutely hate that.

So when I started the series I made a conscious effort that it was going to be like we'd come into the middle of a series, and a load of things had happened in the past, and all the characters know about them – because obviously they've lived through them – so they don't discuss those events unless it's relevant to what's happening. Logan starts out completely scarred before we've begun, because of a case he dealt with before the first book opens, where he was stabbed lots of times, and it doesn't really tell you much about what happened or where it happened or why it happened or any of the facts.

Have readers asked for a few answers to all those open questions about Logan?

I got an email just yesterday saying, 'Oh, I think you should write the prequel. I would really like to know what happened.' I don't want to write the prequel. I have no intention of writing the prequel. I have dropped hints throughout all of the books. I mean, we even meet the guy who stabbed Logan in *Flesh House*. He makes a brief appearance where he's trying to do a Hannibal Lecter impersonation and Logan calls him on it and it all falls apart.

I only did that because at that part of the story I thought: 'What would really screw with the investigation and put a horrible amount of pressure on Logan?' And so you get a tiny snippet of his history with the guy who stabbed him. Over the course of four books there's just enough information to piece together maybe what had happened. But unless it's relevant to the story that I'm writing at the time I won't be giving away any more details. For example, I've got a big character in the first four books called DI Inch, and it wasn't until the fourth book that I needed to use his first name. Up until that point I didn't know what his first name was.

Did he tell you?

Yeah, it's David.

Is that you being witty – giving him the name David when he's clearly more of a Goliath?

Ha! I also quite liked the fact that he would then be DI D.I. But of course nobody picked up on that so in the current book (*Dark Blood*) I have Detective Inspector Duncan Ingram who runs the Sex Offender Management Unit, and the people who work for him are often referred to as 'didi-men' but it's never explained why they're called 'didi-men' – it's because he's DI D.I. If readers pick up on that then great, but chances are no one ever will.

A lot of your writing would seem to be similarly tongue-in-cheek. Is it fair to read Flesh House *as a tribute to Stephen King?*

Stephen King and James Herbert and all the crime / horror

writers that I used to read when I was eleven, twelve, thirteen.

Was setting it around Halloween a hint?

Yep, and nobody ever picked up on that. In fact, even my agent didn't pick up on that until two months ago when I told him.

It seems like quite a common trend amongst Scottish crime writers, and you certainly seem to enjoy the odd reference to literary history and pop culture, don't you?

Most of the time nobody notices. For instance, the comedian Victoria Wood did this series called 'Dinner Ladies' which my wife and I absolutely love. It's so cleverly done. The characters are great, it's all very well observed and the dialogue is superb, but it's not what you would call the sort of thing that dark, Noir-style crime writers are meant to enjoy. So in one of my books there is a huge homage to Victoria Wood running through the book even to the point that there's one character whose son has run off with a marine biologist called Marcus. I always assume that someone out there would say, 'Ah, I know what that is. That's homage to Victoria Wood.' Well, no one has ever spotted it, and this is the first time I've ever told anyone that they're in there. So, I think, really, we just dick around a lot.

And yet you've said of yourself that you're appalled by real-life violence –

– Yes.

So is your dark sense of humour a way of dealing with violence in fiction?

Well, I'm trying to be true to the actual characters who are in it. This is a very immediate example:

I did a presentation at the Edinburgh Science Festival with two forensic specialists. One was the leading forensic scientist in the UK, and the other headed up evidence labs where he looked at lots and lots of murder cases. Our pathologist had dropped out – he was called away to an actual case so he couldn't make the presentation – so we slipped something in at the last minute we'd never done before to fill in his bit. As part of it I read out an actual transcript of a 999 call. The audience wet themselves with laughter all the way through it, because it was ridiculous. I know that sounds bizarre. Basically, it's a guy who's gone to buy drugs. He's gone into this flat and discovered that his friend and a random stranger have died in a fire. As far as he's aware someone has killed them and set them on fire –

– *déjà-vu?*

It's weird just how much stuff you make up and then comes incredibly close to the truth.

But that's the situation. It's this horrible thing; he discovers that his friend is dead along with somebody else. But the transcript of the 999 call, when read out, is funny. It's ridiculous, and if you can separate it from the *context* people do find it funny, and that's what I think a lot of the professionals who work in the police and forensic sciences have to do – they have to make that separation. They will laugh at incredibly dark things, because that's the only way that they can get through life. I mean, imagine you're a pathologist and every day your job is to deal with human misery and suffering and death and the most horribly violent acts that people can inflict upon one another. If you can't distance yourself from that with humour, how on earth are you going to cope?

So the whole point of the humour in the books is that it's a coping mechanism for the characters. It's not that I want to write a comedy crime novel. Apart from anything else, they're a really tough sell for publishers. The humour comes from the characters dealing with what they have to deal with. Does that make any sense?

If you're saying that you accord your sense of humour to a group rather than a single comic voice, yes.

Well, they're books based on teamwork. Logan is not a lone wolf.

Is he not named after Wolverine?

Logan's actually named after my nephew who's named after Wolverine. My brother denies it to his wife but he's always been a huge *X-Men* fan so we know for certain that that's why Logan is called Logan. And I named the character after him, because he's my nephew. So it's true, it's just one step removed.

On the strength of that evidence one would have to assume that you share a similar world-view.

We both have beards.

Case closed. You're essentially the same person.

Except I'm slightly older and much prettier. So, as you were saying, Wolverine is this big, lone hero and Logan has never been a hero. He's not a heroic character.

Is that his tragic streak – his name is larger than his nature?

Hmm, I've never given it that much thought. It was more the fact that I wanted him to be an everyday character. His nickname is Lazarus because he died on the operating table, which isn't really a badge of honour for a police officer. 'You've been so good at your job that you died.'

He did come back, though, didn't he?

Yes, and he pretty much regrets it all the way through. But yeah, he was never meant to be this big, heroic character. He was meant to be a normal guy doing the best he could in a challenging job.

Is he a local?

I don't know. I've never said. I've never even described him.

But he's rather attractive to a certain type, isn't he?

Damaged women.

And just like that you've made my next question imply an insult. Well… How much of your wife is in the female characters?

Ha! Very little actually.

Good for you. But how much of yourself is in Logan?

Not a vast amount. We share a key characteristic which is that we're both incredibly loyal to the point of it being a character flaw. He is often loyal to the wrong people and he knows he is but he can't really help it; he's picked his side so he has to stick with it.

You don't give away much, do you?

That's the thing: Unless it's relevant to the story I'm telling, I don't make stuff up about him. I don't know where he went to school … I'm not being secretive, I genuinely don't know.

Do you keep a file on your characters to make sure you keep getting them right?

Well, when I write I keep a little document and every time I introduce a character it has their name on one side and how I've described them on the other, but I don't have a big dossier on Logan, no. I actually know more about the characters in each book that *aren't* part of the core cast than I do about Logan. So in the one I'm writing at the moment, for example, I know loads of things about the victim, much more than I know about Logan, because I don't need to tell the reader. Unless it's relevant to the story it's not a detail that has to be included in the book.

So your point of view is the same as Logan's?

Sometimes it's mixed third person, but it's becoming extremely close, and my goal is to get to the point where you can almost just swap the pronouns, and then it should be as close to writing first person as possible in a third person structure.

Are you going to write one of the next books in the first person then?

I've thought about this as a technical exercise. I have a very good friend called Allan Guthrie who writes really, really, really good novels. He spends a hell of a lot of time working on language. We very much share common values when it comes to writing. It's through talking to, and arguing with, him that I have formed my core beliefs of what novels should be going towards, and the books have been changing as I've been writing them to come closer to that ideal.

I am beginning to wonder if it wouldn't be easier for me to write the next novel in first person and then go through it afterwards and change every 'I' to 'he'. I wrote a novella a couple of years ago, called *Sawbones*, for a little publisher called Barrington Stoke, and it's designed for reluctant readers – adults who have had bad experiences with reading in the past – to get them back into it. It's a very adult book but it's written to be accessible to somebody with the reading age of eight, which apparently is half the squaddies in the British Army. The same is true of the people in our prisons. It's appalling that we're failing people to that extent. So the idea is that these books will encourage people who want to get back into reading but can't find any adult books that are accessible for them.

So I wrote all of that book – sorry, this is all very meandering – from the first person perspective. Normally my books will take me twelve to fourteen months to get through from starting the first draft to getting it off to the printers. A first draft will take something like four and a half months. With *Flesh House*, for example, the edit took me eight months, because there was such a huge amount I wasn't happy with. That's what I was talking about before: I usually do two drafts but it's not a quick spit-and-polish on the second draft – it's a major sodding about with absolutely every sentence and every word getting fiddled with ... *Sawbones* took me two weeks to write. I did my rewrite in two days.

How long is it?

18,500 words.

And the average length of your novels is?

It varies between 120,000 and 157,000. I think that's the longest one: *Blind Eye*. But *Sawbones* was quick, I enjoyed it from start to finish, it was fun, it flowed ... I'd been across to Iowa to visit some friends and they'd bought me a 'Star 102.5 Sounds of the Seventies' tie-dye swirly T-Shirt, and I'd put on my soybean baseball cap and write this thing, listening to American rock music, because the book's set in America. It was so much easier to write that I am beginning to wonder… Also, *Sawbones* was present tense, which makes a huge difference to speed. It's all very immediate, very action-driven. I loved it. It's my favourite of all the books, which is why I get all excited talking about it.

If writing to you means you immerse yourself in your subject matter, how does the cultural context come into your work when you write stories set in Aberdeen?

Well, I'm sort of surrounded by that so I don't have to immerse myself in it. The thing I'm most conscious of is that I'm slowly trying to build up the amount of Doric in the books. That's the local dialect in Aberdeen and it's very distinctive but I've shied away from doing too much of it because I don't want to get into that position where people get to the end of a sentence or paragraph and think, 'I have no idea what the hell has just gone on.'

In the one that's just coming out, for example, there's a small part where a serial rapist is being interviewed, and one of the characters says, 'How are you doing today, Richard?' He answers her, and then someone else comes in and asks the same question, only he says, 'Fit like 'i day?'

And how is that the same question?

In Aberdeen 'fit' and 'what' and 'how' are interchangeable. Well, it also means 'feet'. So if you have a shoe you can legitimately ask someone, 'Fit fit does this fit?' It's trying to get some of the flavour of the language in while still saying: this is exactly the same question as the first person asked, so you should be able to tell what it means.

So you're educating your readers in Doric?

Well, hopefully being slightly more honest to the characters but trying not to alienate the reader at the same time… There are Doric dictionaries online, you know. I didn't make this stuff up – it does exist.

Do other Aberdonian authors popularise the local culture

as much as you do?

There was Grassic Gibbon who wrote *Sunset Song* and *Grey Granite*, and they were set around that area. The only other author I know who lives around Aberdeen is Bill Kirton who wrote *Material Evidence* and who I used to do emergency role-play with.

Ha! Of course you did. Research for Broken Skin, *was it?*

He's an actor! And I had a small period of time dabbling in the acting field. I remember being quite impressed that I had met a real writer.

Which brings us back to my previous question.

There was a question?

Well, you might call it innuendo. Speaking of which, Allan Guthrie said, 'The success of Scottish crime writing is due to McIlvanney making it sexy, and then Val McDermid and Ian Rankin continuing to keep it that way. Sexy equals internationally marketable.'

He's a very clever fish, isn't he?

No doubt about that. What I'd like to know is whether you consider the strong sense of place and accent particularly sexy?

Well, they don't imply tumescence to me, but, you know, each to their own.

Ah, who's being diplomatic now?

Thank you. Well, you see, it's not sexy everywhere. Certainly not in America. But Germany is a big consumer of Scottish crime fiction. They get it, I think.

Do they get Allan?

They just don't know him as we do. They've never seen him in his pants.

So he says. But might there be another reason? Are all Scottish crime writers expected to write like Ian Rankin now that he's exported a particular Scottishness?

God bless him.

Ever the diplomat. In other words, what's it like to be marketed as 'Tartan Noir'?

Tartan Noir doesn't exist. It's a very convenient umbrella under which to promote crime fiction that is written in Scotland. It's another 'God bless' – this time James Ellroy for coming up with it. Scottish crime fiction is incredibly varied. You can't look at it and say it's all of a 'type', because it's not. It's all over the genre. It's a huge spread from very gritty hardboiled stuff like Ray Banks and Allan Guthrie to much gentler styles of crime writing like Alexander McCall Smith and Aline Templeton. You can't pick up a 'Tartan Noir novel' and expect to get the same thing every time. They are just going to be incredibly different. But it's a wonderful marketing tool to sell the books outside Scotland.

Do you see any common denominator?

Well, there are some key parts of the Scottish psyche... They're not universal, by any means, but there's quite a black sense of humour that runs through a lot of Scottish life – possibly to do with the weather. We have an extremely healthy disrespect for authority, which probably comes down to our political nationhood over the past forty or a hundred years, possible longer. We are incredibly 'thrawn' as a culture. It's a Scottish word that means if you tell us to do something we will do exactly the opposite, given the opportunity. That is how we are.

An excellent example of that is every time England gets into the world cup or the Rugby final or whatever, there's this big thing where we're all told by the BBC that the entire nation is behind England and we all have to support them and how great England's chances are... And because we're all thrawn in Scotland, we go, 'Who are they playing against? Brazil? Ah, we *like* Brazil.' We just don't like to be told what to do. We like to push back. I think that comes out a lot in the kind of crime fiction that I could identify easily as Scottish crime fiction.

Does that mentality predispose Scots to crime fiction, a genre that is all about the tension between constitutional justice and the protagonist's sense of right and wrong? Does it explain the popularity of a guy like Rankin's Rebus who will put his career and more on the line –

– because he likes to push back? Rebus is a perfect example. I mean, there are books that I've read and thought, 'Rebus is really just being shit because he thinks he's right.' It's not because he's going out to save person A or because he's on this big crusade. It's because, as far as he's concerned, he is right, and he refuses to be proven wrong. Not in all the books, but in some of them it feels to me as if what he's doing is he's proving that he's better and that he's right: that he's the man. It's what makes him so identifiably Scottish … I probably shouldn't have said that – I will also say that I do very much admire Ian Rankin's work.

Don't we all?

We don't want the Edinburgh mafia coming after us.

Funny you should mention organised crime. Stephen Fry recently opposed the notion of 'the Church as a force for good in the world'. He was rejecting the very concept of infallibility and –

– a God-given right, perhaps?

If so, isn't it ironic how pop culture has replaced religious authority only to champion the cause of an individual's higher sense of what is ethically right?

I don't know if it's even connected, to be honest. But of course I'm speaking from an Aberdeen perspective which, according to census records, is the most secular city in Scotland. It has the lowest percentage of people in the UK who proclaim to belong to one religion or another. There are loads of churches, but as a city it's incredibly irreligious, and has been for a long time. So I possibly have a different perspective on it, having grown up there, than you might do in another part of the UK.

Is there a noun for 'thrawn'?

I don't know … thrawnity?

Did you say thrawnitude? That makes it sound like a virtue.

It does. Let's call it thrawnitude! You know, possibly the difference is between organised religion – which personally I don't feel is generally a force for good – and disorganised religion which is much more appealing, and which is where the characters like Rebus sit. It's not part of an organised belief structure; it's an individual belief structure. I think that might be what makes it more appealing.

We have to trademark 'thrawnitude'. That's a good word.

It might even make a good title.

Oh God no. I get in enough difficulties with the marketing department as it is.

Is that right?

Oh yeah. Here's something I found really weird: when I sold the first book I was told by my editor, in all honesty, 'Yes, we like the title – *Cold Granite* – that's good. And the Marketing Department likes your name, too. You can keep that.'

That was generous. Then again, your name is as Scottish as they come.

The only thing it misses is the word 'Hamish' somewhere. Apart from *Cold Granite* the only book title they've liked since then was *Halfhead*, and that was written before *Cold Granite*. Every other one has been this huge back and forth trying to find a title that fits the book and that marketing and sales are happy with.

Do you have a working title in mind when you write a novel?

I used to. I know now that any title I give a book isn't the title it's going to get published under.

(Stuart's wife, Fiona, joins us.) *Ah, good. Let's hear some testimony on the man behind the name. I understand Stuart switches in and out of accents.*

He doesn't really do the accents much in public.

– Just at home to entertain her.

How about the audio books, is your musical ear helpful when you do various voices?

Well, not a musical, a whore's ear ... It can be complicated. There was one scene where there were seven different people from Newcastle and one Estuary Englishwoman all talking in quick-fire dialogue, which is easy to do in writing. Reading out loud was a challenge.

Are you enjoying the popularity of the audio books?

I don't really know. I'm contemplating whether or not I'll do the next one, because, as with everything I do in writing, I can't see any good parts in my own performance. I will only ever focus on the bits that I think I should have done better.

Do you read your own books once you're done with writing them?

No. Fiona proofreads and catches some quite remarkable mistakes I've made. I'll have been up to my ears in the book for almost a year by that point, and the editor will have been dealing with it for probably eight months, and so will my agent, and the proofreader will have had it for a number of months, and Fiona is the fresh pair of eyes that comes at the end and goes, 'You do know that when the word "cypress" is mentioned here it's meant to be the country, not the tree?' – 'Oh, that's a good point. We should change that, shouldn't we?'

Do you catch yourself waiting for a reaction when she's reading your books?

I try not to be in the same room. – **Yeah, you are sort of hoping it's going to entertain.** – Well, apart from everything else, you're my wife. I hope what I do is worthy of entertaining you. – **It certainly would be disappointing if you didn't.** – But, see, that's reading. The writing is finished at that point. No, I try to write to please myself, because I'm the biggest critic of my own work I will ever have. It's an absolute bastard, because it means I'm never happy with anything.

Do I want to know what we'll find if we go down that road?

DRINK!

Ah good. Isn't that what a lot of Scottish crime fiction comes down to?

We're Scottish.

Is there more to it or are you writing about self-medication because readers expect it?

It's not coming from being clever about it; it's because they're very team-based books, Logan isn't a loner and there are all those other people who play parts in the book and as a team they go out to drink. And that's only because I worked in teams all my life up until the point where I stopped to become a full-time writer. And that's how the teams that I used to work in behaved. So all the banter that goes on between them is how I expect a group of people, who have to work towards a common purpose, to interact with each other. That's just my experience.

How about that change of scenery – if even Billy Connolly is struggling to keep his material fresh, are you concerned that your team banter might start sounding scripted as you run out of firsthand experience?

That's one of the reasons why I'm doing these 'Murder, Mystery and Microscope' events. Not only is it a huge opportunity for me to spend time with high-class forensic professionals, it means that I'm back working in a team again. We go out for a drink after an event, or for lunch before an event: it's great to be doing that kind of thing with real people again. I know them well enough that I can take the piss out of them, and they do the same to me. We have that team-based dynamic thing where we can all have a laugh and go off on bizarre tangents.

I filmed a trailer for the new book, which was a vast undertaking, because instead of doing the usual – having someone talk to the camera or maybe dramatising a small part of one scene – we approached it as if it were a proper movie trailer so there are scenes from throughout the book. There are petrol bombs being thrown, there's a riot at one point, there's violence, there are sledgehammers … and doing that had to be a big team exercise. So I'm engineering scenarios where I can be back working in a team again in order to keep the banter going, because I do worry that if it's just me in a room on my own all year writing a book it's going to get to the point where I'm going to lose that spark between characters because I'm no longer used to doing that in real life. – **Oh, he has me to talk to. And the cat.**

Ha! With that daily experience of performing to crowds, how do you feel about having to do ever more tours and publicity events?

It's the same thing the music industry went through. I remember before videos there was a big debate about why musicians should have to become actors. That's not their job; their job is to make music. That was when there were a lot more unattractive people making records than there are now. We now expect musicians to be entertainers and performers and we expect to see them on television and do videos and act.

Will readers soon be expecting – or perhaps getting – such all-round customer service?

There's a big debate around the future of writing that is very much related to that. But I think in the short term, as far as crime writing is concerned, it's never really going to be a big showbiz thing because you're only ever performing to, well, in some libraries you'll be lucky if you get sixty people. It's not as if you're broadcasting your image to millions of people on prime-time television. As writers we're not that interesting as far as the media's concerned, which in a way is nice because we get to maintain our anonymity.

A lot of people are now saying that the future of writing is that we are going to see people who had been doing all right through bookshops begin to disappear. As the long tail of the midlist starts to drop off, people move their book buying away from bookshops into places like supermarkets where obvi-

Stuart MacBride

ously the choice is much more limited. That's just the nature of the beast; supermarkets can't have six hundred different titles so they will just have a range for a fortnight. We'll end up in a position where the easiest way for publishers to get books into supermarkets – and it's a *very* competitive game to get your book into a supermarket – is pairings of celebrities with actual writers.

Publishing is increasingly becoming about *platform* – along the lines of, 'I co-wrote this product,' where the word 'co-wrote' is flexible, James Patterson being a prime example of that. You can look to several 'celebrities' who have their name on the top of very well-selling books.

Is that an option you would consider?

I would prefer not to. I hope that by the time that happens I'll have enough of a following that my publishers feel they can sell the books on the back of me being an established author, as opposed to some writers who are maybe not in that lucky position of having been supported by a big publishing house as I have.

Seeing as you're attracting visitors as well as readers, have you considered collaborating with the tourist board on a MacBride-McRae package holiday?

Ha! You know, there are German readers who have emailed me to say that they've come over to Aberdeen just because they've read the books. There's also a digital tourism that goes on. There are several people who read the books with Google Earth open so they can follow the action with the satellite imagery of Aberdeen.

Does setting your fiction in real places make these novels documents of social history?

I think it depends on who you are as a writer. I am mostly writing about the place where I have lived since I was two. It's on my doorstep; it's a place that I know. If I want to do any research I can just get in the car. Quite often, if I want any inspiration, I just go for a walk around the streets, and see

61

things, and pick them up, and incorporate them into books.

That said, I did a range of short stories that were all set in a fictional Scottish town called Oldcastle. I have a standalone coming up after I finish the book I'm writing, that I'm planning on at least partially setting in Oldcastle, because you can just make shit up. **– And nobody's going to email you and say you got a street name wrong or that doesn't exist any more.**

Wouldn't you be losing the sense of familiarity that allows readers to relate to your stories?

Yeah, people quite like that, don't they? People are always saying that at events. – But you also have slightly more freedom. There are things I can't do in Aberdeen, because I would get sued if I were to suggest that this corporation or that organisation or this part of the government was involved in x, y or z. You've got to be very, very careful and that does sometimes limit what you can do.

Do you like Aberdeen?

Yeah!

Chris Brookmyre –

– doesn't like Aberdeen. He *really* doesn't like Aberdeen. In *A Big Boy Did It And Ran Away*, he just goes off for about three pages on a rant about how crap Aberdeen is and how crap Aberdonians are. It's got lines in it like, 'They call it the silver city; you can call it silver in the same way that a turd can be considered copper-tone.' That's the start of the rant and it gets worse. It's just a vitriolic recording of how much he hated his time in Aberdeen when he was staying there. The press absolutely ripped him to shreds in Aberdeen. There was a hate campaign…

Is that not better publicity than anybody could have bought him?

Well, the thing is he then felt that he couldn't come back to Aberdeen until last year; he was invited to the Word Festival. We went and saw him and took him out for a pint afterwards – and he was quite surprised that he'd ever been invited back.

Isn't slagging and ranting part of the charming culture?

Well, the difference is that he was an incomer. He was from Glasgow and he came to Aberdeen, and he slated Aberdeen so –

– it's all right if you do it?

Well, yeah. I've described people in Aberdeen looking like a casting call for *Deliverance* ... **– As murderous and inbred, and that didn't go down too well.** – It was fine though. I haven't had that backlash because I live in Aberdeen, I'm from Aberdeen, it's my hometown, and I can get away with that. Let's face it: no-one ever truly, entirely, one hundred percent loves where they live. There's that love-hate relationship; you love some of it and other days you just loathe it and wish you were somewhere else, and I like being able to do that in the books.

Is it that 'love-hate relationship' that gives your work such a strong sense of place?

If it works that's great, and if people email me to say, 'We moved from Aberdeen when I was six, and I found *Cold Granite* and I was lying on the beach in Bondi reading all about the snow and the rain and the wind, and it took me right back to my childhood' – that's lovely and it's really nice to have made that connection, but I try not to over-think it.

You mentioned emails you got from German readers. Do you think any of the Aberdonian and Doric flavour gets lost in translation?

The German translator I have is apparently one of the best translators of English-language fiction into German. So much so that the publishers held off publishing *Cold Granite* for a year so that this person would be available. They've really got behind the books, which is great. As I understand it he takes the dialect and he places it into the context of the culture that's going to be reading the books. **– Schwaben, isn't it? It's a sort of country accent and you could do that in different languages.** – But I think you need an incredibly good translator to do that.

Global access to local identities – do we compensate for feeling estranged from our own cultural traditions and community spirit by reading about a place that is alien and yet intimate?

That reminds me of Stephen King's idea of time travel and place travel. All writing should be about experiencing something through the eyes of the point of view character, and if they're based in their hometown then that's the experience you should get from it. You don't get that through Street View on Google Earth, you don't get that through visiting the place, you're never going to get that experience unless you're local, and that's a perspective you can only get through literature.

Is 'local' place-making something you enjoy sharing with your readers?

Hopefully it's something that they can experience depending on the quality of my writing and the quality of the translation. What I would hope is that it would be more immersive, that you would empathise with the characters not just watch what they're doing – you would actually be in that position with them.

Do you often get that as a reader?

I've become a very bad reader. I find it very difficult to switch off my editing brain. It's quite unusual for me to pick up a book and just let go. I'm always picking holes.

Whose books do you still enjoy?

Definitely Allan Guthrie. I absolutely love his work. – Zoe Sharp, I like her stuff, even though I picked up one of her books, I think it was *Second Shot*, and within about six or seven pages she's introduced this whiny American teenager and I thought, 'Ach, Christ, I don't think I can face reading an entire book about this whingeing little git. Oh well, let's have a go.' Within two chapters I actually cared whether that character lived or died, and I think she does that incredibly well. – Val McDermid. Yeah, I like her.

Do your reading preferences reflect a shared writing style?
No. Allan is very much steeped in Noir, he is a proper Noir author. I write police thrillers.

How do you define Noir?
I think in Noir your protagonist is doomed from the start, and although there may be the hope of redemption it is small and it's very rarely realised. It is a rollercoaster to hell and everybody is getting fucked on the way, and not it a good way ... They're not making love on the rollercoaster. If I were to write a proper Noir novel with Logan I couldn't write a follow up to it, because he would be dead or he would be irredeemably screwed. That's the ultimate Noir ending – your point-of-view character cops it. I think Logan isn't a doomed character, because he has always been an everyman. He's just meant to be a normal guy, and the events that he gets drawn into are larger than life and the stakes tend to escalate. That is basically the pattern for a thriller.

He's not James Bond at the start of it, and he's not James Bond at the end of it. He's a policeman. In between the books time always passes and things always occur but those aren't the bits that we want to have a book about. Logan arresting seventeen people for car theft or not returning their library books isn't a novel – it's just his day job. It's only when the extraordinary stuff happens that the camera starts rolling.

Of all that 'extraordinary stuff', what moment are you proudest of?
The one I haven't written yet. I'm always hoping that the next one will be the one where I think, 'I've actually done well with this book.' And so far the only one that I can actually say that about is *Sawbones*.

Which one of your own would you personally recommend?
Well, all the books are meant to stand alone. I have been criticised by some reviewers in the past: 'You have to read these all in order because he doesn't tell you the backstory.' But the start of the series will read very much as if it was the

fifth or the sixth in the series. So if you want to start with the fifth you're probably not going to be getting any information about the earlier books, because unless the previous cases directly relate to what's happening now they won't be mentioned. *And* I don't want to spoil the previous books if you haven't read them: I'm not going to give away big chunks of plot or who did what.

Because all the characters do change in the course of the novels – DI Steel is not the same parson now in book seven that she was in book one – there is an evolution. People do change as they go through, so if you want to follow them on the bigger journey then starting at the start is a great way to do it. If you just want to see if you like the books – buy the new one.

What do you think, Fiona?

Everybody likes different things. *Broken Skin* **is the one I liked best.** – That's because it's the dirty one. – **Ah, I wouldn't know.**

Nor would I, Stuart. Our minds are pure. (Fiona starts laughing as we turn in time to see a lady in lycra cobble-wobble out of sight.)

Well, we saw worse yesterday. – **Stuart's always been appalled by the state of women walking about.**

Which finally brings us to your notion of tragedy, Stuart. According to David Corbett, 'Tragedy is nothing but the dramatization of how man's own nature betrays his self-idealization – how his realities undermine his illusions.' That definition almost seems a tighter fit on your work than her tights. How do you feel about that kind of 'tension'?

Ha! That becomes much more difficult to sustain over a series if it's the same illusions and flaws he has to overcome every single time. You'd have to have a stack of flaws that you work through one by one until he becomes perfect which obviously is never going to happen. So the overcoming a flaw thing can be true of one book but once you get into a series you're going to be repeating yourself. So I don't think it should apply to a series.

Did you set out to write a series?

No. When the publishers saw the first draft of *Cold Granite* I was offered a three-book deal but it had to be three Logan books. They had to be set in Aberdeen, and they had to be at least 120,000 words long.

Why did they insist on Aberdeen as a setting?

Because they saw that as being a big part of the voice of the book. That's what they loved about it: that it was set in Aberdeen. It hadn't been done before in that kind of way. You know, you can't throw a brick in Edinburgh without clobbering at least half a dozen fictional detectives. Glasgow is very much the same. Aberdeen is an open playing field.

Did you consciously stake out your territory with remarks on the surrounding cities?

The thing is everybody assumes that the experts from Edinburgh are going to come up and be a bunch of dicks and rough up the investigation. The characters expect them to come up and be pricks. But they're not; they're just policemen like them, except for the profiler who is a dick. To be honest, I always make the profiler a dick. Nobody believes what the profilers say but when you get to the end of the book and go back to look at what the profilers actually said, most of the time they are very close to the truth.

Is that a dramatic ploy or an authority issue?

Certainly the way some of the characters act makes it much more difficult for them to be taken seriously or even liked because there's just that personal animosity. I think there's also a dimension to the characters that by dismissing what this guy says, just because he gets your back up, you're being unprofessional because you're reacting to him on a personal level... It could just be that Scottish thrawnitude.

Ha! That's certainly a virtue you share with Ian Rankin. What did the critics make of you mentioning Rebus in your debut?

So much was written in the reviews about, 'Oh, the young gun is coming up and he's giving Ian Rankin the nod.' All because in *Cold Granite* I had a police officer who had to sit outside a hospital room for hours and hours so I gave him a book to read. And because I know the police like Ian's books, I made the officer read one of the Rebus novels. That's all it was: just a logical conclusion of what a character in that situation would do.

Let me ask you about another logical conclusion of your team-based narratives: Have you thought about co-writing a book?

I have approached Allan about doing just that. We've talked about writing a novella together. We might get around to it next year when our schedules loosen up a bit, because I would really like to collaborate with somebody and do something completely new. We've talked about the genres we'd quite like to work in and thought about some ideas, and I think that would be really fun to do.

For Harrogate this year, because I'm chairing the crime festival, nine or ten crime authors are writing a round-robin novel with completely new characters. I did the first chapter and I'll do the last chapter – which is probably going to be a nightmare, trying to make sense of everything. It's a big experiment on that front.

Do you enjoy that sense of community among Scottish crime writers?

To be honest, the more crime writers we have in Scotland the better. It's a genre I enjoy.

What does it hold for your own future?

Well, I've just signed up for four more books: two standalones and two in the series. So Logan will at least live to the eighth book.

Are you interested in him beyond that?

I don't know. It depends on what happens in the books.

If he makes my life miserable, I will make his life miserable.

Given that Logan is aging in real time, could his retirement become a problem?

I know Ian has always said that the biggest mistake he feels that he made with Rebus was making him so old to start with. I don't quite have that restriction because obviously Logan is a much younger character in the first place, but I think that having the break between doing the series and standalones should keep it fresher.

The thought of having to write about the same character for twenty years straight would drive me mental. I've been living with Logan now full-time since 2003. Being able to take a break after the seventh book in the series and write something just completely different from it – which I think might be a PI novel because I'm not very fond of PI novels – I'm hoping I'll be able to come back to the eighth book in the series feeling, 'Okay, what shall we do now? It's been two years.' Things will have changed; I can fiddle with stuff.

Do you like Logan?

Sort of. I created his world. I fuck with his life. I am his God.

On that final note, does he like you?

I don't think he likes me very much at all, no. But one interesting thing is that he is always 'Logan' to me. We are on first-name terms because he is that everyman character – he thinks of himself as Logan. Rebus thinks of himself as Rebus. Morse thinks of himself as Morse. To me he is always Logan. We are on first name terms: I call him Logan. He calls me God.

Karen Campbell
Copper Dreams and Paper Cuts

Karen Campbell was born into law enforcement in 1967. Strathclyde Police having given her two parents, a husband and a career, it seems hardly surprising that she would pay her dues by making a home for herself and two daughters in the Scottish capital of crime, Glasgow. Before motherhood redirected her professional life into Glasgow City Council's Press Office, she did five and a half years of active service in the city's 'A' Division as a uniformed police constable. Naturally, all this would have furnished Karen with enough diaries to fill a library, never mind the shelves of Scottish crime fiction.

Yet hers would be a less intriguing story, and those shelves hardly the treasure chest they are, if such popular assumptions weren't one and all taken to task in the following interview. Karen did not turn her real-life experience of crime into tales of 'Gangsters as seen on Television', nor did she reach for crime fiction as other newly housebound mothers might reach for the G&T crutch. In fact, Karen didn't reach for crime fiction at all. Unlike most of her fellow officers she got herself an MA in English, Drama and French before joining the force, and unlike most of her fellow writers she lived the life she is now writing about. What's more, she got herself another MA with Distinction from Glasgow University, this one in Creative Writing, to make sure she wouldn't be typing reports but writing novels.

These novels, of which her debut earned Karen the Best New Scottish Writer Award in 2009, have since established her as one of the country's most acclaimed literary talents. Strictly speaking they are not typical crime fiction, though, and strictly

Karen does speak when she calls them 'contemporary novels about people who happen to be cops.' There is a distinction here that has little to do with professional vanity and everything to do with the current state of marketing, especially the risks of generic thinking. Karen will happily talk about both.

When we met for this interview in the summer of 2010, her third novel was about to be published. Featuring Sgt Anna Cameron, the charismatic protagonist of *The Twilight Time* (2008) and *After the Fire* (2009), *Shadowplay* offers that rare reading pleasure: loyalty to the series is rewarded by Cameron's courage to face not only the costs of her promotion but also the demands of the job as suffered by those entrusted to her authority. Much to her credit, Karen continues to explore issues that would send any fainthearted feminist back to the couch, and all along her work is rehabilitating for those who have experienced violent crime and edifying for those who have been lucky enough not to.

Mark Billingham, a man who would hear and call her on any false note, has described Karen's work as being 'gritty as all hell, shot through with black humour and with enough pace and atmosphere to give the likes of Denise Mina a run for their money.' When she talks about how she writes about what she knows, Karen is as quick with a laugh at her former delusions as she is certain to assuage any doubts that she might not have the distance to write with honesty and humour about the politics of policing and the city she has served in so many ways. The Glasgow that gradually moves into focus around us in the following pages is a strange place, although both familiar in its existential jaundice and endearing in Karen's obvious affection for it. It is, like her writing, the real thing.

~

Rumour has it you don't like being called a crime writer. Why is that?

I'm a Scottish writer. What I have found is that I've been put in a crime bracket and it's the antithesis of what I set out to do, because I'm a former police officer and I wanted to write a book about what it was really like to be in the police. I felt that most times, in any form of fiction or TV or any media at all, the police always come over as pretty stereotypical. There's not an awful lot of depth to them. You'll have the racist, the misogynist … and it's not at all my experience of real-life cops. So I thought, 'I wonder if I can just write a contemporary novel about the police that'll stand on its own.' And I've discovered that no, as soon as it's about the police it becomes a crime novel with all the connotations that brings, which was what I was trying to get around. That's what the publishers decided should happen. I wasn't comfortable with it.

Do many readers bring such limited expectations to your books?

Well, I've certainly had some reviews on Amazon that say, 'Nothing much happens in this book for a long time. There were lots of people talking.' If I were them and had bought a book thinking it was about dark and mysterious murders in the red-light district of Glasgow, I'd probably feel short-changed myself, because the first book wasn't about that. So I can see where they're coming from, but that's just how the book's been packaged. At the same time, my editor's very good at letting me write what I write and there's no censoring of the content. But when it comes to the marketing of it, 'crime' is put on it all the time, and that's not been the place I've been writing it from. I don't have a background in reading crime fiction and I feel on the one hand, yeah, it can heighten the appeal I guess because it's got a label on it, but I think it can also diminish the appeal. If you're looking for a pretty accurate portrayal of modern Scottish policing I don't think you'd pick up my book, but to me that's what it was about.

That's what's limiting about being put in a genre: an assumption is made before the first page is even turned and it's very difficult to be given a fair and unambiguous reading of something that's already come packaged in a certain way. I've got a degree in Creative Writing and it irks me a wee bit that it's 'one size fits all' and it doesn't matter what your literary background is or your knowledge or your learning and different influences and all the rest of it: it boils down to what it says on the tin, which I do find frustrating.

You also mentioned your own police background. How does that fit into your writing life?

I did English at uni before I joined the police, so being in the police was probably the aberration, and the writing has been the constant in my life.

So what brought you to the police?

A variety of things. Both of my parents were in the police, and I was getting fed up with studying, to be perfectly honest. I thought, 'What am I going to do with my life?' I've got friends who are teachers because their parents were teachers, so it's always an easy route to go into a profession that you know a lot about, and what appealed to me about the police was the fact that I didn't really know what I wanted to do and it opened up a whole range of opportunities because it's the sort of job in which no two days are the same. You're not limited in any of your aspirations at all; it offers an awful lot in terms of the different specialities you could go into; everyone starts at the same level and then it's down to merit how you get on. All of that really appealed to me – and the excitement of it as well.

When you write about that now, do you deliberately give your readers a less romantic notion of police work than most other crime writers?

No, I think all my books are quite slow-burning. They're much more about the relationships and about the effects that the cops' jobs have on them than they are about any investigation or crime that happens, and that is the truth of policing – that you don't take your work home with you, you don't have a one-man crusade against the world. You couldn't function as a professional if that's what you did. You have to do the best you can do on any given day … and then forget about it and move on to the next thing. Obviously, there are always one or two things that come through, and for the sake of fiction I have to have a narrative strand as well, so there has to be a particular something that irks one of the cops that then becomes a more prevalent part of the story.

At the same time I did want to show that there can be a very quick switch between seeing something quite horrific and making a really sick joke about it – which I don't think is normally shown, but that is the truth of how human beings process unpleasant things. You know, you don't tend to brood in a darkened room for ages – you take the piss out of it. That way you puncture the tension and then you can do what the professional part of your task is. You may well go home and think about it… One of the scenes in the first book (*The Twilight Time*) involves a cot death, and the cop dealing with that has a small child of his own. He goes home at night and takes his baby out of the cot because he wants to feel the livingness of this child. Cops are human; of course you do that, but in the main you just deal with it as an incident and then you move on.

Also, a lot of the time you're not doing an awful lot. I worked in this division in the city. Days would go by when, other than dealing with shoplifters and other minor stuff, you didn't get big, exciting, glamorous things. And obviously I'm not writing a diary either, so I haven't written how boring seven nights of night shifts really can be. But at the same time I didn't want to glamorise or over-egg the pudding because that's not what it was like. I did want to write a book about how it felt to be a young, inexperienced female, aged twenty, plunged into a city where you become very visible wearing a uniform. You can't run away from anything: you're it; you're where the buck stops. You're straight out of university – you're crapping yourself.

Certainly, I thought when I joined the police, I'd be promoted in a couple of years; I'd sort this lot out. And very quickly I thought, 'I've got no common sense at all.' I couldn't even drive. I didn't know my way around the city. You know, when you're dealing with a NED, a smart-mouthed guy who's sort of running rings around you … you learn very quickly; you have to or you don't survive. But initially, nothing can prepare you for that onslaught of the undercurrent in the city that you thought you knew – but my God, you don't know anything about it. When you're really there in its underbelly and have to deal with it and get your hands dirty, you can't just think, 'Hmm, I'll walk on the other side of the street and leave that behind me' … Because folks see you in your uniform and you cannae run away.

Visibility and accountability are certainly experiences that readers can avoid. Has your police work heightened your social conscience in a way that now informs your writing?

To show what it's like? Possibly, actually. I've been surprised that some of the reviews I've had have talked about my love of the visceral. I find gratuitous violence repellent and I can't even watch slasher-type films. I just think the world's a horrible enough place without making that into entertainment. So I was quite surprised at that, and then I thought about it and I talked about it with my husband who was a serving police officer – he's actually just retired now but he was for twenty-odd years – and he said, 'It's what your reality is. You become familiarised with it but to other people it's pretty gross.'

I talked about strip-searching a prostitute, where you actually have to look inside her to see if she's got anything concealed about her person, and that obviously is disgusting to most people. But it became a thing that you just did routinely. Again, you had to depersonalise it otherwise you'd be like, 'Aw, that's a wee shame. I can't do that to that girl.' Then they'd come in with knives and something terrible would happen in the cells so you'd have to dissociate yourself from things like that. But then when I write about it and try to make it as accurate as possible I think people can be quite repulsed and think, 'Oh, you're sick.'

Have you ever toned it down when reality would have seemed stranger than fiction?

I don't think I have. I think it's what you overdo, though. I mean, I would never dream of overdoing a knife plunging into a body or something like that. That's the kind of thing that turns my stomach, because I've seen it really happen and it's horrible. I don't think I overwrite things but I certainly don't shy away from depicting a whole process from beginning to end whether it's dealing with a fatality or ... none of it is glamorised, but none of it is made such that you couldn't watch or read about it either. I don't think. It's invented – not embellished.

Is it fair to say that you are avoiding an aesthetic of violence?

Yeah, I think so. Absolutely. It troubles me that there are almost no holds barred now in society in terms of what we describe, what we depict and how quickly we then move onto something else. The reality is that any crime has an impact on people. Even if you've had your house broken into or your car screwed you've got anger, you've got frustration, you've got fear, you feel a sense of violation. You multiply that with having a scar on your face for the rest of your life, you're frightened to go back to the college you were at – all of those things have a huge impact. I'm not trying to be a crusader but for me personally my raison d'être is not to try to mine that misery that I've seen and make it into juicy stories. It's to tell a story about these cops, and if a situation arises, to be honest about it but not be brutal, and then move on.

You certainly write with dignity about an undignified topic, and yet the genre seems to have upped the ante. Does it make you wonder –

– where it would ever end? I've got absolutely no interest in doing that. You know, I didn't ever say, 'I'm going to write a crime book.' So I have no desire to try to match them in terms of violence or depravity. It's not where I want to be and it's not what I'm interested in. I've just finished my fourth book and that'll probably be the last book I write about the police. I feel I've said all I want to say. What I wanted to write about is policing issues and the way the service has changed: the structures and the business ideas that come in instead of the public service ethos, which I think has had a big impact on how the service is delivered. Issues about, 'Should the police be armed?', 'What do we expect from our cops?' – those are the things that interest me, so I never look at the newspaper saying, 'Oh there's a really gory crime. I think I'll replicate that two books down the line.' That's just not my thing, and I'm not casting aspersions at anyone who does that – it's just never been my mindset.

Do you feel that way in deference to how much drama one set of characters can experience before they become clichés?

Yeah! It's like when you watch something like *Eastenders*, the soap opera, you think, 'How many things can happen to one family on one street before it becomes so absurd it's just not at all tenable?' I mean, we all know it's a fantasy anyway but … absolutely. What I've done with each of the four books is create a two- or three-year gap between each one, so that you can see one of the characters that I follow mostly progressing through the ranks. She's promoted at each stage, and I did that to show the changing face of policing but also so that there was time for her character to grow and develop and for there to be an actual timespan that she had lived in between things happening in the books. If anything, she has become … not *broken,* but the idealism that she joined the police with has been tempered, and I think that's a truth that happens to a lot of cops. Most people's idea of a police officer is a quite cynical and quite callous, chewing the gum …

In my experience, everyone I know that joins the police could have been a social worker. You tend to join because you want to do some good for society. You have this idealism about you. It's not about beating up minors; it's about thinking, 'There are bad folk out there. I can physically and strategically do something about that to make my community a better place.' But then quite quickly you start to realise that it's a neverending cycle and you'll kill yourself if you try to solve the world's problems. All you can do is do what you can do, and with each year that passes you become a wee bit more inured to the bad things that are happening, and a wee bit more cynical, and a wee bit less mindful of what the reasons were that you joined. That's what's happened with my main character, that she's kinda like, 'Ah, I'm scunnered with this.' As opposed to broken or damaged in any way, she's just shut down a wee bit.

When you decided to approach police work as a humanist, did you think you would have an opportunity to point out the limitations of our corrective system?

When I started writing I hoped I would have, but I don't know. I think people read a story and they move on. I don't think people are hugely influenced. Again, maybe it's the crime genre thing; it's like, 'Oh, it's throwaway.' People don't take layers of meaning from those books. You don't get debates in *The Guardian*, do you? There should be, but there aren't any at the moment.

My second book (*After the Fire*) is all about policing and firearms issues and it's incredibly topical in terms of the Jean Charles De Menezes case a few years ago. What would happen if one day a cop was actually charged with murder? That is what will happen one day. I got a few reviews when it came out but it is, I think, topical in terms of what happens in society at the moment and where we could be headed, but it's never deemed as that.

Don't you think that by virtue of engaging with these issues in crime fiction there is a change of our intuitive response to what is deemed permissible today?

Do you think? A sort of slow drip-feed … yeah. All I can equate it to is that people, when I was a cop, were always interested in finding out about the work that I did, and I think crime fiction offers that same opportunity to learn about a world that you kind of know goes on but don't really want to know about. You get an immersion in something that is safe really, but is giving you a door into this darkness … but you know you can come out at any time and close it. I can only talk for myself but I don't think that's where I would turn to for a moral compass. Having said that, I don't know where I would turn.

I suppose what you're saying is true, though. It's after you read a book, isn't it? You don't think, 'I'm going to read this book to get something out of it.' It's at the end that you think, 'Oh yeah, that's made me think differently.' So maybe on a subliminal level it filters in.

Speaking of the force of the subliminal, what do you make of the marketing label 'Tartan Noir'?

I think like any label it depersonalises. It's a one-size-fits-all sensibility when it covers such a range of different styles of writers, different backgrounds, different subjects that they write about. Other than the geography of where these people come from and where they are writing, I don't know what the big connecting factor is.

I guess if you like one then it might encourage you to read others, but equally, if you don't like one it might discourage you to read others because you think, 'Oh well, they must all be the same then.' I don't think it's fair to any of the writers that are put in that bracket because they're all different with their own different audiences and their different take on life.

What would you call it?

I would call it contemporary Scottish fiction, of which there are some fantastic examples. To me the best writing that is going on in Scotland at the moment is about holding a mirror up to society – I mean, our country is changing with devolution and things like that – and it's reflecting and commenting on the world that we live in at the moment.

Is it about the ways in which societies can and do fail their weakest members – and might that explain why Scottish crime fiction is such an international success?

Yeah. I think Scottish fiction has a tradition of doing that anyway. Scotland's always punched above her weight culturally and in terms of inventiveness and discoveries. Whenever you look at Scotland you think, 'My goodness, for a wee country there's an awful lot of talent there.' So I don't think it's particular to a particular type of writing. I think it is just that we've got the archetypal Scottish cringe – we don't like to shout about things. It does surprise me that there's such a proliferation of artistic and academic talent in Scotland, and yet we've always got this feeling that we're not worthy and we don't really do that much. Oh God, 'the best small country in the world' was a slogan that the Scottish government came up with. When you came off the planes at airports it was, 'Scotland, the best small country in the world.' That was our aspirational strapline, you know. I think we need to be more proud of what we do and not be apologetic about it.

Why we're popular abroad or outwith our own confines? I don't know. To be honest, I've found that I use quite a lot of Scottish idioms and Glaswegian idioms in my work and there's been criticism about that. Folk can't understand it, but to me that is how people speak here and that's how it should be written. Someone like Christopher Brookmyre – it's brilliant that that doesn't seem to be a barrier for him. I noticed some other review recently about Denise Mina – somebody was saying that she'd lost the colloquialism that she had at the start. Now I don't know, I've never spoken to Denise about it, but she has maybe toned things down so that it's more universal, but in actual fact people like the Scottishness of it.

I don't know why... You tell me! You're not Scottish. Why do you think there's an appeal to Scottish writing?

Does the spectator see more of the game? I'd say you've already made the point yourself. My best bet is that Scottish literature has a strong tradition of righteous indignation at social ills. Combine that with what you've called a 'proliferation of artistic talent', a high degree of social mobility and respect for self-improvement, a sense of solidarity and suspicion of authority as results of long-term foreign rule, and it's surely not surprising that you get the authenticity, diversity and urgency that attract wide international attention –

– but also a sense of social justice and fairness. I don't come from a background of having read a lot of crime fiction so I've never thought about it that deeply but just in terms of writing in general in Scotland, yeah, I think what you're saying is right. There's a terrier-likeness about Scots, almost a 'We'll show them!' kind of thing. We don't quite know who the 'them' are sometimes; it's just like, 'The world's out to get us.' And yet there's a fierce pride about where you come from.

Actually, when you pick it apart and analyse it, there are a lot of good things about where you live as well as dark things. I suppose what I worry about is if Scottish crime fiction is seen as the tourist literature, in terms of encouraging it, you know. There's a lot of good, there's a lot of light in Scotland as well as dark, and I wouldn't like that to be the only sort of calling-card internationally because, you know, Glasgow has been plagued by *No Mean City* – a book that was written about the Gorbals in 1935, about razor gangs and things like that – and that became the nickname for Glasgow throughout the UK. There's been a lot of work done to dissociate ourselves from that sense of poverty and depravity and slashings.

Does that make No Mean City *the Glasgow prequel to* Trainspotting?

Yeah! That doesn't define Edinburgh. So I would still err on the side of saying that it's great that any Scottish fiction represents us abroad, but there's got to be a balance. I suppose by even calling it 'Tartan Noir' there's a negativity about that ... well, Noir is black and you need to have light with dark to make the dark work. If something is continually dark it becomes unbearable, doesn't it? Then you can't plough through.

That's interesting. Couldn't the label imply that very paradox – a colourful darkness?

Or a lazy way of branding Scotland. We're more than that, much more.

Isn't it interesting how some seem to get a strong sense of identity from the cultural clichés?

And rootedness and tradition. It's a continuous line rather than a blend.

Would that have anything to do with your warped sense of humour?

Ha! Are you talking about us generically or me personally? I don't consciously think about it. I suppose it gives a pace and an authenticity to the novel. Usually after something awful there would be some humour to puncture the tension of the situation, and it could just be a comment or an action or a gesture or something. I wouldn't ever say my books are rip-roaringly funny but I certainly do think there's a sort of pawky humour in them. I've always lived in Glasgow so it's probably reflective of the Glasgow sense of humour, which could even be listening to banter on a bus.

The Herald newspaper has a diary and this is just a classic example of Glasgow humour: it was about this man on a bus on his mobile saying to his wife, 'I *have* left the pub. I'm on my way home.' And she obviously didn't believe him and he's saying, 'I'm promising I'm on the bus. I'll be home in ten minutes.' And then he said, 'Look, listen!', and he held his phone up. These two NEDs had obviously been listening to his conversation and they started shouting, 'Right, mine's a pint, mate!' and making all the noises of a pub, and he's going, 'No! No!' to his wife. Total strangers felt that they could just intervene in this guy's life – and that happens all the time in Glasgow.

There's a bit in the second book (*After the Fire*) where they've set up a sterile cordon because there's a firearms incident taking place. It's behind a chip shop and a couple of guys are walking down there eating their chips and the cop's saying, 'This is a sterile area!' And the guy's like, 'Aw, nae bothers, I'm sterile, I'm a total Jaffa (i.e. seedless orange) by the way – I've had the snip!' You know, he's physically sterile.

So those things happen all the time in my books. I tend to hear and see stuff; I don't plot things very much so the cadences and the humour and the nuances just come in as it's being enacted in my head. If you try and shoehorn that in it doesn't work. It just comes out naturally as you're writing it.

Do you have a fictional cast of actors in mind as you write?

I haven't actually, no. I heard Alexander McCall Smith talk about that once and he said he only sees a shape and the size of a person, he never sees their face, and I thought, 'I never do that either.' There's just a cloudiness where the face is because … I don't know. I just think, 'If it's not broke, don't fix it.' They're alive in my head the way they are, like shadows almost, and I don't want to see their faces. At the moment they're still my creations but they'd kind of have a life of their own if they had proper faces and were like people in the public eye; they wouldn't be mine.

That seems to be quite a common experience among writers who have had their work adapted and then found their creative vision impaired. How would you feel about seeing your stories and characters on screen?

Oh, the first two books have been optioned but that doesn't mean anything will happen. Would I watch them? Yeah, I would. Absolutely. I had that debate with my agent at the time when there were three companies interested, and obviously I wasn't going to turn down an option. She said, 'Would you want to push to be involved in the screenwriting if it got that far?' And I said, 'No, actually, I wouldn't because my creation is the book. Anything that's done after that is another product and it's a different thing.'

I find editing quite hard, when somebody else says these words that I crafted will maybe have to be moved about, so I imagine with TV the whole process may mean we have to lose a whole character or merge two books together. I couldn't do that. I think you've got to dissociate yourself from that and just think, 'Yeah, that's great that they're doing this but it's not really my work any more.'

You said that these characters are alive in your head –

– only when I'm writing. It's not like they come knocking at tea time. I'm not mad.

That said, how has your relationship with your characters changed over the years?

Not at all. I think it's the same. I never lose sight of the fact that I manipulate them. You know, I'm the puppet master. But certainly when writing the second book (*After the Fire*) it flowed a lot quicker because I already knew the characters from the first book and I wrote with an entirely different dynamic. The main character in the second book wasn't the main character in the first book (*The Twilight Time*) but I knew his backstory, I knew his history, I knew his relationships – so it was like I knew him when I took him off the shelf again, and it made it a lot easier.

As you get to know them better, do their personalities ever get in the way of plot?

I think I become more aware of what I would expect them to do or not to do. I don't really plot particularly much but there have been times when I thought, 'Right, this needs to happen.' And then the closer you get you think, 'She just wouldn't do this.' You know them better as people by then and you think, 'This would just be out of character and inappropriate.' And then you have to rethink, but that doesn't happen very often.

With the third book (*Shadowplay*) I did it all from one person's point of view whereas the other ones have usually been a two- or three-hand job. By the end of that third book I'd enjoyed the process of doing it but I think it was too long in one person's head. You know the light and dark thing again; everything was channelled through her eyes so with the fourth one I thought, 'No, I'm going to go back to mix again.' Not to say I wouldn't do another one with one character but I think with the sort of books that I'm writing it does dip into different places and there's a lot of domestic stuff in it too while the work stuff is quite often secondary. With other characters you see things differently and you can present things differently. With one character driving everything you can't; it's all down to her so I definitely got to know her very well by the end of it. But I think what happened with her is that although she has changed, she's also changed positively in that she's embracing other aspects of life a lot more than she did at the start.

Is she on her way out or have you got tired of her?

I'm not tired of her but I think she's served her purpose – certainly in terms of what I wanted to do in writing these books.

Which raises an interesting question: Would you ever bring protagonists back on account of their popularity rather than your own interest in them?

No, definitely not. It's your business driving this book and if you start to accept outside influences and temper how you write and what you write and who you write about it's not what you did in the first place, it's not the work that people like, the work that you produced and that was all from you.

You know, when you write the first book you don't expect it to get published and there's a freedom in that because you think, 'It's just me in a spare room, typing … wouldn't it be lovely, but it won't happen.' When you start writing the second book you are aware that there'll be an audience for it, and people will comment on it, and some people will like it and some people won't. The more you let yourself be aware of those things – 'What's your mum gonna say?' – it's so inhibiting that I just don't think of any of it at all. I couldn't write otherwise.

Do you have an ideal reader?

I think you write the book you want to read yourself, don't you? The first book (*The Twilight Time*) was predominantly written because I had never really read about what the reality of motherhood was like and I wanted to write about how it felt to be at home with two toddlers and no job. You'd been in an exciting job that folk were interested in. Then all of a sudden you were somebody's mum without even a name of your own, and I thought, 'You never read about that. It's always rosebuds and happy mums – you have a baby and then ... happily ever after.'

I wrote *The Twilight Time* for mums who felt they'd lost their identity having had a child and that they'd been subsumed by that child. It's like a rebirth for you as well. What you were before has gone. That person, well, doesn't exist and what you did before – any achievements – people aren't so interested in when you're mums and toddlers. But then you become aware that everyone's in that situation and all of them had lives before, and you're in an environment where, other than the fact that you've all had children, you really don't have that much in common. But equally, you're meeting interesting people you wouldn't otherwise meet. So that was why I wrote that first book and it so happened that the workplace of two of the characters was the police. That's why I was so flummoxed when the publishers were like, 'Yeah, it's crime, because it's about the police.' I've never deviated from that. I mean, I certainly always write from a feminist perspective.

So your politics are present in your writing?

I don't think you can dissociate that. I certainly don't when I write. If I'm writing about social issues, which all of my work is about, even if it's a character who I don't agree with, somewhere in the background – I'm putting those words in their mouths – there will be a frisson. I don't think you can ever be totally anodyne and uninvolved in what it is you're writing. In the second book (*After the Fire*) I have one of my characters talking about women wearing the veil, and then in the third book (*Shadowplay*) I have another character who is a Muslim talking about how she felt. It's not a dialogue that's happening at the same time, but I thought, 'No, I want to give another perspective on this but in another book. Just as a sort of casual aside.' Nobody's got black and white views about anything, so it probably gives writers a chance to talk about the grey areas that you don't have black and white views on, and you can posit two different sides of an argument.

Are shades of grey the new black?

Certainly any writing that I enjoy tends to be layered and quite ambiguous even to the extent of how a story ends. I hate things that are tied up and done and dusted because that's the sort of thing you close and you forget about whereas it's the ambiguity that lingers, isn't it? It's the unansweredness of things that you want to know about or it comes back and niggles at you. So, yeah, I'm all for shades of grey. In fact, I wanted my third book to be called *Fade to Grey* but the publishers didn't like it.

How much say do you usually have in the choice of your titles?

None. All three of them have been changed so far. Each title, having said that, I still chose. I mean it was never imposed on me. All of them were collaborative, based on what my original title would have been anyway. For the first book (*The Twilight Time*) my title was *Backshift* because the backshift is the longest shift you can do – it's afternoon into evening, it kinda drags on, and it's quite a confusing time because most

87

folk have gone home or are going out so you're in this limbo. To me that was reflective of the two women characters and their sense of, 'Have I made the right choices in life, and do I wish I could go back and change the way I made choices?'

I thought *Backshift* summed all of that up but they thought it would sound more like a fire brigade novel. I think that film *Backdraft* had come out recently, and I don't know if 'backshift' is a Scottish term and maybe in England it's called 'late shift', but it just didn't mean anything to them. So when I was explaining what it was my publishers said, 'Twilight time – you just said it there. It's *The Twilight Time*.' It wasn't my first choice but it sums up the same sort of things so, 'Okay, I'll go with that.' Nothing's ever been, 'This is what you're getting.' There's always a dialogue – a long dialogue.

You just mentioned second thoughts. Do you think you would write the same book today or would you maybe write those women and their self-analysis differently?

No, not at all. I would definitely write the same one.

That sounds like you're where you want to be with your writing. Are you?

No, I don't think so. I think I always want to try new things and move on. I don't want to stay with the same characters, definitely not. I think that would just drag me down eventually. I like new challenges. Like I said at the start, that's why I joined the police. I like things to be different and to not know what's going to happen and have that anticipation. I think if I kept writing about the same characters all the time I would lose that, and there wouldn't be that excitement at the start of each book which there has been just now.

I'm happy with what I've written, very happy, but I'm not where I want to be in terms of subject matter and place even. I don't want to necessarily set everything I write in Glasgow. Writers should always challenge themselves, and I worked in Glasgow, I was a police officer … that's what I've written about. Okay, in the second book (*After the Fire*) I wrote about a guy going to prison – never done that. But I did interview a cop who had gone to prison so that was very helpful and I got that as authentic as I could. But I'm not a diarist so I want to write things that challenge me and maybe take me further away from Glasgow.

Which of your books would you recommend to a first time reader of your work?

Well, it's hard to say with the third one because it's not that long finished and I don't know how I feel about it. I think the second one (*After the Fire*) is probably more fast-moving if people are looking for that sort of thing, and it's about one guy's life turning upside down. He shoots and kills somebody, it turns out they weren't armed, he's a firearms officer, and the media are baying for his blood because there have been several instances like this and somebody has to be accountable and he has to go to prison. So it's about how his life turns but also how his family's life is transported: the girl's a policeman's wife and then she's a prisoner's wife. It's about how her children cope in school and how a cop survives in prison. I did a lot of research into that and I spoke to firearms officers as well about the reality of firing a gun and the sort of training.

So that's probably much more 'police-y' if you like, and the first one, I would say, is much more about women in their early thirties wondering about where they are in life and did they made the right choices. One of them happens to be a cop. Obviously, because of her job she deals with crime but that's not the driver of that story.

Given all the research, do you ever worry people might recognise themselves in your novels?

Not really, no. Any friends that are still in the police that have read the books have really liked them because they recognise themselves – not personally, but the banter, and the fact that cops don't all call each other 'Sir' and 'Ma'am' or address folk by their surnames. Some former colleagues that

I've not kept up with have got in touch and said, 'Is that bit about me?' It may just be a nickname or some small anecdote and they recognise themselves having been there and that it's about them, and I'll say, 'Yeah, it is.' But they're always, 'So when's the next book out, and can I come to the book launch?' I think people like that. None of my characters are based on any one person; they're fictional but there are elements of me, I would say, in both of the two women in the first book. The guy is a total standalone character, and other people are amalgams of bits of people that I knew.

You mentioned a spare room as well as your dislike of external influence. I take it you write on your own, no music –

– Yeah! No music, usually when the house is empty. Every so often I do emails or whatever but I don't have the internet on all the time. The last two weeks have been school holidays and I've found it quite hard to write because I've got two teenage daughters and they've both been at home. It's not that they're playing loud music – although, they probably are – it's just knowing that there's the potential for being interrupted. I could never work in a busy café. I need silence, definitely.

So do you have a set writing routine?

Not really. I usually walk the dog first, get the kids out to school and be at my desk for about ten. I'll stop at lunchtime and walk the dog again, and that in itself is quite good because it makes you take breathing space. Something meditative like swimming or going to the gym or walking the dog... I find that's when things will settle in my head. I can sort out problems. At the screen I couldn't but I can when I'm away from it and I'm thinking, 'This wasn't right or that bit of dialogue wasn't working.' It'll come when I'm not thinking about it if you know what I mean; you catch the thought when you're doing something else. So it's usually good to do that and then I'll go back and write for another few hours. I tend to stop when the kids come home from school.

I sometimes write at the weekends if I'm nearing the end

of something and it's gaining momentum and I can't really stop. I don't write in the evening, though. It just doesn't flow for me at night at all.

How long would it usually take you to write an entire novel?

The first one took a couple of years, the second one a year, and the third one a year and two, three months maybe, and I'm just finishing a fourth one now, and that's been about a year and two months as well I'd say.

Is it distracting to talk about last year's book while you're writing a new one?

Well, I suppose to me it's still a momentum, because I'm still working on another one. But yeah, it feels weird to be talking about a book that I finished a year and a bit ago. But equally, that one hasn't been born yet so even though I wrote it a year ago it'll still be new because I haven't talked about it. When you've been doing a year of talking about one book you're ready to start talking about the next one.

Being a book ahead, does the less favourable criticism not touch you as much?

It doesn't touch me in terms of what I write, definitely not. I think you need to have a vision of what you're doing and be positive that that's what's right for you. But yeah, of course it affects you personally. It's like somebody saying, 'You're baby's ugly. That's a right ugly wean you produced.' And you think, 'It's beautiful!' Yeah, bad reviews bother me, of course they do.

So how do you read reviews? All at once, in company –

– Oh no, alone. Alone and very rushed at first and then I go back and read them again. But initially it's like, 'What are they saying?' But to be honest, it's just good to get any review really because it's so hard to get coverage. There's less and less book space for literary criticism in the broadsheets. I had very little coverage down south, which is why I'm interested in this whole idea of Scottish writing being internationally recognised, because in my experience it's been quite limited. The Scottish press have been very supportive, I have to say, because there was a news angle in the fact that I was a cop so I got some really nice, good coverage, but I've had virtually no coverage down south at all.

I got a lovely email from a guy in Sweden, who owns the only English bookshop there, basically saying, 'Karen Campbell rocks! Best book I've ever read.' That was lovely that somebody abroad had read it and bought it and that the Glaswegian-ness of it wasn't an inhibitor at all, because I kinda felt that maybe it was to begin with. But these things are maybe a slow burner.

Have you decided what to write next?

After the fourth book I want a break from writing about the police. I've got a few ideas for books; one's set in Scotland, one's set in South Africa and a third one that I've done a wee bit of work on is set on the west coast, Oban way, so I've got three options when I've finished this fourth one. And although I say I've finished the fourth one I've still got to edit it. I can't work on two things at once, so when I feel that the fourth one is done and dusted I don't know which of those three I'll go with, but I've certainly got three ideas bubbling at the moment.

How many rewrites would you usually go through?

Not many. I do one draft. I tend to edit as I'm writing. Each day I'll go back and look over what I did before and maybe work a little bit on it but I don't do an awful lot of editing. I'll go over it once when it's finished and then send it to my editor and then we usually have lots of to and fro. It tends to be predominantly about Scottish words. It's not about the structure; it's about... 'What does 'gallus' mean?'

What does it mean?

This is the problem. A lot of the time I don't put in Scottish words to be awkward. It's because to me it's the most appropriate word. You know it would take five words to say what this word means. It's a Glaswegian trait of being a bit wide – you think you know everything; you're a bit of a smart arse, a bit dodgy, overly confident but in a slightly sinister way maybe ... lots of words to sum up what 'gallus' means. So yeah, that's what the editing process usually is; it's an arm-wrestle between me and my lovely editor.

Have you considered appending a glossary?

The decision we came to was that if I was absolutely emphatic it had to go in, and I argued my case, fine, but her feeling about a glossary – and mine too – is if you're referring to a dictionary all the time it sort of breaks the spell of the book. You should be able to glean the meaning of a word from the context that it's set in – as long as it's not in every second line.

A glossary is a tacit admission that this isn't the right word and I have to explain it whereas to me, well, that is the right word. I shouldn't have to explain it. Does that make sense? That is the language that I speak in and that is the book you have chosen to read. I think putting in a glossary is almost an apology for having that verisimilitude. It's like, 'Yeah, I know you noticed that word and I'm sorry but here's the real word.' No, the real word is 'gallus'.

Your commitment to writing about the real Glasgow goes further, though, doesn't it?

I think so. The third book I've written is very much about power play and the politics with a small 'p' and a big 'P' that influence policing. Your role as a police officer is to guard, watch and patrol, and to protect life and prevent crime. That's what they tell you when you join. More and more I feel that policing is becoming overly politicised. There have even been moves like police divisions being restructured along local authority lines so it's the same councillors that control everything. There's also been talk about having elected police commissioners, like they have in America, which I think would be atrocious because it would then not be a serving police officer that was in charge of policing; it would be an elected politician with their own wants and needs.

You just have to look at Glasgow City Council at the moment and the turmoil it's in because the leader has allegedly been taking cocaine... I used to be a press officer at the Council – I should never have said that. But no, it's been in the papers and there's been all sorts of suggestions about cash for certain positions or certain quangos that have come up more and more. It used to be far more democratic and everything's behind closed doors and executive committees, and the police to me seems to be going the same way. And that's something that should concern the public, too, because there has to be 100 % public accountability about how policing is delivered and how it's resourced and financed and how it develops and changes.

One of the strongest messages I wanted to get through in my books was that police are not separate from the public. My husband lives in a house the same as I do. He wants his children to be safe at school; he goes to the bank, he goes into town for a drink; he drives a car... Cops are members of that society, too, so it's not in anyone's interest to have a police state or the overt and covert surveillance that goes on now in the name of fighting terrorism. I don't want to live in that sort of world – cops don't either.

I'm glad you've raised this issue seeing as we rarely consider those whose professional responsibility it is to police our society in accordance with the Terrorism Act. How do you feel about the state of our civil liberties?

Very uncomfortable – very uncomfortable because I think it's not just about blowing things up that means that terrorism is having an effect. It's about the panic and about the fear that's engendered and about how we develop a siege bunker mentality. It's what you were saying earlier: what is acceptable in our name gets blurred and elongated, and with each turn of that screw we lose something; we lose a sense of right and wrong. That alarms me hugely. The 'identity card' is another thing. I feel with these things there's no going back once you've gone down that road. It says something about us as a society that we're just allowing it to happen.

Do you write in the hope of creating greater awareness of these gradual changes?

I would love to think it would, but I'd be flattering myself to think that I would make that sea change. But definitely! That is a driver for me. It's about me giving voice to my fears and my concerns and maybe in some way trying a sort of elegy for what's being lost.

I remember the fire brigade were on strike a few years ago about their pay and conditions. Nobody really cared. The changes were made and it just passed by. It made me think a lot about the police service because I bet they were protesting about the same sort of things. A lot of a police officer's power is in their discretion and their ability to give somebody a second chance or make a judgment quickly, and certainly down south some of the police forces are going the way of, 'There is no discretion.' That hasn't happened here yet but there is a steady Anglicisation of the police service here in terms of methods. We are a separate country and I don't think one size fits all. Take crowd control for example: a lot of policing here is done by discretion and a bit of banter and a bit of, 'Come on, boys!' You don't need to have the riot gear and the sticks; you don't need to be like that at the start and I think we're tending towards that.

Strathclyde Police are going to start piloting the use of Tasers. At the moment a firearms officer is the only person authorised to use a Taser gun and its deployment is treated in exactly the same way: i.e. you have to have further authorisation to be allowed to take it out and use it, and you'll have to justify why you did it. Strathclyde Police are now talking about piloting Tasers as standard issue for beat cops. I think that's appalling and I would love to know what the evidence is for them deciding that. 'Oh, assaults on police have gone up.' But cops have always been assaulted and that's part of your job. It's not a nice part but it's part of your job.

If you've got a cornucopia of different tools about you and you're in a dangerous situation you're going to go for the most effective one first, of course you are. The most effective one is your voice and your ability to diffuse a situation. That's what you'll do. But if that fails, and the situation escalates, your second option would be your baton, then CS spray. If Tasers are readily available as well, there's a real risk you're going to go for that first. No matter what your training dictates, reality and being a human being will make you think, 'I've only got one chance to calm the situation down. I'm going to use this. I'm not going wait for them to up the ante.' They say these Tasers will be a last resort but they're hanging from your utility belt as a matter of course, and that's something that worries me a lot. It's another one of these margins that's just rubbed away and then that just becomes the norm and the standard that's acceptable to all.

Are you expressing a conscientious objection through your writing?

Yeah. I've certainly tried to in the fourth book.

Does that have a title yet?

My title is *A Small Bright Proof of Life*. I don't think it'll go as that but that's what I'm having.

And which of those issues are you addressing in this fourth book?

I have a protest at George Square which develops into a riot. That's one of those issues and that was prompted by – I remember there was a case of a Sergeant down in the MET who struck a protestor and he just recently went to court. He was shown striking her. She came up to him twice – unarmed – to protest about him stopping her from going wherever she was going. The second time he turned round and struck her with his hand, and he was charged with assault. That prompted me to write this scene – not to be an apologist for police violence, but to describe how in a situation like that when you're being assailed on all sides and you're aware of a threat you don't have five minutes to turn round, make an assessment, write down what that threat is, consider what to do … you react – wrongly, as he did – but you react. It doesn't mean you're a vicious bastard; it means you're a human being who's been pushed to the limit. It's quite right that you're held accountable for that.

You know, none of my books are saying, 'Poor, misunderstood police.' They're just trying to show, well, this is why these sorts of things happen.

Are you saying that you're more concerned with the primary causes – the stress – than with the stereotype of drink-fuelled self-loathing?

Yeah! Of course that stress can affect you however much you try not to let it, but you just find different ways of coping with that and part of your coping mechanism is what gives rise to this police stereotype. You come over as very professional and very inhuman but that's not the reality. It's a coping mechanism.

Is it fair to say that you write about the times when coping mechanisms fail?

Yeah. I remember my husband talking about a fatal road accident he went to. It was a mum and a dad who were perfectly fine and their four-year-old boy who was dead. He didn't have a seatbelt on and he just went right through the window when the car stopped. My husband had to take him to the mortuary and he was still warm and he was only four.

I wouldn't say it affected him in that he couldn't do his job but I know he thought about it on and off quite a bit. The actual fact of having to pick a small child up when he was still warm and felt alive and wasn't – it's a horrible thing to have to do. And it's not gory. It's not visceral. It's just that you wouldn't be human if that didn't affect you … the futility of it.

It could have been prevented and they have to go about with that grief for ever. And for a split second you've shared that grief with them in a very direct and immediate way.

Does that suggest a way of reading your work – should such integrity have the last word?

I hope it does. It's not a crusade. None of my work is about, 'The police are all great and you're bastards for not seeing that.' Not at all. I do show up the pettiness and the politicking and there are some right bastards that are cops. But there are also an awful lot of good, decent people as well. That was my real driver: to try and show that breadth of characters – obviously in a narrative framework, so there has to be conflict and there have to be investigations and impact of crimes and things like that – but they kind of frame the people; I don't think they drive the stories, definitely not. At least, that's not how I've tried to write them.

At the end of the day it's important for any writer that you're not on a soapbox. You're there to entertain people and you're telling a story. You have to tell a story that's interesting about characters that you can hopefully believe in even if you don't sympathise with them. If any other of your messages or hopes or whatever come out from that that's brilliant, but the main reason that you write is so that other people will read it and have a connection. I wouldn't like my books to be me standing on a soapbox saying what I think about the world. They're just telling a story and trying to present the facts as I have experienced them as a cop. Then people can make up their own minds.

Neil Forsyth
Read This At Your Peril

Neil Forsyth was born in 1978. Bob Servant was not. Although destined for Dundonian fame, and despite popular belief, Bob is not a co-authoring pensioner. He is Neil's brainchild. Clarifications such as this may strike some of his true believers as wanton sacrilege but, as Neil has learnt the hard way, when your alter ego becomes a local hero chances are you soon appear 'schizophrenic … or a fraudster.' Speaking of which, before Bob Servant there was Elliot Castro. When he doesn't invent them, Neil investigates men of criminal charisma. This principal fascination, more than any consignment to genre or method, would seem to define the appeal of his diverse writing in both fiction and nonfiction.

It is worth mentioning that Neil's thematic catalogue, though commercially successful, is not the calculated effect of his career. It is the original cause. After all, he was first gainfully employed as a teenage journalist working for a Dundee United fanzine, and would later enter an even more colourful world as a nightclub promoter before graduating from the University of Edinburgh and the New York Film Academy. Yet lazy thinking often suggests that to recognise criminal charisma is to encourage it; hence some rather predictable indignation. Not only did *Other People's Money* (2006) receive instant popular attention and wide critical acclaim, but Neil's bestselling debut was also serialised in the *The Guardian*.

As for the debatable controversy of the book's subject

matter, *The Sunday Times (Scotland)* was quick to suggest a remedy: value judgments rather than research accuracy ought to have dictated Neil's approach to the true story of Glaswegian fraudster Elliot Castro. In light of such criticism any book is poor in taste relative to the extent of a writer's resourcefulness. Writers such as Neil, who have chosen to reveal the truth at the heart of much prejudice, have to depart from conventional research methods to arrive at the full story. Of course, this may well be found wanting as a morality tale for the easily corrupted whom the last remaining evangelists of news agencies have sworn to defend.

Alternatively, if the license taken with pedagogy is overlooked, the truth of the rendering alone will strike us. Neil read about Elliot in *The Scotsman*, visited him in prison, and gained his permission to write a book about his life story. *Other People's Money* has since been released in seven countries and, with or without poetic justice, the film rights have been purchased by the producers of *The Last King of Scotland*, so the fiasco this book reveals is unsurprisingly uncomfortable. It is also highly entertaining. Not only do our own fantasies about the financial sector flash through the joints of biographical facts, but we also learn about the fantastic scams that got Elliot into – and his story out of – the joint.

In Neil's second book, *Delete This At Your Peril* (2007), we meet Bob Servant, Scottish Don Quixote de la Internet. These email exchanges with scammers the world over have drawn even the admiration of those who make a living of cult characters, most notably Irvine Welsh, who selected Bob's book as his choice in a poll of the Funniest Books Ever Written. Neil has since written a radio adaptation for the BBC and the sequel, *Hero Of Dundee*, was released in October of 2010. 2009 saw the publication of *Let Them Come Through*, Neil's third exposé of criminal charisma: a failing TV medium. Having spent a year researching several psychics, including eminent sceptic James Randi, Neil was praised once again for his darkly comic approach to a comically dark subject.

Neil's journalism has appeared both in gentlemen's magazines and international broadsheets in which, to name just one example, the most detailed study of amnesia victim Benjaman Kyle has earned him a certain reputation. So when we met in an Edinburgh bar for the following interview I was expecting the wryness of the reporter who has written it all and seen worse. Is that the man I met? Fair to say, he would trump that image with a sense of humour that is yet another specimen of his originality in self-knowledge, and with a talent for storytelling that seems suspiciously at home in a pub.

~

Welcome back, Neil. You've been away for a while, haven't you?

Yeah, I went to New York. I did a lot of journalism for some of the big American mags but I was also supposed to be writing a book over there which never actually came off. It was a biography of a war photographer. I got sent over there, commissioned to write a proposal, got there, wrote it – it wasn't a particularly good story to be honest, but I just stayed anyway – and then I went to the New York Film Academy and did a screenwriting course, which just finished a month ago.

Did you enjoy it?

Loved it… But absolutely hated it for the first two or three weeks. I didn't have a fucking clue what I was doing. It's very technical. It's a very structured style of writing: the three-act structure and eight-sequence approach. It's kind of the opposite of prose writing.

Does it help to have a background in journalism?

Yeah, but I don't have any qualifications or anything. I got into journalism to write books, because that was how it worked. I started out in football writing, actually, because that was the only place to get published. I was in Edinburgh six or seven years ago and I started doing match reports with *The Scotsman, Scotland on Sunday*, some interviewing, some features, and then from there I got work with the men's mags, so I wrote for *FHM, Maxim* … all the ones on the second top shelf. It was while I was writing for *Maxim* that I found Elliot Castro. He was originally the subject of a feature I wrote. Then I got the book deal from that to do his full biography.

Would that be your standard methodology?

A lot of the things I do are nonfiction stories that I find and then think they could maybe make a book. So what I do is I sell it as a journalism piece to someone who'll send me off to do it, because most of it is foreign. For instance, as a result of *Other People's Money* I get an email every month or two from a crook. That book's very popular in prison. About a month or two ago I got an email from a guy in Canada called Gerald Blanchard who wrote this semi-literate email to me saying, 'I'm just out of prison in Canada but I read your *Other People's Money* and I thought you might be interested in my story.' He sent me all these articles about himself. He was a fraudster and a jewel thief, and his most famous crime was …

There's this castle in Vienna. He went round there with his wife and his father-in-law on a holiday and there was this famous jewel called the Star of Assisi which was one of the Austrian royal heirlooms. They were getting shown it and he though, 'I've got to nick that.' So he met a guy in a bar who was a pilot and about a week later he parachuted onto the roof of this museum in the middle of the night, stole this jewel and it became this famous crime. That's a good example because I then sold that article, and I'm going up there to interview him. I don't think I've got another book about a single criminal like that but I'm going up there to sell it as journalism and see what happens.

So yeah, I use journalism to fund me to go and find the stories and once I find the story I decide if it's worth a book or not. Crime's got a very dedicated audience, and true crime especially.

Having worked as a journalist in the UK as well as the US, do you see any differences between the two approaches to researching, writing and editing?

It's very interesting, the difference between writing for British or American titles. Say I write a piece for a British magazine, usually the editor will just phone me up and he'll be like, 'All right, how're you doing? What are you up to at the weekend? Oh, listen, about the article, is that definitely his age and is this where he was born? All right, no bother. See you later.' It'll come out in the magazine a month later.

In the States it'll go through two or three editors, then a copy editor … the editing process is longer than the writing process and it's fucking torturous. I'll write something about the interview subject like, 'He said this angrily,' and they'll write back, 'Was he actually angry when he said this?' That's the level of detail that they go to. They'll do a line-by-line edit. I don't know why it is. It's not for litigious reasons because the freedom of speech law in America makes it very hard to sue. It's just the editing philosophy. It's very interesting, a huge difference, and a very different style of journalism in America. It's very impersonal, very hard for your observations to remain in the copy by the end of the edit, because it's not substantiated. That's what it's all about: fact checking.

How did you go from that to Other People's Money*?*

I was a freelance journalist at the time, so the mindset I was in was finding stories, repackaging them, spamming them out to the magazines and trying to sell them. I read this article about Elliot in *The Scotsman*. I was living in Edinburgh at the time. I got up in the morning, had a cup of tea while I was reading the paper, and there was this small article about this Scottish fraudster that said how he'd been caught in this hotel and spent all this money. It was a curious story. They didn't really have much information. They didn't have any quotes from Elliot. They had a quote from his mum, which was a bit odd, saying he's made a few mistakes, and it had a few quotes from this detective who'd tracked him down, Ralph Eastgate.

I went out that day and was walking past a garage and I saw the front page of *The Daily Record* – 'Catch Me If You Con', with a photo of Elliot. So I bought the paper and they had a bit more information, *The Daily Record* being a bit more dramatic about it all. I thought I could easily sell this story so I wanted to get in touch with him. All I knew was the court he'd been convicted in, which was Isleworth, so I phoned up the court and said I wanted to get in touch with this guy and what prison was he in. She says, 'Well, I can't tell you that, but anyone convicted here goes to Wormwood Scrubs for at least the first few weeks until they get processed.'

So I wrote to Wormwood Scrubs prison – didn't have his prisoner number – and just wrote on the envelope 'Elliot Castro, HMP Wormwood Scrubs' and sent it off. I didn't expect it to get to him. A week or two later I got a reply from him on notepaper; a very cautious, short reply, all block capital letters, very impersonal: 'I'm not sure why you want to speak to me. I don't want to glorify my story.' So I wrote back to him, he wrote back, and onwards like this. He then got moved to an open prison, which was fucking astonishing. He was a felon with a history of running, so they put him in an open prison. He probably talked them into that.

Then he wrote back to me from the open prison and we talked on the phone. Now this was the best thing: he was in an open prison and he managed to get himself a job in the prison office. So I got this letter from him and it was on personalised paper that he'd made up on the computer and it had all these graphics. It was a prison address but he'd made up personalised notepaper like he was running a business. So we talked on the phone, got on well and eventually he said, 'Right, you can come down.'

In an open prison you can get taken out for the day on a

Saturday if it's for a constructive reason, which this was, of course.

Of course. Reformation complete.

Yeah, the lies stopped. So I sold the story to *Maxim*. I went down with a photographer to this open prison just outside Brighton, Sussex. I said to him, 'Right, you wait around the corner,' and Elliot walked out. This was the first time I'd met him and I didn't really know what he looked like. I spent the day with him in Brighton and he told me his story. In retrospect, some of it was bollocks, but he was protecting himself in certain ways, which is understandable. But it was a great story. I mean, amazing. I only had a few hours with him and that was like a highlights reel.

Then he went back and I spoke to Ralph Eastgate, the detective. The fact that he was willing to speak to me made a huge difference to the story because it validates a lot of it. So I went back to *Maxim* and said this was just a great story and there was so much more to it. I started to get phone calls from a few TV production companies, so I went on the internet and found a huge list of British literary agents. I put together all the features that I'd written, Elliot's story, a bit about me that said I wanted to write this book, and I emailed that to a hundred literary agents over a period of a few days.

I got about half a dozen replies back, positive. Two of them I went to see in London, and one was David Riding at MBA, a young guy, very into the story, very into me and developing me as a writer, so I signed up with him. He taught me how to write it as a book proposal. I then wrote two opening chapters, getting material from Elliot while he was in prison, which wasn't easy.

How did you manage to get enough material for a book proposal?

Various ways … I probably shouldn't say much more than that.

Ha! You're probably right. So once you had the material,

was it difficult to find a publisher for a book that could have become a professional liability?

We had a lot of interest from publishers and then they started falling away one at a time ... just got scared off by various aspects. But Macmillan was still interested – big publisher, good deal – they were just very excited and they were the only ones left. Then I got this email: Elliot had been caught years before on a train doing something ridiculous. He had the credit card of a doctor and was on a train going from London to Glasgow. The conductor comes round and he doesn't have any cash but he's sitting in first class. Elliot was about eighteen at the time. So the conductor was fine with it, but obviously took notice.

About an hour later they're going past Carlisle and there's a thing over the tannoy saying, 'Someone's taken ill in the carriage. Are there any doctors on board?' Elliot's sitting there laughing, going, 'That's funny. I've got this card.' Then he saw the conductor coming up pointing at him, 'You're a doctor, aren't you?' Elliot had to go, 'Yeah ... yeah.' He went, 'Can you come and have a look at this woman?' So Elliot had to go up the carriage to this woman who was hyperventilating in the corner, and the conductor's going, 'We've got a doctor! We've got a doctor!'

Elliot got led through, sat there and went, 'Right, what's wrong with ye? ... I think you're having a panic attack.' Then this other doctor appeared and said, 'Oh, she's having a panic attack,' and Elliot went, 'Yeah, I thought so.' To cut a long story short, they stopped in Carlisle, an ambulance came, and the woman said, 'Can you come with me?' to Elliot because he'd been so comforting to her. So he's like, 'Right, yeah, fine.' He's sitting in this ambulance, went to Carlisle hospital, they got more and more suspicious of him, and he just legged it, but they caught him on the way back to the train.

He got charged with impersonation of a doctor which is a 200-year-old offense that no one had been charged with for something like forty years. And obviously credit card fraud. So when he got convicted in Carlisle he got in quite a lot of papers, and most of the papers did it as a quirky story, but a couple of tabloids did it as sexually motivated. What they didn't know is that Elliot is gay.

Macmillan did a Google on him and found one of these stories, so the publisher emailed me saying, 'Look, we can't go ahead with this book. This is just a bit weird, a bit creepy.' I said, 'No, no, that's not what happened,' and I told her. She said, 'Well, we don't know how he's going to come across.' So I said, 'Look, how about this? We come and meet you and if you don't want to go ahead with the book, fine.' We agreed on that. So Elliot came out of an open prison in Buckingham-shire, got a train to London, me and my agent met him off the train, went straight to Macmillan's offices, he had his stuff in a bin bag, handed it to a woman at reception, said, 'Look after that for me,' went up to the meeting and I said, 'Listen, do you understand that this is all or nothing in this meeting? You've got to really perform.' He just went, 'I'm a con man. It's not going to be a problem.'

So we went into the meeting and he just ran the whole thing. He was introducing people to each other ... Honestly, it was like he was the MD of Macmillan. We got the deal the next day.

What a story ... Well done!

The story is just fantastic. I was just so lucky to stumble across it and the more I worked on it the better it got.

Do you remember how long it took you to write the book?

I wrote quite a bit of it while Elliot was in prison and then another six months and three months of editing. I wrote it quite quickly. I did it full-time, pretty much.

Did you notice your writing voice change?

Yeah. I had to do something on it recently – a public reading – and I looked at it again and I think the voice is quite consistent throughout, actually, which I was surprised about because usually with someone's first book, towards the end is where they get confident. So I probably had quite a good understanding of him early on. The big thing for me was having Eastgate, the detective, taking part because that just made such a difference.

Instead of me having to go and check every fucking thing Elliot told me I could just speak to Eastgate. He had all the paperwork and I had all the paperwork, because in a fraud case the defendant gets all the paperwork as well: credit card statements, faxes between the airlines, and Eastgate saying, 'You've got to catch this guy!' It's fantastic.

So there was a bit of research and then it's just chronology really. He'd only been active as a fraudster for about four or five years, but because of the life he was living and the completely dysfunctional nature of it and the travelling he was doing, he couldn't remember where he'd been when. So I was using these credit card statements from the trial to map his progress around the world. I put them into years, worked it out, and he'd go, 'Oh fuck yeah, that's right! I'd forgotten I went there.'

It was a great book to write because when you've got that you've got a very natural structure, and then you've got Eastgate to throw his contribution in every so often to back things up, and then I'd use my own voice on occasion as a means of introducing Elliot's mum, for example. So it was a great book to write, and a quite easy book to write as a first book. The story's there; you just have to find it.

Let me ask you about the other side of success: the come-down. Was it hard when it came?

Well, yeah. When it got published it got huge publicity. For two weeks we were based in London getting sent here and there by the publisher. Elliot was on 'This Morning' so we had the populist edge, loads of coverage in the papers, and then *The Guardian* serialised it, which for me was the big thing because *The Guardian* is somewhere that holds good writing.

It was more after the publication process that the come-down came. That's when I was like, 'What am I going to do now?' There was a period when I was desperately looking about for a relatively similar story and none of them were as good as that. It's very hard to find that kind of story. I'd be surprised if I ever find a nonfiction story that good again. That was when the comedown came, I guess.

And then you had the book optioned for film. What did that feel like?

That was very exciting. We were down in London getting taken around the big film studios and we got signed up by Charles Steel who co-produced *The Last King of Scotland*. Yeah, that was fantastic; a really exciting process.

What happened?

Well, we sold a two-year option to Charles Steel, then we sold him an extension, and then we actually took the rights back a few months ago. Not a huge amount happened. We got very close. It's a weird business the film business, and it's all about timing.

Are you worried it might now seem too much like I Love You, Phillip Morris?

I was worried about that when I saw the description but, to be honest, there's no great correlation. It's a very American story. The guy is like forty and he has a big gay thing in prison. I wasn't too worried about that. The worry is *Catch Me If You Can*. So what we did was we took the rights back – very amicably – and we got other people interested. We could easily sell the option again for two years but what I said to Elliot is, 'Give me six months to write a script and then we'll see if anyone wants the script. If not, we'll sell the option.'

So I went and did this screenwriting course and I've started writing the script. By the end of August I'll have a script written and we'll send it round. Even if people don't want the script and want to rewrite it, it's just more material for them to see, and I want to show that the story is different from

Catch Me If You Can. It's a very filmic story, it's a British story, and it's a true story. We've had a lot of TV interest. Donald MacIntyre's going to try to do something on it in a different strand, so I think we're going to do that just to get something going and then keep going with the film.

How did you go from that to other people's stories?

I started the novel ... and then wrote myself into a level of confidence. The novel took a long time because I was doing it off and on as I was doing a lot of journalism. The Bob Servant book came out next, but I started writing the novel first, then did the humour book, and then went back to the novel and finished it. Yeah, so I just got involved in other projects and I'm very glad I did because I would have been very quickly pigeonholed in that nonfiction area if I'd gone straight into a similar story. Now I've done three books in three genres and can go anywhere ... if people are interested, obviously, but it opens things up a bit.

Have the recent developments in publishing influenced you in any way?

Yeah, I've not made any of these choices on a commercial basis, but I'm aware of the need to diversify – not really for a commercial reason, but for myself, because it develops me as a writer. If I start churning out biographies of criminals I'm not developing in any way. In fact, I'd be stagnating or getting worse, whereas I knew that writing a novel would develop me enormously, which it did. It was by far the hardest thing I've written because it's a relatively different but much more demanding thing to write.

But you've got to balance the commercial thing with it. I guess I'm lucky in a way because I have the journalism and also I'm not married with kids. I know a lot of very good writers who are basically going job to job – a lot of editing, a lot of ghost-writing – because it pays.

Are so-called 'victimless crimes' a defining interest of your work?

Exactly. I mean, a lot of people would call Elliot's stuff a victimless crime, which it isn't. Yeah, it's definitely an interest I have. *Let Them Come Through* is about a medium and I take a very dark view of it. It's written from the medium's point of view, it's all bollocks, and he shows the reader how he does it.

Is he a fictional Derren Brown?

Well, he's different because he doesn't present himself as genuine. He's very open about the fact that it's bollocks.

Don't both expose the industry?

Yeah, we're very similar in the position we're taking. What inspired me to write the novel was going to see a famous psychic. He does all the... 'Is it Mary, Mandy, Mark?' A few of us went to see him in Edinburgh and it was fucking hilarious. It was just so blatantly obvious that it was bullshit, but what I couldn't believe was – first of all him – but second, the audience, and how they just went along with it. They were wanting to believe so badly, but he was all over the shop.

I'll never forget he said to this woman in the top row about her late husband: 'Yeah, yeah, I've got him ...' He managed to guess something here and there and then waved around his chest where basically all your vital organs are: 'Did he die like this ...?' You've got about an eighty percent chance. Anyway, she went, 'Oh, yeah, yeah!' He says, 'God, I can see your whole life. I've really got you. I've got your whole personality. I can see everything about you,' and she went, 'Oh, that's wonderful!' He goes, 'Stand up so we can see you,' and she went, 'No, no ... ' So he went, 'Come on, stand up and let everyone see you,' and she says, 'I can't. I'm in a wheelchair.'

We were wetting ourselves. But even after that, at the next thing he says the audience are on the edge of their seats again, and I'm looking around going, 'He just didn't know she was in a wheelchair.' I just found the whole thing absolutely incredible and I'd wanted to write about this, so I thought about doing it in a nonfiction sense. But it's quite hard to do that – it would be an exposé sort of thing and that's more of a magazine article – so I just started writing this novel. I took as my starting point, 'How the fuck does someone end up doing that as their job – standing on a stage speaking bollocks to people, mucking about with their dreams and their hopes and fears?'

How did you make sure your indignation wouldn't spoil the effect?

Dark humour, I guess, but humour all the same. I mean, a lot of people are getting something from it. I think it's outrageous the money they make from these people but there are worse crimes committed than that, so it wasn't a book I wrote running on indignation but rather on disbelief and great interest in how it actually works.

Which raises questions about the potential of a likeable character. Do you see Elliot as such?

He is a likeable character and in real life he's a likeable character. I mean, he's different from the book, as anyone would be, but the flaws he has aren't serious and aren't any different from the flaws most people would have.

Did he agree with your portrayal of his life and crimes or did he make editorial changes?

The stuff that he would want to change in the book was never stuff that made him look bad; it was things that would make the family look particularly poor, for example, because they're a very proud family as many Scottish working class families are, so it was things like that that he'd want changed. He gave me a huge amount of trust and I appreciated that.

Certain critics seem to have ethical concerns. Do you share any of them?

No, I don't have any ethical worries at all. I think my duty is to the story and that's it, and if people are using that book to decide whether credit card fraud is bad then I would suggest that they're already wavering in the first place, so I don't have any ethical concerns. In fact, I'll tell you a story: I was in Waterstone's on George Street about three months

112

after it came out and they had a big pile of them, so I said to them, 'Do you want me to sign them?' She went, 'Do you know that that's the most shoplifted book in Edinburgh?' I was loving that, because we still get paid. In fact, in the hardback I had a thing in the back where I wrote in Elliot's voice something like, 'If you've bought this book and commit crime we can't stop you.' When it came to the paperback they just shot that straight away. But Elliot gets messages through MySpace from crooks.

What's he up to these days?

He's in Glasgow. He DJs, he does some stuff for banks and companies, and he speaks at events. I've done a couple of things with him actually. We've spoken at a couple of big fraud events in England. It's good fun.

Would you say that this book has changed your perspective on banking and finance?

I think it was a great story of the time because the profligacy and complete recklessness of the banks were very obvious in Elliot's story. Elliot was a convicted criminal and was doing his fraud, and meanwhile was getting offered credit cards in his name by the banks. He was a criminal and they didn't make him do it, but their complete recklessness and their complete lack of checks and balances with Elliot reflects well, I think, the whole ethos of the time. One of the hardest things for Eastgate when trying to convict Elliot was getting the information from the banks. They didn't want Elliot's story to be told because it was a complete embarrassment for them so they were actually incredibly resistant, and one of the reasons Elliot got convicted for so little was that the banks just wouldn't give the information to Eastgate. They had it – they knew what he'd done – so he got off fucking lightly. There's no doubt about that.

What do you make of the propositions you've been getting ever since Other People's Money?

I do them as journalism. One of the guys who read the

book is the press officer at Prisoners Abroad, so any story that comes to him that he thinks is decent, I get a phone call. So I got a phone call, for example, from an English guy living in Bangkok who was a drug smuggler, got caught and put in prison in Japan. I met him in London and he looked like a city banker. He was in a linen suit, very well turned out, very smart, very posh, I had a drink with him in a bar in London, and he was drawing on a beer mat how you can hide hash in suitcases within five minutes. He said, 'Come out to Bangkok. I'll introduce you to some of the dealers out there. You'll get a good story out of that.'

So I went to Bangkok, got out there and John's nowhere to be seen. I'm out there on the paper's tab and can't find the fucker. He's not answering his phone. He'd said to me, 'I'll get you into Bang Kwang Prison to meet the main dealer.' Eventually he phones me: 'I'm in the jungle in Venezuela. You can probably imagine what I'm doing.' So he's at some fucking cocaine factory in Venezuela, I'm in Bangkok, the paper's going fucking berserk, and I said, 'I thought you were going to get me into Bang Kwang.' He said, 'No problem.'

He phoned me up the next day and said, 'Neil, a couple of guys are coming round. They've got a false passport for you and the photographer and they'll take you to Bang Kwang.' I went, 'I'm not doing that,' and he went, 'Well, they're coming round, Neil. A passport is usually ten grand. They've done it for free. They're not going to find that very funny.' So I went, 'All right, I'll be here,' hung up, phoned the photographer and said, 'We're fucking going!' We packed our bags, legged it out of the hotel, went to another hotel, stayed one more night and flew back. I sold it as a travel piece.

He emailed me about a week later and I said, 'Look, I wasn't comfortable,' and he wrote back saying, 'That's no problem. I'll be in touch.' Two weeks later I got an email from Prisoners Abroad: 'Sorry about Bangkok. John is in prison in Japan. He will be for some time.' Never heard from him again. So that's the calibre of person I deal with.

Have you come to trust your instincts on those close calls?

Yeah, you kind of get a feel for it. I told Donald MacIntyre that story and he's obviously done a lot more of that than me, and he said he just gets this sixth sense.

Was there a moment when you wanted to go through with the plan anyway?

There's a group of expats over there who go in and give chocolates and newspapers to the Western prisoners, so I went in with them the day before and interviewed a couple of British guys through the bars just to get a bit of background. I told one of them what I might be doing and he just went, 'You're fucking insane. I wouldn't try to sneak in here for a hundred grand.' I was like, 'Yeah, maybe you're right.'

Another time an English guy in prison in India got convicted for drug smuggling for ten years. He's in prison in the north of India, rural India, and someone got me in touch with him – Fair Trials Abroad or something – I interviewed his parents in London and then I went out to India. I smuggled myself into that prison with a Swedish photographer, and that's the dodgiest situation I've ever been in. We went and told the governor that I was his cousin. We bribed our way in. He was on one side of the bars, we were on the other. I had a dictaphone hidden in my shorts, the photographer had a camera hidden up his T-shirt, there was an armed guard walking up and down behind us, and every time he got a certain distance away the photographer would take a shot. Every time he did that both me and Patrick nearly had a heart attack.

I said, 'Listen, this is going to sound a bit odd but I need you to talk into my crotch.' So Patrick's leaning down and we did the interview like that, got out and just fucking legged it. Anyway, Patrick had said, 'I've done these paintings for my dad. Can you take them back to London?' But we legged it in the end and were so scared we just bribed our way out, and I was like, 'Fucking hell, I forgot to pick up his paintings.' I was in a real moral quandary and decided I needed to go back.

So I went back to the governor and asked for the paintings, and he said, 'Ah, you … stay here.' He came out with one of the guards, took me around the corner and said, 'What's your job?' I said I was a doctor. He'd Googled my name and said, 'You're a journalist. We know who you are.' And I went, 'What! What? Me?' It's got my fucking photo on my website. He said, 'I know you're a journalist.' So I just took out all the money I had and went, 'There you go.' There was this horrible silence. Then he grabbed the money and went, 'Don't ever come back!'

I just legged it, met the Swedish guy at the hotel, didn't even stay that night in the town, and paid one of the kitchen staff to drive us to Delhi, which took twelve hours, just so we could get away … So that was another guy who came to me as a result of *Other People's Money*. Yeah, you get good stories from it – no doubt about that – and it's very interesting; anyone's fascinated with these stories.

Why do you think that is?

There but for the grace of God go I. Elliot's story … if I was from his background, if I didn't have any real opportunities, and if I found a way of doing his fraud, I would do it. The guy in India – that could have easily happened to me. With these stories it's voyeurism. The big attraction to Elliot's story and the reason that it's popular is the voyeurism of unlimited funds, unlimited travel and no responsibility. Who wouldn't want that for a period of their lives, especially when they're young?

For me it's a finite attraction. It's definitely worn off. I wouldn't do another book similar to Elliot's because I've just done that, but I'm definitely attracted to the darker side of human nature. I think anyone is. That's what you want to read about. There are more books written about Hitler than about Jesus. People are interested in flawed characters, and books about flawed characters have got durability.

Is sympathy for the underdog typical of the Scottish?

116

It's a funny thing with the Scottish. It's sympathy for an underdog until they're no longer an underdog and then there's no sympathy whatsoever. Elliot gets recognised in Glasgow and it's not always a positive experience, but there is a lot of the idea, 'Good on ye, nicking the money of those fucking banks,' which is a morally corrupt view. There's definitely an element of that.

It's strange; the only negative stuff we got when it came out was *The Sunday Times (Scotland)*, which went for us a couple of times with negative articles, whereas elsewhere coverage and reviews have been very positive. It's not sympathy; it's more that people are enjoying the story and not having some hang-up reaction to it.

Does Other People's Money *travel well? For instance, how has it done in America?*

I wrote a big adaptation of it for an American magazine that got huge coverage and I got a lot of emails from literary editors in America asking had the American rights been sold. Americans are quite open to it; they don't really have the class concerns that the UK has so they would appreciate it just as a story. I mean, there are writers in the States like Ben Mezrich who makes his living off these stories. I think it's really quite an American kind of story: you can do anything you want, which is the American dream ... apart from the crime. I think it's got a great international appeal. It's a bit of an everyman story really, but it's in Britain that it gets the abuse because it's about one of our own.

As a debut writer, how were you received by the Scottish crime writing community?

I didn't really have a huge interaction with them. Irvine Welsh was the guy who read it and came back positively and actually gave us a quote for the cover. He was the only other author who really got behind it. It was ignored by the Scottish literary magazines and editors, which is fair enough – it's not a literary book – but they were very positive about my novel

117

so it wasn't held against me.

The problem is I don't live in Scotland and it sounds very parochial but that counts against me hugely. The Bob Servant book – I'm writing a sequel just now – is being republished by an Edinburgh publisher in October. BBC Scotland are adapting the emails and that's going to go out in October as well. There's going to be a lot of coverage around then so I'm going to come back and spend a decent amount of time in Scotland then, but in terms of a Scottish movement I don't feel part of one at all. I've got some level of profile in Scotland, I guess, and it would probably help me professionally to be here, but it's just the way it's worked out.

How would you define the Scottish novel?

A lot of humour, definitely. Irvine Welsh is one of my biggest influences, without a doubt. I think in Scotland you get a lot of great writers with huge experience. What I like when I read a novel is the idea that the novelist has put a bit of work into it and not necessarily personal experience. For instance, my novel with the medium: I wanted people to come away thinking, 'That guy has immersed himself in the world of the medium.' So the reader feels educated in some way, thinking that there's either some experience or work behind what you've written. That's what I think is quite a Scottish trait ... that you feel there's a bit of pain and heartache behind it.

I think writing a book is a very cocky thing to do and being cocky in Scotland isn't something that's appreciated. That then, through osmosis, affects the writing. People are writing and trying to flaunt what talent they have, but couching it in a self-deprecating way which affects the writing style and the characters. You don't get the grand, sweeping American novel that the author writes from a position of total confidence.

How do you write?

I go away for three or four days to places with no internet; the internet's the big killer for me. About four days is the

optimum for that; then you start to go a bit mad. My friend
has a cottage on the Isle of Wight so when I lived in London
I'd go there for four days – no internet – and do a good ten
to twelve thousand words, and I'd do the same in some other
places. I try and write to a decent standard but really get to
the end and then start editing. Writing is rewriting.

Do you ever reread your own work?

Yeah, definitely. It can be quite motivational. I mean, with
Other People's Money I go to prisons quite a lot and do
readings there.

Like a latter-day Johnny Cash?

Ha! A Dundonian Johnny Cash ... which is good fun. Yeah,
I reread the books but they all hold up well. I mean, you spot
flaws but I don't find anything to cringe at. I can see with
Other People's Money that I was writing it in the position I
was in then. It would be a better book if I wrote it now. That's
the great thing about writing: you know that the more you do
the better you get. So rereading is a good motivational thing.

On that note, who have been your greatest influences?

Irvine Welsh, Martin Amis, Kingsley Amis, George
MacDonald Fraser, James Ellroy ... The books I read when I
was young – in my early teenage years – were the Perry Mason
books by Erle Stanley Gardner, but *Trainspotting* was a life-
changing experience for me; the same with *Money* by Martin
Amis, which I probably read once a year, and *Lucky Jim* by
Kingsley Amis ... very much male authors.

Do you have a favourite scene?

Well, yeah. Talking about scenes, I was at a music festival
in California last month and I was separated from my mates.
I was in a bar, turned round and bumped into Kevin McKidd
who played Tommy in *Trainspotting*. He was with his wife. I
was chatting to him and was pretty pissed and went, 'This is
better than when Archie Gemmill scored against Holland in
the 1978 World Cup!' You know, the scene in *Trainspotting*
where he's having sex, and he went, 'Fucking hell, I haven't

heard that one for a while.' That's a favourite scene, from the movie, not from the festival.

What have you most enjoyed about writing?

The praise that Irvine Welsh gave two of my books and the praise that I've had from a couple of other writers and artists is immeasurably more exciting than getting a good review from a freelance journalist who's reading three books a day and then writing a hundred words on it.

Speaking of the vagaries of literary criticism, what do you make of the genre debate and recent popular crossovers?

I think you have to be very careful. I'm sure that people are largely reviewing these books on the perceived quality, but there's such aversion for people trying something outwith what they're known for. That was probably one of the reasons that I deliberately went biography, novel, humour – because once you've done one they can't say, 'Oh, he's trying something new,' whereas if I'd written five nonfiction books and then tried a novel I'd have been billed as a nonfiction writer trying a novel. You're instantly graded like that.

So what made you choose the Bob Servant book as a follow-up?

I just loved the character, and I'm writing a very different book. I'm not doing the emails but his memoirs ... Bob Servant came about as a total laugh. I'd read about these people who were writing to scammers and called themselves 'scambaiters', but they were a bit nasty with it. They were getting Nigerians to dress up in fancy dresses and stuff like that. I wanted to write to them for a magazine article, so I just opened an email account as Bob Servant so I had a different name and scammers couldn't track me down. As I was writing to them I had to make things up because I didn't want to write anything that would identify me so I thought, 'Fuck it! I'll make him a 62-year-old former window cleaner from Dundee,' and then the character just grew through the emails.

Anyway, it was far too long for a magazine article so I

wrote a few of them and sent it all to my agent who said, 'We'll sell this as a humour book.' As I was writing the book the character just got bigger and bigger. Then I wrote the blog and then the book came out and the character got a great reception. I love the character and I want to do other things with it. I'd have no problem if I became known as the writer of Bob Servant because I think he's a fully formed character and I'm not churning out within the same medium each time.

How has your relationship with Bob changed?

I'd been away from him for a long time and I just went back to write his autobiography a month ago and it was quite hard at first getting the voice again. Now I'm just flying. It's absurdism I want; constant absurdism. Every time it looks like he's being a bit conventional I throw him a curveball. I really enjoy writing Bob... It becomes worryingly easy.

Can you give me an example of what makes him special to you?

The book is basically a collection of Bob's grievances through his life: why he doesn't think he's got the respect he deserves in Dundee as a man about town. The entry I wrote today was 'Not Having Black Pals' and Bob's anger about never having a black pal, and how hard he's tried to get one because it would make him look exotic when he was looking for a bird. He's like, 'It's impossible because Dundee just doesn't have the mix. When a black guy turns up in Dundee it's like Beatlemania; we're all over him and someone else will take him as his pal.'

He talks about how he went to the hospital once with Frank, his neighbour, because he'd dropped a bucket on Frank's head when they were window-cleaning. The doctor was from Kenya and Frank would try and nick him as his pal and then Bob would try and nick him as his pal. Then Bob started hanging about the hospital trying to find him and then started to get on the guy's bus home and suggest they go for a drink. The guy just fobbed him off and Bob says, 'If

I could just have got in with him, my whole life would have been different. People would have known me as "Bob with the black pal" and I would have been exciting for people.'

So when that never worked out there was a Turkish guy who worked at a bar. He says, 'I spoke to him a bit but always as part of a larger group. It was never just me and him...' That's what I love about Bob: his absurdism.

When your point-of-view-character is a man twice your age, what experience do you draw on?

When I was younger I worked in a pub in Broughty Ferry, the area of Dundee where me and Bob are from, and the clientele was just eccentric, heavy-drinking old men. Bob's an amalgamation of a lot of them and the absurd things they would come out with. There was one guy who looked exactly like Lester Piggott, the jockey, and he just wouldn't accept it. For years people would come in and say, 'Mate, I'm really sorry to bother you, but you look exactly like Lester Piggott,' and he'd say, 'No. I don't.' He just wouldn't accept it, and I found that so funny I would encourage people to go and tell him.

I remember one really self-important guy came in who worked down at the docks spray-painting the legs of oil rigs. He's a pompous buffoon who'd just been to Rome and I asked him, 'How was it?' He said, 'Oh, wonderful. That ceiling in the Sistine Chapel, it's just incredible. I mean, broadly speaking I'm in the same business.' Hah! I said, 'That's fucking broadly speaking all right.' He paints the legs of oil rigs and says, 'I can understand how technically it would be very tricky.'

So they were my inspiration ... guys like that. The great thing about being a writer is that you can pass almost any behaviour off as research. Bob Servant is certainly a guy I'd like to stay close to.

On that ambiguous note, who is Bob Servant?

He's always presented as genuine in all the stuff. When Bob came out I got a lot of emails and calls from *The Daily Record* and people like that saying, 'I'm really sorry to come to you for this but can you give me Bob Servant's phone number?' and I'm like, 'I'm sorry to tell you this but he doesn't actually exist.' I get loads of emails to Bob so I was in this quandary. I had two options: I either write back and say, 'Look, Bob doesn't exist,' and basically shit on these people's dreams, or I write back as Bob, and then at a later stage they find out that Bob doesn't exist and think I'm a schizophrenic ... or a fraudster. So these are my options. Look like a dick in one way or the other.

Christopher Brookmyre
Red with Something More than Blood

Christopher Brookmyre was born in 1968, and born again in 1976: a St Mirren fan. Most of his readers would argue that this explains his frequent references to Scottish 'fitba.' Some believe it justifies them. Anyone who has seen the club play football, however, instantly understands the artist's soul. One may read his books again and again and each time forget that one already knows the outcome, for the competition of heroic hope, vitriolic indignation and loyalty to an idea remains as unpredictable on the pitch as in his work.

Chris is the author of thirteen published novels to date. Having assembled a cast so memorable any one of them could command their own series, he has said of his most popular and frequent protagonist, the investigative journalist Jack Parlabane, 'I always adored the idea of a character who cheerfully wanders into enormously dangerous situations and effortlessly makes them much worse.' Ford Prefect, Robin Hood and Noam Chomsky rolled into one – this John Lapsley Parlabane may be most profitably read as a comic allegory on anarcho-syndicalism and the state-sanctioned manufacture of consent. The miracle is that the hilarious battle of conventions and conspiracies he gets caught up in is at every point a serious criticism of our times.

What makes this lastingly interesting is the fact that his concern is with the calculating selfishness of the disabused. What makes it lastingly entertaining is that he can be an ironist without being a moralist, radical without being ridiculous, and gentlemanly without being genteel. What makes him lastingly successful is that he has lost neither motivation nor momentum. That and the generosity of history which has insisted on supplying enough material to inspire an award-winning line-up of 'white collar villains', such as homicidal NHS Trust managers (*Quite Ugly One Morning*, 1996) and rogue secret service chiefs (*Be My Enemy*, 2004).

Christopher Brookmyre has been conceded comic genius often and willingly enough, and yet he remains a source of surprise in that part of the reading public where reputations are considered settled. However, this may have less to do with his merits than his literary identity. Having won the Critics' First Blood Award for Best First Crime Novel of the Year, *Quite Ugly One Morning* was dramatised by ITV. *Boiling a Frog* earned Chris the Sherlock Award for Best Comic Detective Novel in 2000. 2004 would see him take the prize again for *Be My Enemy*, and, as the only writer to have won two Sherlocks, he went on to win the seventh Bollinger Everyman Wodehouse Prize for Comic Fiction in 2006 with *All Fun and Games Until Someone Loses an Eye*.

On accepting the award, Chris said, 'My favourite PG Wodehouse quote is: "It is seldom difficult to distinguish between a Scotsman with a grievance and a ray of sunshine." Today I'd like to think that I resemble the ray of sunshine.' During the following interview in the sun of the Edinburgh International Book Festival, it wasn't difficult to agree with Chris, nor was it difficult to see why he had received the Glenfiddich Spirit of Scotland Award for Writing in 2007. What *was* difficult was to resist overtures to his singular sense of humour while asking for stab after stab of his sharp wit. Thankfully, Chris is a devotee of the telling as well as the suggestive phrase, and there is little more rewarding than letting him speak for himself.

~

How do you feel about your reputation for expressing extreme feelings in your writing, such as frustration with society as you or your characters see it?

Perhaps people identify with some of the sentiments I've expressed in my novels that are kind of deliberately exaggerated and rendered grotesque just because I was always setting out to write a larger-than-life, self-consciously escapist fiction. I suppose I invited people to interpret the opinions expressed as being identified with me, particularly in my early work, because a lot of the time it was true. But subsequently that was less true, so I was exaggerating the opinions of characters as a kind of shorthand of where they were coming from or their motivations, particularly in a character like Simon Darcourt. I wouldn't say it was so much any frustration on my own part, just a desire to have your own say.

If our culture still has an ethical centre, it no longer seems to be defined by traditional authorities and a didactic church or state. Is it fair to see your protagonists' actions as reactions to this development?

I wouldn't say as a didactic exactly, but it does come through. I was asked recently what an antihero was, and I was trying to explain that it's hard to explain because there are hardly any heroes left that would fit the traditional description – so it's almost as if the antihero is more common than the hero, because we generally, in crime fiction, don't like the white hats and black hats any more.

Certainly in my work I've painted a lot of institutions as morally ambiguous and if the moral codes endure it might be painted as admirable, but I'm not dependent upon subscription to a particular ideology. They're not authoritarian codes. They're not handed down. They may be developed by individuals and they'll get them through circumstances that may actually require them to reject the other codes that they've lived by and codes that have been handed down to them, specifically a religious and political framework. Institutions are held up to be revealed in my work.

Is that another way of saying that our traditional value systems require modernisation for a modern world?

No, I wouldn't say that this is necessarily a modern phenomenon. Value systems are constantly evolving but at base a lot of them have been enduring for most of civilisation. We keep ... not so much *reinventing* them, as often certain institutions are very good at pretending they invented them or pretending that they're tied to a set of values that they happen to subscribe to. Most of these values remain common in most societies and most cultures; certain things will be taboo and certain things will be required for evolutionary purposes.

There's a fairly common morality about a number of things that has endured across societies and centuries. I wouldn't say that we are morally more complex in our days than in any others. Maybe we're looking that bit closer at the moral complexities, but they were always there.

What do you make of an increasing obsession with those who transgress?

I have a problem with a section of crime fiction that thinks that people are obsessed with crime or obsessed with violence. In my case – I can't speak to any trends, but in my own work – I'm more interested a lot of the time in the rules of a game rather than any rules of society. You know, the ways in which characters will be trying to play each other, and the ways in which they will try to deceive each other.

Crime fiction allows that. It sets down a framework of rules and also a framework whereby the crime itself suggests something is wrong with society. In a perfect society there is no crime. I feel like every crime, even murder, is going to suggest something has to be addressed. Even if it's just personal jealousies, personal vindictiveness ... some of it you can say isn't blamed on a larger group of people, isn't blamed on society, but certainly gives you a very good starting point to examine aspects of that society.

Christopher Brookmyre

Crime novels seem to reflect global issues in a local setting. Does the genre give you a better sense of a larger crisis?

A lot of people read it, and a lot of people write it, initially, to get an entertainment. That aspect of a game being played with sudden revelations and sudden twists of fate. It begins with that. Crime writers are more immediately engaging with some of these social issues because they're always looking for the next story and the next plot. They're less concerned with writing something that they think is going to be read in universities in a hundred years time. Although they maybe wouldn't admit it, a lot of writers are thinking that way. They think that if I respond to a more immediate news story or a global issue it will date my work unless this particular global issue happens to last and becomes the defining issue of its age. So I think crime writers are less concerned with their place in literary posterity in that respect, and it frees them.

Do you think the genre is more timely than literary fiction?

There's a split whereby readers will always want escapism and yet want to read something that will relate to them directly. Certainly a lot of people say that what they like about crime fiction is that the characters or the locations are things they can relate to. They find it exciting to find characters they can identify with in a larger-than-life situation and solve a crime that they've only seen in Hollywood cinema. If you suddenly bring that to locations that mean something to them then that adds to the excitement. It makes it a wee bit less outlandish.

You suggested earlier that a crime is a symptom of a greater social malady. Does writing about individual crimes allow you to show that criminals can be victims of structural violence?

Sometimes you can point the finger – with a particular target in mind – and you can definitely stack the deck in your favour in terms of how you tell the story so that it identifies a threat or an institution or a trend that you blame for a recurrent or potential wrong. In *Boiling a Frog* I was conscious that, after the opening of the new Scottish Parliament, it was going to be

128

an important new institution in Scotland, so immediately other institutions would have a concern that readers can relate to.

I noticed that the churches were completely aware that having the new parliament would essentially fuck them and to a certain extent marginalise the position of the churches or certainly create another body that they'd have to compete with in the State. There was a lot of sabre-rattling going on, of institutions working for position and reminding everyone of their own relevance so that they would continue to be perceived as an important estate in Scotland.

I could see that as a result of this the quickest way to get that attention was to allude to a sexual morality, for instance, and that's what the churches were rattling their sabres about. And I thought, this is a dangerously small country. For one thing, the churches were being given a greater influence than they were due in terms of how many people in this day and age subscribe to their religion. But also in that the relationship between what is the churches' place and what is their play in the other estate, in the media, was skewed by the fact that if they talk about abortion or homosexuality they'll get more play than when they're talking about God, for instance. So in that respect I wanted to write a book that identified this relationship and showed the ways in which it was potentially damaging in a small country.

Do you see the irony of using populist methods to point at the threat of populism?

Ha! I don't know if my novel is sufficiently populist for it to be perceived as on the same level. I don't think anybody would support that kind of irony, to be honest. I suppose in thinking in terms of satire, it's a very self-conscious satire in that it constantly seeks to remind the reader that this is a work of fiction, and usually an outlandish work of fiction. There's not a lot of verisimilitude to it; I'm not trying to say this is reality. A critic last year – when he asked me about my latest book which is technically science-fiction – said he actually thinks all of my books are science-fiction, since I write about a world that isn't quite our modern world. You can recognise our modern world in it but it's not really our world.

Isn't that the special quality of genre fiction – that it contrasts our social realities with a more stylised authority structure?

Some of it does. I think there are certainly some people who want a kind of crime fiction that reinforces the idea of social control and reassures people not only that if crime is committed the perpetrator will be caught and punished, but in some cases reassures people – go back to the classic cosy English Home Counties of Agatha Christie-style crime fiction – that if the underclasses get out of line and cause trouble they'll be put back into their place. That's certainly the underlying message in a lot of the traditional 'whodunit' mysteries.

I think there's a very discreet division between readerships in that respect. Some want reassurance about order and others perhaps want crime fiction that acknowledges the fact that a lot of these supposed orders are illusory or are in their own way slightly corrupt or capricious. I don't think you can come up with a singular prescription for what people who read crime fiction are going to interpret as crime fiction's moral universe.

Interestingly, Naomi Klein speaks of political shock doctrines as stupefying us into apathy. Are some of us turning to crime fiction for its promise of people who make an actual difference?

Probably everybody likes to think that they individually, if they wanted to, could make a difference. There's a childhood psychological aspect to it, as well, when everyone liked to think that their dad could save them from anything. They have a belief in the idea that one individual can make a difference but to me that's the heart of the escapist feel-good aspect of it.

It's also the part that I'm conscious means you're living a fantasy. To an extent, I'd like to be able to write something that rests on social issues and has a character who takes these things on, but part of me would like to acknowledge that that wouldn't happen or show the ways in which that only works in fiction. Generally it doesn't work that way.

At the same time, it often only takes one person to step outside the social and moral framework to call that into question, and sometimes that is as much as you do. There's an equilibrium usually reestablished by the end of the story; the world hasn't been changed in most crime fiction but there's maybe a point or two in which the world could be changed.

Can you be too morally didactic by providing a melodramatic notion of 'justice served'?

I feel there's a danger in that, in fact. Somebody once asked me whether there's a cathartic element to writing about ideological aspects of my fiction. If you follow the ills that you want to address, in a way that's satisfying to yourself and the reader, there is a danger that, once the bad guy has been put back in his box at the end, the anger disappears. People will get a cathartic experience from it, and don't feel quite so motivated to engage with that issue. That's a danger, but at the same time I think that if you make someone aware of the issue they might identify what it is that annoys them about it at an earlier stage in future, so they recognise that kind of behaviour or opinion or ideology from something that they've read.

Are you saying that you're not just pointing out wrong answers but also wrong questions?

My first few novels were written when I was in my mid-twenties and are far more simplistic in their outlook for a number of reasons. I suddenly came to realise that by the time I'd created this Jack Parlabane character, I invited readers to identify with him and his opinions, and so when I ran away with that I was actually trying to play with it. When I pained the reader to identify and go along with the character of Simon Darcourt I subverted that by telling it through the villain. You realise how often you think you agree with him and then you realise how far he's taken the many petty, egotistical things that lie beneath his opinions.

It's certainly true that I've always had this self-conscious aspect to my fiction and also wanted to pull the rug out a wee bit from where the reader thinks it's pointing.

Is that what you enjoy most about writing – the ludic element?

Sometimes that can trump painting expectations: pulling back to reveal purely for the stylistic impact, to tell the tale, to surprise the reader, to give him a visceral entertainment. For me that always has to be the main thing. I don't want to have an ideological agenda that in any way dictates the structure. Sometimes, I admit, if I thought it was going to be hugely effective but went ideologically against my own position, I had to find a way in which to pull it off but retain the questions over it all, even if the resolution wasn't necessarily the happy ending or the one that seems ideologically most convenient.

How do you feel about readers who enjoy your work because it sounds out differences between their own experiences of the world and the ideological views of your characters?

I'm always slightly wary of readers who write to me saying that what they most identified with were ideological positions, because I think that sometimes I've written them in a deliberately exaggerated way to comment on the characters, whose opinions they are, in a Brechtian sense rather than necessarily *advocating* their positions. I don't want to be too closely identified with them. I think, as I get older, I feel less driven by ideological motivations. My recent book is as morally grey as anything I've ever written. As I grow older that becomes what I'm more interested in.

Are shades of grey the new black?

Ha! Or the new Noir, wouldn't you say? For me, I've never felt my writing to be very Noirish or as black as it's perceived, because I've always thought of it as escapist and I've always thought of it as humorous. Therefore the good guys tend to win. For me Noir is far more honest about the tendency not to win and not to offer resolutions that answer all the questions, so I've never thought of myself as Noir. You're definitely not going to get me on record saying, 'Grey's the new black.'

Ha! How about the status quo that you so rarely re-establish at the end of your novels – are you suggesting it isn't worth the trouble?

I think you want to suggest that the status quo has been ruffled and is not quite the same and that that's the attraction of the ending, which suggests that there's plenty still to be resolved for those who are maintaining the status quo, for institutions or sometimes just for individuals. That's something I'm more intrigued by.

I used to wrap my endings up very neatly and I'm trying to move away from that a wee bit more, just because it used to be satisfying to me and now it seems more satisfying if there are more questions. It's not just a question of saying you want to leave these things unanswered because you might write a follow-up. It's more that readers are finding it more satisfying if they're left to make their own postulations about a number of issues.

Obviously not too many, because readers will feel a bit cheated if you don't give them a certain degree of conclusion, but not a conclusion that ties everything up too neatly, because if you tie it up too neatly, you also remind readers of the extent to which it's all a kind of confection. So you want to still give the book a 'diegetic afterlife', if you like, so that the world the story is set in can continue somewhere in their heads – somewhere in the writer's head it's still going on – whereas if you close it all up too neatly it's the end of a fairytale and the book's closed.

Are you deliberately denying your readers the satisfaction of scratching them where they itch?

Yeah! From a crime writing point of view, I think that anything that troubles the reader after the final page has been read is one of the things you're aiming for. Obviously I like to make readers laugh and I like there to be a certain degree of gratification. A certain degree of reader stroking must go on, but if you can give them something that's slightly troublesome after the fact then that's all to the good.

So is there any point in paying academic attention to crime fiction?

I'm thinking that when I was at university about twenty years ago I studied Film Noir for a while, and it had obviously been considered just a black cult genre. It was only the cinema of the sixties, and what they did on American Noir movies and Noir fiction that began, through a degree of academic study, to uncover the way in which this was probably the best social document of that part of American history that was available.

I suppose to that extent an academic study of modern crime fiction would perhaps deliver that. It's certainly going to deliver us a body of crime fiction that allows us to see what we're concerned about on a day-to-day basis rather than themes that are universal or themes that are timeless.

Which brings us back to the question of dating your work – not just romantically. Does that make it a document of social history?

Ha! I think it does. I've had people ask me about even some of the pop culture references, 'Does that worry you? You know, that instantly dates your book.' Well, it dates the book but there's a difference between being dated and it being anachronistic in six months' time. Sometimes it functions as a social document because it will record these minutiae in a way that other forms might not. So we will look back to certain books in twenty years and look at trends, whether those are trends you see in crime or things like joyriding and road rage, and when these terms were coined, and say, 'Does this still exist?' The fact that we've got a document means

134

that we can ask, 'Did this morph into something else or are we identifying something that was always there?'

I think it functions as a social document because it's happy to put down on record what we were talking about and what were the buzzwords. Genre fiction will record these things more effectively than a lot of literary fiction, because that consciously avoids anything that dates itself.

Can you give me an example of this service to posterity?

When I wrote *A Big Boy Did It and Ran Away* a lot of people seemed to think it was about terrorism. It wasn't. It was really about gaming and gaming culture and the fact that it was the steam age of online gaming. Nowadays you buy a console, plug it in and you've automatically connected to the internet. In the writing days it was more complicated and unreliable. I was involved in it at the time and I thought there were a lot of coinages that were arising from gaming culture, phrases or words or vernacular, and I wanted to put these down. I knew that this was going to date but I wanted to write about this culture as it was emerging.

I'd be interested to see whether some of these terms went into popular usage, and I think it does a service to posterity in that respect. Well, you could say it's not going to be crucial to know where the term 'leet' first appeared, for instance, and it might not last, but it functions as a valuable document to see how language evolves. I'm always interested in etymology and where words and expressions come from, and often we have lost the root of them.

It's only through things like literature – and often pulp literature, genre literature – that you'll see the popular phrases. If you look at the pot-boilers of bygone ages, that's where you'll see more of the phrases the man in the street was using, rather than in the higher art literature that was trying to create the language it would like people to be using, or the best language one could be using – the Shakespearean ethos.

Is it fair to say that your novels – when read as documents

*of fluid identity politics – offer a record of extreme crisis points
defining who we are at that particular time in history?*

Yeah! Go back to the Aristotelian view of drama that
it should be about 'persons of importance' and how that's
been misinterpreted by people to mean 'aristocracy' when it
actually means 'remarkable men'. I think it teaches us most
about ourselves when it's about the extreme points in our
lives. I guess that's true of a lot of fiction.

In a way, modern literary fiction retrospectively skews
its perspective. In the past more highbrow fiction might
still have been about these big things, but nowadays we've
got a literary fiction that's quite happy being about – ha! –
absolutely nothing. If anything dramatic happens in it it's
almost regarded as vulgar, and too showy if you've got a
murder in there. The biggest thing that's going to happen is
someone's going to have an affair. Crime fiction is about the
big themes, the big archetypal things that happen to us.

*Does the genre chart the course of social and political
philosophy by making readers pick sides with regard to a
given morality?*

That may be a product of the form rather than the perspective of the writer or the reader. Narrative by its nature
is linear, so a lot of the time you're going to reach a junction
from where there are two possible directions. I don't think
anyone necessarily sets out to render choices like that. It's a
product of the way a story forms itself. It may be something to
aspire towards to write a kind of fiction that has a branching
system that allows a greater multiplicity of options.

*Does that mean the popularity of crime fiction is relative
to the reassurance of seeing fictional characters tested in their
moral fibre?*

I think the keyword you used there was 'reassurance'. On a
day-to-day basis, I don't think people are full of doubt about
the choices they've made or the positions they hold and they
don't challenge them very often either. They will generally buy

a newspaper that conforms to their own point of view and a lot of the time people avoid fiction that they think is going to present them with a set of values they don't like.

I think what we like in crime fiction is the reassurance that our choices would have been vindicated, and sometimes the vicarious excitement of seeing someone else take choices we wouldn't have taken and seeing whether they'll get away with it or are punished for it – or thinking to yourself, 'Actually, the choices he took I wouldn't have had the courage to take' – and seeing what lessons you can draw from that.

It's the chance to see someone else having a dry run at it as there are no consequences ... the chance to learn from someone else's mistakes or just to see a hypothesised model of moral choices ... sometimes to be told that the choices we would have made were the right ones or that our values are correct ... sometimes to just play a wee bit of 'what if'.

Does that include the wish to live the bohemian life of the protagonist?

I think there's a kind of ... not quite class tourism, but vicarious escapism there about spending time in the company of a literary avatar, being someone that you would never be like, someone you'd actually cross the street to avoid. I've never been drawn to the too-damaged protagonist because a lot of the time they're a misery. I don't want to write characters that are miserable to be around.

Do your characters show readers how to cut the 'commercial umbilical cord' – do they offer a glimpse at what life might be like if we chose the hard road?

Yeah! First of all, there are no consequences. If someone's in a job and the thing they'd like to say or the course of action they'd like to take would be a bit more maverick but they have a mortgage to pay, they've got wife and kids, they don't want to do that. It must be exciting and satisfying. Part of the thrill is to see someone do what you wish you had the balls to do yourself.

Christopher Brookmyre

Sometimes that can actually be quite annoying. Sometimes it's reassuring to read about a character that has to knuckle under a wee bit, has to work with the strictures that the framework around him imposes. And sometimes the dynamic can be that he triumphs and gets his man despite working with those strictures, and there's a kind of heroism in that – an everyday heroism that people can relate to.

Is the fringe a creative environment for the Scottish culture of self-investigation?

I've never thought of myself as consciously being on the fringe or on the edge. Sometimes I think about the massive sales in commercial books and then I'll think of something that's far more fringe than myself and consequently not hugely commercially successful. I think the person who writes the real fringe stuff isn't going to change where they're writing to find my market whatever genre I'm writing. You know, I didn't aim for a particular market. This was just my idiom that I felt natural in, so I was never conscious of placing myself towards the end of any particular spectrum.

As for why so many Scottish crime writers have gone this way, perhaps we are more introspective and a wee bit less likely to just go along with something. I can't offer any kind of scientific analysis of this, just on an anecdotal level: my sister is a drug rep and she's worked for a number of drug companies. She went along to all these conferences where all sorts of team-building games and jargon were being handed down. She said that the Scots and often the Irish weren't having it. They wouldn't be using that jargon – like when someone starts using some term like 'silo' as a popular management term. The Scottish people would ask, 'Why are you using that word?' They wouldn't just go along with that, while all the English people couldn't wait to adopt the new buzz word into what they were saying. Her opinion was that for some reason we want to know why. We're not just gonna go along with it because that's the way it goes. Maybe that feeds into the fact

138

that so many Scottish crime writers want to look very closely at what lies behind something...

Publishers are probably happy to publish Scottish crime writers more now than they were twenty-odd years ago. Obviously they sell, so there's nobody in the wider market who's going to be put off by the fact that a writer is Scottish. That might have been the case in days gone by.

There's also the fact that if you've grown up in some rural idyll or some middle-class grid in the Home Counties, you're going to write about that, about what was around you or what you aspired towards or what you imagine was going on around you. If you grow up in Glasgow you're conscious of a different world going on around you and you're gonna write about that. It's not that you grow up with crime going on outside your house, but you may start thinking in terms of the people that you generally meet and they're gonna be from a certain background. The way of looking at the world is influenced by that and that lends itself to a particular type of writing.

Is that social realism apparent to readers as well as writers?

They can certainly see that something set in Scotland is likely to be that bit more modern and immediate and raw. There'll be a perception of that.

Is that perception shared abroad?

Certainly a lot of people in England say that what they like about my writing is the fact that it's very direct. There's a phrase in Scotland, 'You didn't miss and hit the ball.' I remember a professor I studied under at university and he was talking about Scottish and English comedy and he said that essentially English comedy was a 'comedy of manners' and Scottish comedy was a 'comedy of bad manners'. We actually celebrate somebody who's obnoxious or has said something that's really rude. It's a very different ethos.

So there's maybe a directness in Scottish language. There's also a perception that Scottish writing is going to be a bit more working class and English writing is going to be more middle class. So perhaps people, if they pick up a Scottish crime book, are going to expect it to be a hard-hitting crime book rather than a 'cosy', as they call them.

Another expectation would be the comical swearing. As an expert in this area, do you agree that readers who will happily countenance violent crime draw the line at swearing because that happens to be a breach of the social contract they can personally relate to?

You're right about that. It's strange how many black comedies there are where it's all right to joke about murder but you couldn't possibly have a black comedy about rape. Killing people there is okay because you can't relate to being dead ... even if some can relate to bereavement and gross spectacular injury. But everyone can relate to being raped to the extent that it couldn't become something humorous. And you're right, that's why people can object to swearing in a book about serial killers.

Do you see readers of crime fiction become less ignorant about violent crime in the same way that black comedy has made us less pious about it?

I don't think crime fiction really will ever be able to have that degree of immediacy about it. The odd aspect of a book that might make it successful will be the way in which it brings something home what otherwise is purely in the realm of fiction or something on the news that happens to other people. When you can bring it right in for a short period of time, that's when it's probably at its most exciting. The problem is, by the end of the book that immediacy may have faded.

Is that why you like to end on a suspenseful note?

I don't always end on a suspenseful note, but in a terribly corny showbiz kind of way it's like you always want to leave them wanting more – like the story's never been completed ...

Paul Johnston
Think Hard with a Vengeance

Paul Johnston was born like this; he had no choice. He was born with the gift of a thrilling voice. In 1957 his father Ronald, also a thriller writer, tied Paul to his fate in the city of literature. So he could go to Edinburgh's private schools all he wanted, could study Greek, both Ancient and Modern, and even gain an M.Phil in Comparative Literature at the University of Oxford. He could work on a newspaper and teach English in Greece ... In the end, he became a writer. They don't let talent like his escape, not from the city of literature.

So although Paul lived on the small Aegean island of Antiparos when he wrote *Body Politic* (1997), his first novel is a book about Edinburgh, and although the quintet of Quint Dalrymple novels is set in the 2020s, it is the product of the Scottish Enlightenment as well as Greek philosophy. 'Think of Plato's *Republic* with a body count,' is how *The Sunday Times* put it. Ian Rankin praised the debut as 'a thrilling hunt-the-psycho novel with countless twists,' which not only won the CWA John Creasey Memorial Dagger for the best first crime novel; it also established Paul as an expat who eloquently aches in the places where he used to play.

Paul's conscientious objection to his country's gentrification and his genre's conventions got *The House of Dust* shortlisted for the 2001 Sherlock Award for Best Detective created by a British author. With his second book in his second series, *The Last Red Death*, Paul won the prestigious Sherlock Award for Best Detective Novel of the Year 2004. The three novels, which follow Private Eye Alex Mavros around Greece as he investigates endemic corruption as well as personal and

141

family values, have made John Connolly assert, 'The very best crime novels are those in which location, character and story combine in a single, powerful whole... Paul Johnston stakes his persuasive claim for a place in that pantheon.'

After an involuntary sabbatical, during which he under-went chemotherapy and beat two unconnected bouts of cancer, Paul also beat the odds of writing a third bestselling series when *The Death List* was published in 2008 and shortlisted for a Barry Award in the category of Best British Crime Novel. Introducing Matt Wells, crime writer with a stalled career and ego, Paul's third debut has been followed by two more thrillers set in the UK and eastern US, and while the novels reveal a man's loss of his 'mortality cherry', as Paul is fond of saying, something new and wise has entered his writing. The crime writer seems to have made peace with the tension between his personal fears and his professional exploitation of them.

It is hardly news that Paul understands violence. What is new and rare is that he has come to show his readers how to understand vulnerability. Yet if he owes a debt of gratitude to his time spent on a PhD in Creative Writing, he has so far refused payment in style. Thankfully, Paul insists on being subversive. If you recognise this as the crime writer's code of honour, chances are he'll buy you a pint so, with or without poetic inevitability, we met for the following interview in the hallowed halls of The Oxford Bar where, in place of Scottish top dog Ian Rankin, Allan Guthrie was holding court. Several hours and ales later, Quintin Jardine, yet another Edinburgh crime writer, didn't even have to be present to be preaching to the converted: 'Paul is a prince of our craft.'

~

After three series set in three different countries and cultures, would you say that the issue of voice has been significant in your work?

Interesting question. Let me think about that… Particularly in the first book, because you never know whether it's going to get published, you're looking for a voice that's different. I'm trying to cast my mind back. See, because my first novel was the first in a series of five set in Edinburgh it was probably more foundational than most writers' debuts. I was definitely looking to do something different within the genre. *Body Politic* was first written in the third person. Having written that book I was happy with the setup of the story, but it just didn't seem to work as a piece of fiction to be read.

So I rewrote it in the first person. It obviously wasn't done by changing 'he' to 'I' but by imbuing the text with the voice of the narrator, and he's in many ways the classic PI. Quint (Quintilian Dalrymple) understands his society but he's also an outsider because he was kicked out for being a revolutionary type in an authoritarian state. I deliberately didn't make Quint particularly macho, though it's inherent within the Noir genre. He had to be a lot more cerebral, so yes, the issue of voice is very significant, particularly in that book.

Speaking of Noir masculinity, don't your gender politics make Quint an unusual male lead?

Yeah! That's fair comment. I was also interested in that when I was writing the female characters, especially in casting his on-and-off girlfriend who's in many ways a far more in-your-face character than he is.

Which casts an interesting light on those pivotal moments of male bonding, doesn't it?

Absolutely. That's another integral part of the genre. Quint and Davie have a fairly spiky beginning but gradually come to trust each other, and that's certainly a dynamic that continues through the series. Masculinity and strong women – there are a lot of them, not just Katherine. In the first book the senior guardian is his mother so there are issues for everyone.

Is Tyler Durden right – are we a generation of men raised by women, and is that a question you address by looking at male attitudes towards violence?

Well, a lot of crime fiction is content with traditional notions of masculinity but that's not something I'm particularly interested in so I've problematised it in all of my three series. Being a *Guardian* reader for years I'm aware of feminist theory, and most readers of crime fiction are women so this is a complex area for such questions, particularly after 9/11, Iraq, the London bombings ... news has become much less retiring. During the second Iraq war very graphic scenes of violence were broadcast, so I think the violence issue has turned a bit.

I think it's interesting that people have started complaining about violence in fiction because they've become sensitised by what they're seeing in the real world. Now to me that's a reason to display even more violence openly, but I can see why some readers feel like it's too much like watching the news coverage, and want to escape into the more traditional mode of crime writing or reading.

Does that mean crime fiction provides an arena in which writers and readers can experience violence and experiment with ways of responding?

I'm sure that's true for a lot of people. I'm wary of generalisations because I'm not sure what one can draw from that. My personal confrontations with violence tend to come through hard fact, whatever that means in a post-modernist world. I mean through reading history and committed journalism, which for me is a lot harder to come to terms with because it's real. I wouldn't want to imagine myself in a situation in which crime fiction was my main way of facing up to the world. It is one way, but for me it's not enough because it's fiction. It's still significant though, and that's one reason I write crime fiction.

I don't like crime novels that don't face up to these issues. Crime novels are almost always about murder, and I don't think it's right, in any sense of that word, not to display the effects of violence. Whether you're writing about a relatively clean death or people being blown up in a terrorist attack, I think it's dishonest not to describe that violence in some detail. So to answer your question, I think a lot of people don't confront these issues because the crime fiction they choose to read isn't as honest as the world it's from.

Do you write violent scenarios to demonstrate the collateral damage every act of violence has?

Yes. Showing the fact that actions have consequences is a very important part of a crime novel. The reasons for these things to happen, and the way in which they do, provide you with the plot and how the characters develop. I think most novelists would step back from the idea of didacticism but in reality most of us do, to some extent, display knowledge that readers are not familiar with, particularly things that are unpleasant, in order that people can perhaps be less glib about them. So yes, I think there is an inherent didacticism in the genre but how you handle that is a tricky thing for each author because if you're too didactic people won't read your work.

Why do you think that is?

People get very involved with characters. As a writer I'm not hugely keen on that. I try to keep my characters at arm's length even when I'm writing in the first person, because I prefer the reader to grapple a bit more with ideas and these issues of consequences and motivations rather than just thinking about the fate of this character, which is an easy escape clause. Not necessarily to my advantage, I'm more cerebral about this than most authors.

Yet if you look at the three categories that most protagonists fall into – the bureaucratic team player, the rule-bender, and the maverick avenger – it seems like most authors can't help promoting their position on these issues. Does crime fiction then come with a moral agenda?

It might well do implicitly. I'd be surprised if many authors would own up to that though. The tension between bending rules and being corrupt certainly provides an interesting narrative drive. I probably go further down that road than most, and I'm not boasting. In many ways it's a heavy cross to bear. But although I wouldn't say I build stories around moral issues, they are implicit and I don't think you can get away from that.

That said, to what extent do genre conventions constrict you?

To me it's a battle with the procedure and reality of police investigation. Unless people are killing themselves in the desert and there's no social structure, there are things you can't just ignore. So in many ways these generic conventions are actually extra-generic; they're social. In the end it comes down to the same thing: how much you want to subvert these conventions or stay within them. I'm obviously a member of the subversive faculty but I daresay most writers in this country are not.

The PI tradition, simply because it is rooted in fact, gives you an inherent opportunity to be anti-establishment and individualistic. I certainly try to subvert as many conventions as I can. What you do run up against then is the basic fact that there are only so many stories, plots and ways of telling them. All you're ever doing really is providing a variation on a theme.

Which begs the question: who has most influenced your writing?

Well, it started off with Conan Doyle. Although he's a Tory and all the rest of it, he possibly unknowingly problematised the darker aspects of Victorian and Edwardian society. Of course there were the opium dens but also some issues about the way women were treated, and his writing is certainly underrated in terms of its darkness and subversion.

Then there were people like Hammett and Chandler. If you're even vaguely interested in Noir you can't afford not to pay attention to them. Jim Thompson was a great writer but his view of humanity is such that you'd never want to read more than one of his novels. I like a lot of contemporary Americans, like James Ellroy and James Lee Burke with their curious blend of lyrical violence.

It seems like your shared concerns might go beyond similarities in style and subject matter, wouldn't you agree?

That might well be the case. I don't have a particularly rosy view of human nature. I broadly go along with the traditional Noir position on that, which is that in a certain situation anyone would behave in an illegal way. But, again, it's important not to lose sight of the fact that crime fiction is a recreation for the vast majority of readers. They want a good story with interesting characters.

Does that facilitate a certain reading process – do we sound out the differences between our personal experiences of criminal behaviour and alternative coping mechanisms?

I think that process does go on, whether consciously or not. There has been a gradual change over the last three decades in how readers view authority figures like policemen, judges, politicians and so on. There's a lot less respect for them in a social sense than there used to be, and that is obviously reflected in fiction where people accept far greater flaws in their characters as long as they're seen to be achieving a degree of justice.

I tend to leave a lot hanging because I don't believe that certain things are susceptible to solutions. A man whose wife is multiply raped and murdered in real life is very unlikely ever to recover from that. In fiction one tends not to find that very often at the end of a novel. That's where Noir is much more convincing in its conclusions of broken lives that will continue although there may not even be a temporary solution.

I'm broadly sympathetic with that position, which is why I have tried to bring in significant issues rather than providing an easy ride that doesn't push readers' ideas of the social and political structures they live in. I think that after the collapse of one's oldfashioned values, the only way to validate your own existence is by attempting to construct some kind of accessory identity that is within the globalised world and at the same time something personal. I think it's also true that the genre often offers false solutions to that problem.

How so?

To some extent the big questions are being devalued by the fact that they're asked so often. They're not shocking any more, which is another reason to describe violence and be hard-hitting about motivation in order to deal with almost taboo subjects like child abuse or organised sex industries, which are beyond most people's everyday lives. I think crime fiction can make people face up to that, but I do worry about the conservative nature of a lot of it by the end of the story.

Might that explain the post-democratic setting of your Edinburgh series?

Yes, that's certainly true.

Why did you place your novels in the tension between authoritarian and libertarian societies, and highlight their conflicting attitudes to crime?

I did it because those ideas interest me, and because they're part of the tension in such stories. A lot of people like to think that they are more tolerant of those who bend the rules than they would probably be in real life.

How does that affect the way you write?

You can write about bureaucrats but to make them interesting you have to make them rule benders. That's actually rather absurd when you've got a novel which is about the reacquisition of justice by someone who behaves in many ways that are not on the side of justice. You've got two issues there: one is that the story has to make sense as a story within the confines of what the characters are likely to do, and the other one is the issue of what people want to read.

It may be that people just accept that society is fucked and the world is fucked but it's still possible to be heroic. I think a lot of people want to find something gold underneath the layers of shit that are modern society. That's also one of the things that worry me about crime fiction though: the effect it can have on the reader ... if it all works in a fantasy world then

148

I feel better about the real world. I mean, I love the genre and am fascinated by it, but there's much more to life than that.

Isn't there a rather old tradition for those concerns in Scotland?

I see where you're heading with that, but one thing that you have to bear in mind is that lots of Scottish crime fiction doesn't provide social analysis. A lot of it is traditional crime fiction seen through Scottish lenses if you like, and there's nothing wrong with that. But I would argue that there are more Scottish crime writers who are interested in social issues than maybe in, well, I'm not going to say Britain, because it would sound anti-English, but you know what I mean. The per capita rate here is pretty good and that probably has something to do with the Scottish education system, the slightly more left-leaning society, the Calvinist background … who knows?

It certainly raises the question of authority. How do you deal with that?

Yeah, Quint isn't much of an authority figure. In effect he is handed carte blanche, so in many ways he is a hero, but he's uncomfortable with that role and is only interested in the effect of all that stuff on the victims.

Does being a 'man of the people' fully account for his modest choice of lifestyle?

Well, in *Body Politic* he's kicked out of his flat by the Public Order Directorate and he can cope with it because he has his blues records. At that stage I didn't want to do the same as Ian, although I'd only read two of his books. But a lot of people like that, and one has to assume that even female readers like that kind of thing. I mean, Rebus is very popular with women. Readers, in some way or another, try to refer back to what it was like when they were young.

Does that suggest a desire to identify with a person who doesn't work a job he hates to buy things he doesn't need to impress people he doesn't like?

Yeah! I myself would like to imagine that I would be able to live like that. I mean, in many ways main protagonists have a lot of sublimations of their creators. I took that even further in Enlightenment Edinburgh because those assumptions can't be dumped on anyone, let alone by society. Supposedly, they all have jobs they like. There's a lifelong learning program. They have their sex lives controlled. Supposedly, the magnanimous state gives them everything.

Having said that, one of the reasons I invented that society based on Plato, Orwell, Huxley and all the rest of them, was my own lack of interest in and commitment to what was then contemporary society, and I would still say the same thing now. When I wrote the first book I was living on a small Greek island, very poor ... i.e. I socially disapproved of – and to some extent still do – the aspirations of contemporary society. But you can't say that openly or very few people will buy your novel ... Intellectuals all borrow from libraries.

Social commentary?

Ha! Crime fiction is all about society. It either calls it into question or ultimately, and often rather abstrusely, ends up supporting it in a conservative way. What I was trying to do was to invent a society that would call into question the society of the 1990s which I imagined would crash and burn in 2003 in a flu epidemic. But that didn't have anything to do with contemporary events. That had to do with 1918 and the end of World War One when millions of people died of the Spanish flu. When you start imagining what might happen, some of it eventually comes true, and people think, 'Wow! That's amazing. How did he imagine that?' Well, by reading history. It gives you a pretty good idea of what might happen in the future.

For me it was about the extrapolation from the individual to the society, and of course the body image of the individual as a part of or against the state was a metaphor all the way through the series. That was almost a signpost to say this is not a normal crime novel, but the problem with that was that a lot of people looked at the back of it and threw it away.

Do you think Quint's uncommon name added to that effect? Most point-of-view characters today seem carefully drawn as clichés for fear individuality might kill the celebrity cult.

I think that's fair comment, but this has really only become an issue in recent years. It wasn't an issue when I started writing. There was celebrity but it wasn't as soul-destroying and all-defining in social terms as it is now. But I think it's fair to say that protagonists today, whether male or female, are supposed to be sufficiently accessible to the reader's imagination of what they themselves could be, and yet there are detectives who are celebrities. I suppose to some extent Quint follows through from Sherlock Holmes. It's an interesting point that there is a romanticism to it, as you've already outlined.

Wouldn't that imply a willingness to leave the protagonists behind when they return to broken lives between adventures?

I agree, because you want to let go of that life, whether it's the violence or the hard drinking or the totalitarianism. You want to let go and say, 'I'm better than that.' I think you have a get-out clause with films in that you can associate yourself with the actor playing the role.

How about the writer – how involved are you in your fictions?

First novels are always over-determined because you potentially have endless time to work on them, so I obviously worked much more on *Body Politic* than I then had time to on any later books. But even when I had to press on to write one novel a year, what I was interested in was Quint's personality in/against/on the margin of society. The basic premise I had at the beginning was – and it's stated throughout the books – that although Quint is anti-establishment the regime is benevolent.

As far as I was concerned, that regime – where no-one is poor and there are no drug gangs – is an admirable society we should aspire to. Of course, I as an anti-authoritarian git wouldn't last one day. But then I like David Simon, the guy who set up *The Wire*. They asked him about how complex it was and how difficult to dip in and out: 'Wouldn't it be very hard for the casual viewer to cope?' He said, 'Fuck the casual viewer.'

That may be one reason why those books of mine weren't bestsellers. I didn't say, 'Fuck the reader,' but I didn't take any prisoners in the society I represented. Many people, particularly ex-pats from Edinburgh, were going, 'Can you do that to our beautiful city?' Well, your beautiful city at one point had the highest heroin addiction rate in Europe. My sister-in-law used to be a GP in Sighthill right outside the surgery where addicts would get their methadone. It's nothing much to be proud of. Sure, you can be proud of the city but at the same time you have to admit this isn't exactly the perfect world here.

But has crime fiction tasked itself with addressing such uncomfortable truths?

Well, it should do as far as I'm concerned. Again, it comes down to numbers. What are – and have been for the past thirty years – the most significant crimes in this country? The vast majority are drug-related. People get killed for wearing the wrong football jersey in Glasgow, but while that's horrible, drugs are the main thing. A lot of contemporary crime fiction isn't addressing drugs, it's blowing smoke up the reader's arse. I can't respect any crime writer who doesn't take that on board.

It's hardly news that crime is the symptom of a greater malady and not some social sickness, wouldn't you agree?

Of course, but that's not something a lot of readers want to have rammed down their throats. They might accept it as a backdrop to the story but you'll have to have a lot more going on to attract a reader before you can slip that kind of stuff in. It's not that people aren't doing it; it's just that a lot of it isn't really *sexy* in a broad sense of the word. People are more interested in the easy hit or a bit of messing around with gender issues. I reckon that the enjoyable story with interesting characters and a happy ending is still the model, and some authors will add bits here and there.

Does that model have anything to do with the anti-intellectual bias attached to the genre, and do you see a potential for that to change if it enjoyed more critical attention?

When I started you could write for a large publishing company and be kept on even if they didn't sell huge numbers of your books. In most cases you'd sell enough to justify your existence with them. Large publishing companies aren't interested in that any more, which is why there are many small publishers stepping in to pick up the slack. The problem with that is that you'll get published but won't make enough money to be a full-time writer. I'm sure intellectual credibility would be a good thing but I'd be very surprised if it led to a change of the bestselling model.

So I'm all for more critical attention to Noir novels and there is no reason why there shouldn't be an academic tradition of studying crime fiction. The lack of academic rigour in the study of crime fiction is actually rather surprising, since it's been the traditional recreational reading of dons. I suppose that's been the distinction: they can't write about it from a critical point of view but they could write it in their spare time. I'm sure intellectual attention would have some effect in terms of loosening up the commercial bonds that constrict a lot of writers. The more diversity the better. But I think the commercial imperatives unfortunately will always out. Certain kinds of crime writing will always only be small print, and that in itself is not necessarily a bad thing, if at least they're being published.

Has Scottish crime fiction been in a position to afford certain departures from the current norm because the country has a history of cheering those who try to go their own way?

I'm sure that's part of it, yes. The issue of social mobility strikes me as being significant. Almost anything goes these days in any Western country, but there is a strong tradition in this country of social routes to self-improvement. I don't think there can be any argument about that. Whether it's the Calvinist tradition of understanding, a hangover from that or a general acceptance amongst Scottish writers and readers that analysis and the quest for knowledge are a good thing, if you went from a farm boy to a professor of philosophy or a captain of industry you are more likely to be aware of the fact that there are still a lot of other people who are poor. There is a greater awareness of the whole social world.

Does that lead to a greater curiosity about the causes of criminal behaviour?

Probably. I very much admire Ian Rankin who started as a coal miner's son and became the success that he is. His combination of genre conventions and a broader awareness of Scottish society is exemplary and hasn't put people off buying his books. There are a lot of people doing that in Scotland and he's certainly achieved that much better than I have. So it's possible to combine the two, and it would be fair to say that he does that more than any English crime writer, apart from Minette Walters who does it from a different political angle.

I was lucky in that *Body Politic* came out two months before the devolution referendum in 1997 and a lot of the stuff in the book was relevant to what was going on in Scotland at the time. There's a lot of interest in the end of empire, and I would argue it's a bit bloody late. That kind of experiment in fiction should have started about fifty years ago, but for various reasons – predominantly the conservatism of publishers – it didn't. A lot of major novelists are taking that on board now, but generally the tendency to go back rather than be contemporary is a bit worrying.

Is crime fiction about broken social scenes and the collateral damage of history?

It certainly is for me. Writing my Edinburgh novels was a way of not only assessing the damage of the past but hypothesising about the damage of the present. From a literary point of view, I am interested in writing satisfyingly plotted novels but I adamantly insist that it is possible to write a novel that is not completely conventional and still exciting and gripping, which is what I'm trying to do with my current series which is not set in Scotland and is definitely more mainstream.

What's been the greatest challenge of writing about Matt Wells?

Having a protagonist who kills people is quite a hard one to get past, because the general view is that the investigators should be on the side of the angels. That wasn't a direct issue with Quint or Alex Mavros, who were fairly intellectual guys, but Matt Wells has to kill people, which goes against that namby-pamby British desire that the protagonist should be more wholesome than that. That's unfortunate, because one of the most essential aspects of crime fiction is that people are placed in extreme situations. That's something I've drawn myself closer to in recent years.

How do you make your readers go along with such extreme measures?

Decision-making happens much more quickly in crime fiction than it does in a real-life investigation, and the skill of the writer is to reduce that responsibility. Often if you sympathise with the character you will go along with his decisions, though. I quite rarely find myself grinding to a halt and going, 'Wait a minute!'

But you haven't only got the location of a crime novel in some social reality – there is a symbolic, metaphorical and literary level of reference as well. In *Body Politic* I was playing around with *1984* and, less so, *The Republic*, because frankly, who's going to buy that book? *Water of Death* very much pays homage to Hitchcock. In *Blood Tree* I was messing around with *Macbeth*, and *The House of Dust* has parallels with *Blade Runner*. Of my current series the first one, *The Death List*, has a very clear structural and intellectual link with

Jacobean tragedy. It's all about revenge, basically. There's a quotation from John Webster on the front because the main villain calls himself 'the white devil', which is one of Webster's plays.

Beyond the individual novel there is the series. Does it help you provide immediacy and context?

Yes, you have this automatic setup if you like. That does help. One of the reasons the genre is popular is that it nails the reader's concentration to a specific point and place in time, and then controls and moves it forward. There is immediacy and there is at least the possibility of a solution, whether it's temporary or whether there are drawbacks attached to it or whatever else.

Is that why more and more 'literary' writers have started writing crime fiction?

That certainly has been happening. There's been a lot of fuss in recent years about John Banville who started writing crime fiction as Benjamin Black. It would be fair to say that that has not been met with a huge amount of enthusiasm either by crime critics or crime writers, and it doesn't help when he does reading events at which he says that it takes him far less time to write a crime novel than one of his literary novels. He claimed afterwards that didn't mean he viewed them as being any less significant aesthetically. Of course he does. Why wouldn't he? He's a Booker Prize winner! It would be easier if he came over and said, 'I'm writing these books because I want to make some money.'

Having said that, doesn't this trend strengthen your general position of welcoming the genre's increasing recognition?

Yeah, I mean I'm preaching to the converted here, but I think it is an issue that a lot of non-crime novelists tend to ignore a lot of important issues. Let me put it this way: there is no question that if you look at the genre globally, and I mean literally 'globally' as well as 'across the board', it treats all the major issues, in different forms and in varying degrees of profundity and seriousness. It makes it encouraging for people like Thomas Pynchon, who has always been very subversive in his own way, to take on the crime novel. My view of life is totally predicated on the idea that crime is an unavoidable part of the structure of the world, so it would be hard for me to write anything that wouldn't refer to or take account of crime in some way. The reality is that I would like to take the crime novel somewhere where it hasn't been before.

Have you considered taking it further into satire?

Yes, I've often thought I'd like to write just a satire, but of course satires, by their very nature, are full of crime so it wouldn't necessarily be a jump in the opposite direction.

Sure, if humour is a perspective on the limitations of the human condition and our inability to reach certain standards of perfection, isn't it quite at home in crime fiction?

That's a very interesting point, because crime by its very nature is not funny. Humour in crime fiction tends to occur when a person is facing a terrible situation. In some ways the integrity of the human being is reflected by the humour. The potential for humour in crime fiction is enormous, and the total commitment to excitement is something that interests me a great deal.

Is it fair to conclude that you have no immediate plans of slowing down, or what do you want to write in the future?

Well, I have this political novel hanging around on the back burner which I'll be working on over the next two or three years, and after the fourth one of the current quartet I don't know what I'll do. It rather depends on how those books sell here and in the States. The Quint novels are going to be re-published one by one over the next few years, and if they pick up a new readership I might get asked to write another one. I have a feeling that I'm more likely to transform the social and political interests into a contemporary crime novel ... I think I've done what I want to do in the future.

Alice Thompson
Portrait of a Femme Fatale

Alice Thompson was born into an educated Edinburgh family. Blessed with the company of three brothers at home, the pleasures of Latin and Greek at school, holidays in the Highlands, and the promise of conformity that only parents who teach for a living can offer, Alice chose an artistic career. That said, it may be more courteous to treat all generational information as an irrelevancy, but since time alone gives definition, to do so would be a disservice to the diversity of her creative work.

Suffice it to say that in the mid-80s Alice recorded an album with the post-punk band The Woodentops and made a number of their music videos highly watchable, but like so many rock stars she eventually decided to leave the bright lights of the stage for the hallowed halls of academe. Thankfully, she didn't quit all her keyboards. Having discovered her passion for books as a little girl, she first studied them at Oxford, then began writing her own while completing a PhD on Henry James. Out to slay the same conventions of life and thought as the grand master, Alice climbed into her attic and buried her early writings in a shoebox. When she came back down, she won the 1996 'James Tait Black Memorial Prize' with her first novel, *Justine*.

Yet rather than taking the show on the road, Alice spent the following two years in pursuit of a new creative direction and was promptly shortlisted for the Stakis Prize for Scottish Writer of the Year upon publication of her second novel, *Pandora's Box*. Alice went on to win a Creative Scotland

Award in 2000, and has since written *Pharos (2002)* and *The Falconer (2008)*. When we met for this interview in the summer of 2010, her fifth novel, *The Existential Detective*, was about to be published.

Ian Rankin called this latest offering a 'haunting, strange, Kafkaesque, poetic mystery set in Portobello.' Walking through this suburb of Edinburgh, where Alice now lives with her husband and son, I have yet to discover her novel's surreal dreamscape. But once we talk over coffee and a view of the beach, an unusual creative process comes into focus that owes much to her infectious enthusiasm. The parallels will suggest themselves throughout our conversation, and she will forgive me for pointing them out here, for to witness the care Alice takes in the art of storytelling is to see James's fine flower of feeling expressed in action. Louise Welsh, keeper of the same secrets, knew all along: 'Alice Thompson has bent the detective novel to her own will and produced something rather exciting.'

Her latest genre shift, her long-cherished love of crime fiction, her thoughts on artistic boundaries, and her experience of teaching creative writing at the Arvon Foundation, all promised that the following interview would be as revealing about the art and passion of writing as about the limits of interviewing. The challenge, as I saw it, was to avoid not only the public-relations language we nowadays adapt to such occasions, but the misleading questions that collapse the character of an author's work into a case to be argued or defended. Thankfully, Alice can be cordial and charged all at once, and her discerning way of reproducing in concrete language the multiplicities of her writing experiences should be a delight to all who meet her in the following pages.

When I asked her to say a few personal words in this introduction, I was reminded of what I so enjoyed about our conversation. Alice doesn't just answer questions, though thankfully she does that as well. She rewards her reader's curiosity with her own desire to go beyond the mere telling of experience; she wants to go beneath it into the ramifications of feeling, fantasy, and inspiration that are concealed from ordinary sight:

'My main feeling about my work is that I have always written as I see things, and all the answers are in the text – you just need to find them. I am never deliberately obscure; it's just that I want the ideas and images to speak for themselves. Above all, I trust the reader. Patronising the reader is anathema to me.' If that doesn't, the following interview says it all.

~

Your artistic background couldn't be more colourful. Do you remember what brought you to writing?

Reading. I learned to read when I was young and it was the first thing that I was really quite good at, and I never stopped. I continued to read and that's really what inspired me to write: my love of stories. I loved the imagery and symbolism of fairytales, and I think that's a huge influence on my work.

Who encouraged you to embrace that 'love of stories'?

I didn't get any encouragement. I was impulsive and consistent.

Do you remember your first story – have you kept it?

Somewhere there might be in a box that first story of a little girl who was a bank robber. I can still remember the felt-pen drawings I did for that story. I've actually kept most of what I've ever written … bizarrely. I started off with short stories and I've kept them. I started writing books in my early twenties, and I've written quite a few that haven't been published but that I've kept.

Do you ever go back to that box to reread your early work?

Never. I hardly ever reread my published work let alone stuff I wrote before.

How come?

Embarrassment. You're never happy with a book you've finished. You can always see things wrong with it and you can never write a perfect book. I think that's why writers just keep writing, because they're always searching for the Holy Grail of the perfect book. Woody Allen said – and that's just how I write a book – he starts a film with the perfect film in his head before he's even started it, and then he does the film, and it's sort of sixty percent of what he envisaged. It's not even a conscious process; you just have this template, which is, for me anyway, totally unconscious.

When you wrote your first book, did you have publication in mind?

With my first book I never tried to get it published. It's quite autobiographical.

Is there a chance of it ever getting published?

No. Not unless I'm dead and someone goes through my belongings.

In the meantime, and after a few moves, you're with Two Ravens Press now. What prompted that decision?

It was my experience of having been published by quite a few publishers. I've been published by Penguin, Virago and Canongate. Virago didn't want to publish *The Falconer*. The great thing about Two Ravens Press is they're Scottish and I've got a new Scottish agent too. It makes for close working relationships.

Speaking of the technical side of the writing life – is the physical aspect of storytelling important to you or what makes your book covers so unusual?

I think it's more the imagery because, as we said earlier, I'm very interested in symbolism. For me what a book represents – the cover – is terribly important, because it gives you a window into the meaning of the book. I think because my books are quite surreal I like surreal imagery. My writing is often quite unexpected, so to have a strange image on the book helps the reader. For me it's integral to the book.

Is the title similarly integral to the book?

Yes, very much so. With *Justine* the title was very easy to think of because it was a revision of de Sade; the title was there. *Pandora's Box* went through different titles at different stages of the writing until I realised I wanted to write an allegory of the myth of Pandora's box, which I hadn't initially realised I was doing. Often I will superimpose a title onto a book once I realise what it's about, because often I write the first draft and don't actually know what I've done, and it's only when I come back and look at it that I realise what the story actually is. *Pharos* was tricky because I didn't want to call it *Pharos*. I thought no one was going to understand it, but I knew that that was the right name for it because it's Greek for 'light'.

Does that concern explain the subtitle?

Well, the publisher put on 'A ghost story', and I quite like that because it reminded me of *The Turn of the Screw*, which I think is the most sinister novella, and in a way *Pharos* is a homage to the ghost story and to Henry James. I like the humour of it as well. It's like with *The Existential Detective*; that title makes me laugh. It's almost tautological. The whole genre of detective writing is about being alienated. It can't have a friendly, sociable, well-adjusted detective, so calling it *The Existential Detective* just sung out to me. But again, it was just a phrase in the book that I'd written on the last page – and which in the end I took out. It was only after I'd written the book that I saw that phrase and thought, 'That's what I'll call it.'

Looking back, does the title give a 'window into the meaning of the book'?

Yes, I think it's very much a state of mind. To me an existentialist is someone who has trouble with society and the laws being imposed on him or her; someone who lives life from a very powerful, subjective viewpoint, and who is at the same time, paradoxically, alienated. It also seemed to work well with my type of writing in *The Existential Detective*.

It's quite alienated and doesn't necessarily invite empathy so I'd like to think that when you're reading the book you're experiencing a sense of alienation yourself.

Does that explain the extraordinary reader responses your books are notable for?

Yes, they're not obviously emotional, and I write my books with huge emotion. Every word has emotion brought to bear on it. Think of T.S. Eliot and the objective correlative and how imagery bears emotion. That's really how I work but the emotion isn't explicit; it's not gone into detail over. The emotion has to be read into it. It's like Eliot said: 'It is not an expression of personality, but an escape from personality. But, of course, only those who have personality and emotions know what it means to want to escape from these things.' I feel that because one has that excess of emotion, if you read it in a certain way the emotion will come out. I don't know whether that works for people or not but I think it's a paradox at the centre of my work.

How did you make the transition to crime fiction?

I've always loved detective writing, and when I say detective writing I mean specific writers rather than the genre. That's why I would never call myself an expert. But with people like Raymond Chandler, Agatha Christie – who is despised very unfairly now, which makes me cross – Erle Stanley Gardner, Paul Auster and even literary novelists like Jane Austen, who you can argue are in many ways like detective writers, it all seemed to come together: my love of detective stories and my love of literary novels which often have elements in them which you have to decipher. So it wasn't such a leap for me at all. It seemed a very natural thing to do and it wasn't a conscious decision.

So how would you describe The Existential Detective?

It's very much an homage to detective writing, but whether the people who are experts in detective writing actually embrace it for that I just don't know.

Louise Welsh would certainly seem to have done just that. What does the praise of your peers mean to you?

Louise Welsh loved it and Ian Rankin really enjoyed it, which means a huge amount to me because those are the two people out there who first responded to it. I was concerned that people would think that this is someone trying to write a detective story ... and she's fallen flat on her face. I could see someone reading it and think, 'What is this?' But obviously they embraced how it dovetailed detective writing and it didn't bother them.

So where do you see yourself in the shady spectrum of 'Tartan Noir'?

You know, it's difficult for me to even think of myself in those environs. I wouldn't even peg myself within the Scottish literary tradition. I suppose because my books are out there on a limb I don't see myself as part of a movement and never have. I just don't think like that.

Yet given your academic background I would imagine you're quite aware of your influences. Can you say who or what has taught you most about art?

Oh gosh, that's a difficult question ... Henry James. I talked about emotion and I think it's very latent in his work. People see him as quite a cold, intellectual, roundabout writer. I think if you read him attentively there's a lot of repressed passion and emotion in his work. He's also highly intelligent so you have that lovely meeting of mind and design. Very few people appreciated James at the time. I mean, he had this huge success with *The Portrait of a Lady* and ever since, as far as I'm concerned, his writing became more and more sophisticated and difficult, and his readers fell away.

His great friend Edith Wharton – who's really a poor man's Henry James – had great success because she was much more accessible and easier to read, but was dealing with very similar subjects. James was all about language and style and implication. He never *stated* anything and that drives people mad.

164

Are we still talking about Henry James?

Ha! In a way that's flattering. I think *Justine* was successful because it was about sex and obsession but I didn't realise that at the time. For me a lot of the import of writing is about language and style, but why I'm more or less successful – I don't know if this sounds self-serving or justifying – in a way it has nothing to do with me. It's to do with publishers and how much promotion you get. In a way it's out of my hands. I don't think my writing has changed or become more sophisticated at all but I do think that I have changed and I'm seeing the world in a different way, so especially with *The Existential Detective*, I would say that it's a more grown-up book.

Which begs the question, did you write your first crime novel in the awareness of different reader expectations with regard to your treatment of violence, trauma and transgression?

That's a really interesting question. No, not at all. I mean, all my books are pretty violent. In *The Existential Detective* there's a torture scene, and I suppose I have a slight obsession with eyes but I've treated violence in a pretty similar way to the way I treated violence in my previous books, which is quite detached and unemotional but, I hope, resonant given the context.

What does violence come down to, as far as you're concerned?

I've always felt that violence comes down to a terrible lack of imagination. In *The Falconer* I look at violence as part of our human condition, how we manage it and are responsible for it.

So is your work mainly an exploration of conscience or motivation?

That's interesting. I would say conscience. That's another thing people perhaps look for in my books: more motivation. With *The Falconer* my agent would say, 'Give a backstory to Iris. Talk about her childhood.' I'm not really interested in backstories. I'm more interested – and I suppose that's quite a Jamesian thing – in the power of thought as it is.

Isn't that rather a symbolist approach to writing?

Yes, which is ironic really. Of course, symbolism attracted Freudian analysis, which I'm very interested in. I suppose it's about story rather than motivation...

Do you have a favourite painter?

I love Magritte. He did a lot of paintings of statues in moonlight, and I love that smooth surface. Henry James is obsessed with that flat look. I don't know how one would analyse it. It seems to me that those types of paintings are about mortality in a way. They're lifeless and yet you bring life to them so they make you feel oddly alive.

Does that perhaps correspond to your writing philosophy?

Well, not consciously at all. But now that I think of it ... yeah it does. Very much. What we were talking about earlier – about the work apparently not having any emotion and how I hope that you can read emotion into it ... it's identical.

So does narrative still draw its power from the confrontation with mystery?

Hmm, yes. This is why I have a slight problem with post-modernism because I think in a way you lose the mystery of story. For me, from a very early age, why I loved stories was that intrinsic mystery – that sense of discovery and revelation that in certain postmodern work you don't get. I think it's throwing the baby out with the bathwater.

Didn't you mention Paul Auster as one of your influences?

He has it both ways, with self-consciousness and a very strong narrative. He sucks you into the mystery at the same time as making you aware that it's an artefact.

Do you see any parallel between The Existential Detective *and his work?*

Well, what was strange there was ... you know, I have the oracle in *The Existential Detective* and I only noticed afterwards that Paul Auster had written a book called *Oracle Night*. This is the magic of writing: you do things subconsciously.

What attracts you to stories told by a single point-of-view character?

I think because my characters will often see strange things I like that ambiguity of subjectivity which you get with one character. You get that sense of their world; wonder how much of it is real and how much of it is imagined. I like that uncertainty, which I think you would lose if you brought in other perspectives. I've always been very much drawn toward that one vision, that singular vision. I think it's nice for the reader to capture that one world.

How do you avoid personal identification with 'that singular vision'?

I suppose that's the Nabokovian position of the unreliable narrator. There is a bit of that when I'm writing about Will. I'm very aware of his failings. I'm not synonymous with my characters at all, but I suppose I would never dare to articulate my own morality in the book. That brings me back to the T.S. Eliot quote, because I think the 'escape from personality' includes my personal position.

Do you worry about the reader's response to all this while you write?

I suppose I don't think about a reader at all, and this always annoys people because it sounds so undemocratic. I try and write my perfect book. It's only afterwards that I start worrying.

Can you tell me a little more about your writing process?

The first draft is handwritten … very unconscious, almost automatic. I like cafés and noise around me but sometimes I write in silence. I try not to criticise it at all, and then for my second draft I will type it out on my computer. That helps to look at it afresh, because it's in a different form. It's not my scrawls; it's now on the screen. In that second draft I'll try to see what I've done as if reading it for the first time and look-ing at the scenes and the structure, probably adding things to bring out points. Then I'll do draft after draft after draft.

How much time passes before you're happy with what you've written?

One year probably for the first draft and then perhaps another year to redraft.

Then what happens?

At that point I might show Stephen, my husband, and he will just say, 'Oh, it's great!' Then I'll show my agent, and then my agent will show it to my publisher, but I won't show it to friends. In fact, my new agent was just round the other day asking me about the book I'm working on at the moment because she doesn't know how I work, and I said, 'I'm really sorry. I just don't talk about my books when I'm working on them.' It's quite a secretive thing for me.

Have you come to rely on a particular set of writing rules?

Only in terms of my routine. Actually, I'd question that. To me my writing is so distinct and each book has its own life, so I couldn't really use any rules that I've learnt from my previous books. Just by dint of having written for quite a long time you practise rules that you're not aware of. I suppose 'sentimentality' is a rule ... as in a lack of. A lot of my writing is paring down and cutting out.

Is it fair to say that your writing is about people who have been forced into the margins?

Yes, definitely. I would say they are outsiders. They tend to be very isolated. In *Justine* my protagonist is obsessed by beauty. In *Pandora's Box* my hero is a scientist, an empiricist who thinks life can be reduced to certain facts. There's a lack of love in his life. In *The Falconer* Iris is emotionally petrified and finds it very difficult to feel. In *Pharos* I have a mad lighthouse keeper who becomes obsessed, and in *The Existential Detective* I have someone who is angsty and not dealing with life in a predictable way. They all seem to find life quite difficult.

It's as if their vision of life doesn't match the reality of it so they try to create their own reality – again, quite Jamesian – because there is a disjunction between their perception of the world and what the world is like, and they find it difficult to cross that bridge. It's about the fiction you create in the book but also within the lives within the book. In *The Existential Detective* Will has visions. His lost daughter, Emily, appears to him as she was fifteen years ago. His inability to deal with that loss creates his visions. His desires create her apparitions.

Would that be what Ian Rankin called kafkaesque?

Yes!

Given the existential individualism of Kafka's characters, do you see your own protagonists as oppressed or empowered by their subjective vision of life?

That's such a big question it makes me feel weak … I would say it's about the inevitable difficulty of being an individual in society. It's about how difficult that is, not necessarily how empowering or oppressive. It can be both. I think it's constantly shifting: the power of one's subjectivity – that incredible sense of omnipotence that you get from having your own vision of life.

Like a writer?

Very much like a writer, yes … creating your own world. There's always a sense in Kafka of being a victim of circumstance. That's that constant movement between various visions that make up our lives. What I'm fascinated about in my own work is this notion of power. You have people with different kinds of power, and often people who don't have much imagination or aren't very sensitive wield the most power because of that very fact. It's the people who have more imagination who find it very difficult to make choices because they're victims of their own imagination, of seeing the various possibilities in life.

With Will it's very sad. In the end he keeps his existential position. He doesn't really learn anything and so he never comes to any resolution in his life. He thinks he's a free agent and yet the critique of existentialism here is that you are caught up in society. So in a way it's a delusion. That sense of alienation from society is sad and it can lead to terrible consequences on a social and a personal level. I mean, he's lonely. The existential position, in the end, is one of acute loneliness.

Is it fair to say you had to do some living before you could write The Existential Detective?

I think so, yes. I can't really put it into words …

Well, you've done better. You've put it into a book, haven't you?

Ha! Yes. But to answer your question I'd have to ask someone to look over my life because I can't really be objective about myself. I just feel that I have changed quite a lot over the past few years and so inevitably the book will reflect that. I'm seeing life more for what it is.

Was it a case of putting enough distance between you and your experience to write about the trappings of subjectivity without falling victim to them in the process?

Yes, very well put.

Thanks! Do you mind telling me how you define heroic qualities?

In literature or in life?

Is there a difference?

Ha! Well, there's that archaic kind of *Beowulf* heroism, and then you have the single mother on benefits in a council flat who's more heroic. I think, on the whole, motherhood is quite a heroic thing … childbirth. I think courage is a heroic quality.

What does courage mean to you?

Not being defeated. For me courage is a mental attitude to life. It's about dealing with difficulties.

Is your close attention to the many ways in which the twentieth century has tested our courage the unifying thematic concern that defines your work?

Hmm, yes. In *Justine* my protagonist is very uncourageous because he really loses himself in his obsession. I'd say Iris was

170

quite courageous in *The Falconer*. It's funny because I haven't really looked at my work in terms of courage. I think on the whole my characters aren't courageous; they're so flawed.

Do you like them?

I'm fond of them. I like some of them. I don't really like the protagonist of *Justine*. I think he's a bit horrible. I'm quite fond of my protagonist in *Pandora's Box*. I'm fond of Iris and I'm very fond of Will. There's something interesting that Louise Welsh said about *The Existential Detective*. She found him unlikeable. I didn't.

Do your characters stay with you once you close the book?

Only when I talk about them. I don't think about them otherwise.

Do they take shape as you write them?

Yes, very much so. I generally have a visual image of one characteristic about them that lets me begin writing. On the whole they very much evolve.

Do they ever surprise you?

The fact that I've managed to write a book always surprises me. I've constructed something out of nothing and then I look at it and think, 'Where did that come from?' I wouldn't say that about the characters specifically, though I know a lot of writers say that the characters come alive. For me it's the whole story that is a surprise.

If the author's task is to construct 'something out of nothing', is writing an act of creation?

It's a very unconscious thing because it does seem to come out of nowhere but there's that weird feeling that the book – like a movie that's being remade – has already been written and you're just writing it out.

Given your visual approach to writing and the fact that quite a few of your books have been optioned, how do you feel about adapting your novels?

Have you seen Polanski's adaptation of *The Ghost*? I love his eye. He's got that incredible combination of storytelling and vision. So if I had a director like Roman Polanski doing my books, I think I would just have to give it away. Earlier on in my career I think I could have adapted but I don't think so any more. I'd rather just hand it over.

Would you want to see an adaptation at the cinema or at home?

I'd like to see it on the big screen to get the visual impact ... I think on the whole you have to look at films as being something very different from novels because it's a visual medium, but that's why I think it would be very exciting to have one of my books filmed. They are very imagistic, and I think they would invite an interesting cinematic interpretation.

If the interpretation of your work is a question of style – and if style is the assassin of polish, the blade of grass that draws blood before the stroke is felt – does your way of writing engage your reader emotionally after the story is read?

I think that's absolutely brilliant. I'd love it if that was the case and yes, I think that often you can only understand my books in retrospect. In that way I think they're quite like dreams. You wake up with a feeling about a dream, don't you? You might not necessarily have had that feeling while you were dreaming.

To extend that analogy of wise awakenings: what have you learnt about yourself and being a writer?

I think it's really important for a writer to lose that self-critical inhibition that everyone has. It's very hard to do, especially with the idea that my parents might read the book. I'd argue that you're never totally uninhibited. Coming back to the idea of existentialism, you can never be free of social expectations, but I've always found it quite easy to slip into that creative state of mind without any help. I suppose what can help me is some conflict in my life, but I don't need that – certainly not now. I think it's about taking a leap into the unknown and that takes courage.

Is that something you can learn?

Can you teach it?

I've never been on a creative writing course myself and I think I learned the hard way how to hone a book. I think you can show people shortcuts, but you'd lose something. Ignorance can initially be creative. What I find when I teach creative writing is that you can teach shortcuts – you can teach people how to edit and show them their strengths. I think the most important thing when teaching creative writing is to respect what each student is trying to do and not impose your own prejudices on what you think they should be writing. It's really about the individual voice and whatever kind of book they're trying to write.

Isn't that the kind of guidance for which writers pay their agents?

I think that's interesting because I've had a few agents but I remember giving a book, *The Perfect Man*, to my first agent. She said she didn't understand it at all so I wrote this letter explaining it. She came back to me asking, 'Alice, why can't you write like this? Why can't you write like the explanations?' She basically wanted me to write a different book. Through my own arrogance – I turned down various publishers, which was stupid at the time – it never got published, but I think what makes my books original is that thing that certain people will say I should take out or change.

Have you taken your own advice – have you identified 'that thing' that makes your books original, and have you fostered it over the years?

That's a very good question. This is the weird thing about teaching creative writing and talking about my writing: I feel a bit schizophrenic. One has to analyse something that one does very unconsciously, so answering your questions is sometimes a bit nerve-wracking. It sounds like it was a conscious decision but it wasn't. I just knew that this is how I saw the world so this is the way I would write.

173

Was choosing to write that letter and not edit your book a career-defining moment – was it a question of resisting commercial advice or sacrificing artistic integrity to make a living of writing?

At that stage I had no idea that that was the choice I was making. All I knew was that that was what I wanted to write … but looking back that's exactly what I did. In fact, the reason I left Canongate was that they wanted me to make huge changes to *Pandora's Box*, and I refused. Then Virago wanted me to make changes and said, 'We'll offer you X amount if you make those changes and X amount if you don't.' I got much less. So these are all decisions that I made instinctively. Looking back, what I would say to my younger self is that Canongate were fantastic and at that point my career could have been very different – but do you know what? I love *Pandora's Box* and when I die I'd rather have that book than a different one, so in terms of posterity – if there is such a thing – it was the right choice. But in terms of career … probably not.

If modesty allows, how do you rate your writing?

I'd quite like to read *The Falconer* again but my initial reaction would be that I'm very fond of *The Existential Detective*, I'm actually fond of *Pharos* and I'm fond of *Pandora's Box*. Though I'm fond of *Justine* I see it as juvenilia, as conceited almost. I don't see it as a very three-dimensional work. Even though it has the most obvious poetic language I see it as my least poetic book. It doesn't have much room to breathe. I like the simplicity of the writing in *Pandora's Box*. *Justine* was like an exercise in a very ornate, Wildean type of writing.

Have public readings changed the way you write? Allan Guthrie, for instance, edits his work for reading events and says that has, in turn, changed the way he writes.

Yeah! Oh yeah. This is the thing about writers who are never happy with their own work. See, that's interesting. My brother would actually say that my writing sounds pretty good when it's read out and I think that when readers don't read the book in a certain way they don't hear the rhythm. I've always, always written hearing the rhythm of a sentence.

Does that vary with your male and female writing perspectives?

I'm very aware of the gender and I find writing from a female perspective much harder. I don't want to associate too much with them, so in a way it's easier with my male characters because I can be more detached. It's like … I'm very glad I have a son because I don't over-identify with him. That little bit of detachment means I'm not projecting my own personality on him, and it's the same with writing. Having a male character is easier because you have to make it distinct in your head that this person is different from you, and with a female character it's more challenging to do that.

Can you say which has been more successful?

That's very interesting. I think because of the way I work I wouldn't say that one is better than the other. Both my male and female characters are very much responsive to events in their lives, so I think they all seem to be reasonably perceptive, imaginative and intelligent. But I can't be objective about that.

On a final note, is there anything you know now that you wish you'd known when you started writing?

Yes…

Are you going to tell me?

Ha! I'd say it's all about publishing. It's much more about how you deal with publishers, agents and the logistics of the profession. The interesting thing about being a writer is the importance of self-awareness. I was never very aware of what I was doing. So I think I could have been more aware of how important it is to develop and cultivate good relationships with publishers and agents. I always thought, intrinsically, that if I just wrote the best book I could write I didn't have to do anything else, but the literary world is a very political world. People are sensitive; they take umbrage. People like to be courted … I just wrote my books.

The advice I'd give a budding writer is: treasure your publisher. Realise that you're not the only writer on their books. Have more communication. Writing is not all that matters. Actually, I would say it's almost fifty/fifty in terms of your career.

From the commercial point of view I'd concentrate much more on a sympathetic hero or heroine, I'd cut out the symbolism ... things like this. See, I know these things now, but in my next book I'm not going to put into practise any of those suggestions. So even if I'd known all these things back then, I'd probably have ignored them.

Allan Guthrie
Darkness at the Edge of Noir

A llan Guthrie was born an oddity. Correction: Allan
Guthrie was born on Orkney. Coincidence or not, both
suggests that he is 'far out' yet rewards those who make the
journey. Since that may well be as adventurous in his books
as on your map, even a seasoned traveller is bound to discover
new horizons from Allan's position in the Scottish landscape,
literary or not. At a time when only headlong advocacy or
bland assumption of aesthetic unanimity would seem to be
encouraged, his position is far from either. That is to say, his
work stands far from most contemporary crime fiction and its
deadening of sensibility. So far, in fact, that it has made critics
claim Allan 'transcends the genre', whatever that may mean.

Of course, there are also those whose praise does not imply
the genre's limitations, most notably Stuart MacBride, Ray
Banks and Charlie Williams. While they may all be eccentric,
not one of them has made the mistake of confusing such
artistic vision with avant-gardism, and while it is true that not
one of them, least of all Allan, has left the crime novel as he
found it, their departure from fashion is not the product of
capricious experiments with form. It is, much rather, the result
of an inner necessity to make the familiar rare. In short, Noir
is not for everyone, but if you are interested in 'noiriginality',
you might just be Allan's ideal reader.

Shot through with Hobbesian hilarity, life in Allan's writing
is solitary, poor, nasty, brutish, and short. And yet his work is
humorously empathetic, at times almost jubilant, in the way
only a true pessimist about human matters could write. It is
because of this curious blend of brutal honesty and reverent

openness towards life that his inimitable style has made him the Scottish authority on the swift passage from life to death. Then again, there might be an easier explanation for his expertise: Allan has spent most of his adult life in Edinburgh. Now, if the phrase 'poetic justice' comes to mind, you haven't read his work.

Justice, especially the poetic kind, exists only outside of Allan's work. His debut, *Two-Way Split* (2004), won a Theakston's Old Peculier Crime Novel of the Year Award. Success followed with his second novel, *Kiss Her Goodbye* (2005), and nominations for an Anthony Award, an Edgar Award, and a Gumshoe Award. *Savage Night* (2008) was met with similar enthusiasm. In the meantime his novellas *Kill Clock* (2007), *Killing Mum* (2009) and *Bye Bye Baby* (2010) have earned Allan further critical acclaim, and the inaugural Spinetingler award for Best Novel went to *Hard Man* (2007) which Val McDermid praised as 'an Edinburgh festival of lipsmacking gruesomeness and black comedy, where every light at the end of the tunnel is an oncoming train.'

Here's the problem: I enjoyed Allan's fifth novel, *Slammer* (2009), as yet another masterclass in Noir. But hadn't the reading public been dutifully warned that Allan's work can stray dangerously close to a literary equivalent of 'torture porn'? With that in mind I was as hesitant to accept his invitation to Leith for the following interview as I was relieved to note that Allan does not, in fact, sell suffering to sickos. Perhaps there is a lesson for those who inflate our critical currency: there is harm and there is no need. Meanwhile, his peers have recognised in Allan a master of the uncomfortable truth. In short, it is safe to say that his work has no business with the easy and the acceptable, and it can only be a question of time until the critics stop holding the novelist responsible for the society he reflects.

~

Tell me about Noir: how would you define your work in particular and crime fiction in general?

Generally speaking: fiction that has crime in it. I'm pragmatic about such things, and I don't even know if it necessarily needs to have a murder in it. Noir, for instance, doesn't have to have a murder... My published novels are not really mysteries and they're not detective fiction because they're not about detectives solving crimes. They're primarily from the point of view of a criminal and therefore crime fiction is the obvious term for it.

Are you happy with that label?

I always wanted to be a crime writer. There are people who are talented enough to write literary fiction but I'm not one of them. I'm very story-based. I like the idea of entertainment being paramount.

What does 'entertainment' mean to you?

I started reading crime fiction as a result of reading a lot of very dull novels one after the other, all of which were extremely literary and I bored myself silly. If I'd had to read another one I think I would have given up reading completely. I was really fed up with it. A fundamental part of what I find enjoyable about reading is the story, the narrative, the drive ... all the other aspects of it are of course relevant, but I want to be entertained first and foremost. I want to see interesting people do interesting things. Literary fiction seems to be full of dull people doing nothing, which is fine but it's not what I'm after. And I know there are exceptions, of course, and I should point out that I love literary crime fiction. Give me a story AND a flair for language and I'll roll over and ask you to tickle my stomach.

It sounds like you turned to writing as a frustrated reader. Is there a story waiting to be told?

I was working at Waterstone's at the time and I said to my line manager, 'I'm having this big problem – I've read about ten or eleven books in a row and hated every single one of them. I just don't want to read any more.' So he said, 'Why don't you read something more … exciting?' and I thought, 'Yeah, I'll try that and see what happens.' That was the tipping point for me.

Do you remember the title of that turning point?

A Philosophical Investigation, by Philip Kerr. It was a tipping point for me because suddenly I got very serious about reading again. I didn't look back, and not only that, I got enthused about writing.

How so?

Previously, I'd thought, 'I have nothing to say, so why should I write?' After my introduction to crime fiction I started to think, 'Well, actually, I may not have anything to say but I have stories to tell; I have characters to write about. So even if I don't have anything to say maybe they do.' I still don't have anything to say, but the characters I write about have their opinions and thoughts and they can be quite interesting, but I try to keep myself as far removed from what I write as possible.

Don't most of your peers date their work by registering social issues and personal politics?

Well, Noir doesn't have much to do with politics or social shifts. As I see it, Noir is about the fact that we're all going to die in the end. Dennis Lehane called Noir 'working-class tragedy', which is quite an interesting definition I think. When you start using the term in a more generalised way, it's a completely different thing, but Noir that derives from the tradition of writers like James Cain and David Goodis and Jim Thompson, they're tragedies, even if Aristotle wouldn't approve.

How do you see your own novels?

I've written two Noir novels but I've written three that I don't think are. *Two-Way Split* and *Slammer* are both Noir. *Savage Night*, possibly. I'm not sure about that one. *Hard Man* I don't think is at all, and neither is *Kiss Her Goodbye*.

They're hardboiled, but that's a completely different thing.

And yet those labels seem almost interchangeable when applied by publishers. For instance, what do you think the genre label 'Tartan Noir' conveys to readers?

It conveys whatever it says on Wikipedia, which is dark, Scottish fiction with gallows humour. I don't know the exact terminology because it's not a term I use myself, but my guess is that that's what it means.

Another byword is 'Ian Rankin'. Why do you think reviewers, critics and publishers are so eager to find 'the next Ian Rankin' even before he has retired?

Now, that's a good question... I've no idea but he said that himself. Why publishers would be looking for the next Ian Rankin? I suppose because Ian Rankin is a very successful writer who makes a lot of money for them so they want to ensure that keeps going, and if somebody finds the next Ian Rankin then they'll presume they're going to make a lot of money from that Ian Rankin, too. It's a business, so that's what they want to do.

Does the formulation imply a changing of the guard?

It's not an assumption that I would make, and when he said that I don't think he made that assumption either. He actually said it in response to a question about me in 2004 when I was unpublished in the UK. What he said was that every publisher is looking for the next Ian Rankin. I'm pretty sure he didn't mean, 'That means I'm done and dusted here.' Absolutely not. What he meant was that they're looking for somebody who would be the same kind of phenomenon and generate the same kind of sales for them.

How's that working out for you?

Ha! That was never on the cards. It's a very nice thing to have said but we're actually very different writers coming from very different places. I'm very influenced by American crime fiction and haven't done any detective fiction.

Aren't you working on something along those lines now?

Yeah … I am. But to date I haven't published any.

If logic-and-deduction narratives are about the desire to find an original cause, is Noir about the drive away from it?

I would take issue with 'drive' in relation to Noir characters because they are frequently very passive. They are people who things tend to happen to and they react to those events. The differences between various kinds of detective, crime, mystery fiction and thrillers I think can be put down in terms of the focal point of the story. There's a crime at the heart of everything. Noir fiction is very frequently about the commission of the crime. Detective fiction is about solving the crime. Thrillers tend to be about preventing the crime. Basically, it's about the different angles that you're looking at a particular crime from.

If it's a matter of angles, what is Savage Night?

I think it's more horror. There's a hell of a lot of blood in it, which is very pertinent to the book, and there are fantastical elements in the hallucinatory stuff that might tip it over into horror. *Hard Man* is possibly a horror novel too by certain definitions, but I think the difference between horror and Noir is a really fine line, and in some instances I would suggest the only difference is the element of the supernatural. If you look at film classifications you'll find a lot of thrillers are called horror movies. *Silence of the Lambs* is horror as a movie; as a book it's a thriller.

What kind of movie would Savage Night *be?*

Depends on who makes it and how they decide to shoot it. Might be a comedy musical.

Ha! So have any of your novels been optioned?

Yeah. *Two-Way Split* has actually been in development for quite a while. It's been inching ever closer for about five years now, and it's as close as it's ever been to actually getting funding. Like proper funding … the whole shebang.

Are you involved in the adaptation?

I co-wrote the screenplay for it.

Who was your co-author?

The director, Simon Hynd. Very talented guy – taught me a lot.

What happened next?

It was picked up for option in 2005. There's been more interest in that book than in any of the others cinematically. Why that is I have no idea. There is just something about it that seems to appeal to movie people. There's an element of the surreal in it which I think makes it quite interesting: a David Lynch aspect that will appeal to certain filmmakers. And Pearce is introduced in *TWS*, and he's generally seen as being my most likeable character.

Was Two-Way Split *as you remembered it when you read it again for adaptation?*

Oh, I didn't read it again.

You wrote your screenplay from memory?

I think so, yeah. It was a very long, tedious process. I mean, at one point we'd written thirty-five treatments that ran to about sixty pages. Thirty-five different versions for different execs! And I don't know how many different versions of the screenplay we've written. It's gone from being quite close to the book – you know, from our memory of it – to veering away almost completely so that you couldn't at any point genuinely say that it was adapted from the novel. Rather that it was loosely based on it.

What was that like?

Interesting.

No precious feelings about wanting to retain it in its pristine form?

No, no … no. I wouldn't even like to retain it in its pristine form as a novel, to be honest.

Would you want to rewrite it?

Oh yeah! I'd love to have a different version of it out there.

Is that in the works?

I can't see anybody being remotely interested in that. It's

only me who's interested in doing anything that daft. No, that'll never happen, but it would be... When I first started writing I used to write quite quickly and I plotted on the hoof. I made stuff up and thought that if I didn't know where I was going and what was going to happen next the reader wasn't going to know that either, which is utter bollocks by the way. Just because you don't know where you're going doesn't mean you're not going to the obvious place. In fact, usually you are.

That's how I wrote, anyway; I would just go with whatever came into my head first. I don't do that at all now. Every time I get to a point where I need to come up with a new plot line, a new direction, I come up with five or six different possibilities, ruminate over them, and go for the one I think is best... and *Two-Way Split* never had that. It has had that considerably as a screenplay, and sometimes the direction I took in the book was right. But not always.

Has screenwriting changed your writing by and large?

I suppose in terms of story it has. One of the first things that you learn when you're writing a screenplay is that dialogue is the last resort. Film is a visual medium; dialogue is not visual. Therefore, the first thing you want to do when you're adapting a novel is strip all the dialogue out and see if you can still tell the story. One of Simon Hynd's early short movies, *Virus,* has no dialogue in it whatsoever and it's a brilliant story, a brilliant piece of storytelling.

That was a really interesting exercise for me: how do you convey the same information in a visual manner rather than using dialogue. When you need dialogue to convey certain things then you do, but your first port of call is looking at it visually so that, I suppose, was the big difference to me – to try and tell the story visually rather than through expositional dialogue or conversation or even internal monologue. Screen-writing without dialogue. It's not intuitive, is it?

You tell me. Have you noticed a structural change in that your books are more action-driven?

Well, what you're writing is action so yeah, they're more visual because action is visual; you see what people do. But most writing tries to be visual anyway. What you try to do is create pictures in people's heads. 'He was mean' conveys nothing. 'He kicked the dog' and you see the picture of him kicking the dog and you know he's mean. That's a very simple example of it.

That 'very simple example' happens to be how Stephen King provoked most of his complaints. Why do you think that is?

People have their boundaries.

Do you like to test those?

I do appear to do that, don't I? But I never think, 'Oh, I really want to test somebody at this point.'

Is it a question of exploring your own boundaries?

Well, I like challenges but the challenges I like to set myself are technical. The way that *Hard Man* is written with character-specific voices, for instance – from seven or eight different character-specific third-person points of view – was totally new for me; and the way that *Savage Night* is written with a fragmented chronology was totally new for me again. Those are the kinds of challenges that I set myself. Exploring boundaries ... I don't know. I like to explore things that interest me but I don't really think of it in terms of it being a challenge I set myself. I'm not really a particularly timid person so I don't mind exploring things, whatever they may be, in the fictional sense. At the end of the day it's fiction: nobody's getting hurt. There's a difference between writing a scene in which somebody has a gun pressed against their head and told they're going to die and the real thing, which I would be very tentative about experiencing myself. But the actual writing of it? Nah, it's fiction. I'm very good at making that distinction between fantasy and reality, and most people are borderline schizophrenic, I think.

Ha!

No, they are. Whether it's a book or a movie, they get immersed in it and think it's real. They get really annoyed about it, and really angry and upset, and it's a contrivance. It's not real. It's a fantasy, an illusion, and yeah, we're trying to make it real but at the end of the day it's not. I've never cried at a movie, for instance.

Have you not?

Well no, it's a movie. Why would I cry? It's not real. I'm not schizophrenic. These characters don't exist.

Isn't that the appeal of art – that although it's not real it evokes empathy by being vicarious?

Ah, but 'vicarious'! Is that not the word? It's not actually happening; it's a secondhand emotion.

If that's true of the cinema experience, how about the more personal relationship we have with those characters whose drama we read about?

I don't really see them as being that terribly different. I would have thought that for a lot of people it's easier to get emotionally caught up in a film because of the visual nature of the storytelling and the fact that a lot of people are not very good readers. So I suppose it depends on the demographic that you're talking about… Ah, I've forgotten the question. What was the question?

Whether art is energy shaped by intelligence, and whether you're trying to give direction to it by means of empathy?

Yes! That's exactly what you're trying to do, which is why the art of writing well is to use sensory experience because that's where you empathise. You're putting the reader in the shoes of somebody and trying to make the reader smell, hear, taste, see, etc., what the point-of-view character experiences. But at the end of the day the reader can look away from the page, they can step out of it, they can turn it off, they can shut the book; it's not real.

Does that not conflict with the notion of the 'page-turner' – readers being so absorbed in the story that they can't just shut the book?

Yeah, but you don't have to be absorbed in the characters to do that. I think empathising with the character and being absorbed in the story might be linked but they certainly don't have to be, because a lot of page-turners are very poorly characterised.

And yet a lot of readers would seem to buy sequels because they feel for the main protagonist. Have you been tempted to write a series?

No. Never.

You mentioned a new direction earlier. Can you say what's different about your next novel?

It's a serial killer detective thriller. I don't want to say too much about it because I'm in the process of writing it at the minute so it could go in different directions. But it's different because it's written deliberately as a thriller, for a start, which is not something I've done before. And it's aimed at a wider market ... in theory. We'll see how that turns out in practice.

People, generally speaking, don't like the kind of crime fiction that you would associate with Noir where you've got antiheroes and the status quo is not maintained. So this new one is written from a very different and possibly easier perspective to ... empathise with, I guess, or want to empathise with. I think generally people do find that they empathise with my characters and then they end up hating the fact that they're empathising with criminals. You know, they don't want to feel that way and have these thoughts and emotions. So I'm trying something different. See how that works out.

Because you've put your readers through enough?

Yeah. I mean, that's the thing with writing Noir: the better you are at it the more you will inevitably disturb people. That's the irony of it. The reason I'm trying something different again is, like I said before, that the challenges I like tend to be ones that are to do with structure and craft elements, in this case, with different labelling. It's still crime fiction but it's something

I haven't tried before and it's a huge challenge to see whether I can handle the police procedural aspects and all the rest of it.

Do you like the research?

No. Hate it! God, I can't stand research. I'm just missing that out and making it up.

Sure, why wouldn't you?

Yeah. It's fiction, isn't it?

So it's safe to say you're not writing for police officers?

No. No, no, no. I'm hoping to appeal to a wider market than just serving police officers. You never know, but that would be the idea. I hate that whole authenticity thing.

Isn't factual accuracy considered a basic requirement by a large readership of crime fiction?

Yeah. Absolutely. I've done my best to avoid it. But fortunately I've had a lot of assistance from Stuart MacBride who is something of an expert on such matters and has spent several years on it. He's been extremely helpful. So any mistakes in the novel are not mine; they're his and he should be castigated accordingly, Dear Reader, because I know cock-all. Mind you, he once put a drinks machine on the wrong floor of the police station in one of his books. Can you believe that? Shoddy stuff.

Speaking of Stuart MacBride, he made two points about you. One, he credited you with the ability to quote long passages of Noir classics from memory.

Did he? Why the hell did he say that? What an imagination he has! You know, he can lift himself up by the ears – no it's true – several feet off the ground. Yeah, he can. Ask him to do it. It's a kind of levitation … And what was the other thing he said? That'll be a lie too, no doubt.

He claims you're writing a book together.

Well, that's true …

That wouldn't happen to be the detective novel you're working on?

Something else entirely; a solo project, this one. I have

written a novella from a detective's point of view. (*Bye Bye Baby*, which is out in digital format at the moment, print version due in 2013). But this is my first novel that's trying to do the same thing.

And you're not interested in a series?

I get bored really easily, you know. No, the thing for me with detective fiction is that I generally find detectives to be pretty dull. I think I may have used this phrase before and I stole it from someone then, but I like books to be about interesting people doing interesting things, and detectives, generally speaking, are not very interesting. I don't associate with detectives at all. They have interesting jobs, sure, but they themselves – as somebody once said to me – are just like you and me. Well, that's really boring because I'm really boring, and I tend to write about people who are not really boring and who are not like you and me. They're interesting. And exploring their characters is fun and that's what I like doing.

So the idea of writing something about this person who I find fairly boring over and over and over again is not terribly appealing to me. And you can say, 'Well, make him exciting.' Which is what a lot of writers tend to do with their detectives, and that's why you end up with a lot of maverick detectives, and I really don't want to write a maverick detective because it strikes me as very unusual that you would get somebody who would have any kind of seniority in the police if he was known to be a maverick.

And also, the whole police procedural thing is just a nightmare, and I've already said that I'm reliant on external assistance in the form of Mr MacBride and his sexy beard for all that. I don't want to burden him with a series. That would be horrendous. I might do another detective thriller but it would be with a different cast. It's better from a practical, mercenary and movie option perspective as well, to be honest...

If you look at anybody who's got a series they can option the series or the series character but, you know, you can write twenty different standalone novels with different characters and you can option each of them. I had some experience of that with *Hard Man* which features a character called Pearce where it was almost picked up as a movie and we had a director, a producer, a screenwriter attached, and the whole thing fell to pieces at the last minute over a particular character rights clause because Pearce is in *Two-Way Split*. It ended up not happening. Not that I'm bitter or anything.

No?

I'm very careful about such things now because it would have worked really well. It was a really excellent team that was put together. I offered all sorts of different possibilities but in the end none of them were workable. So the answer is: don't use the same characters in different books.

What great novels inspire you to keep writing?

Really good novels don't inspire me at all.

Do they depress you?

I think so, yeah. They make me go, 'Well, what's the point?' I had that experience reading some Ted Lewis recently. He's tremendous and sadly neglected. Only *Jack's Return Home – Get Carter –* is published these days in the UK, and yet he was a phenomenally gifted writer. When I read *GBH* and *Billy Rags* and *Plender* I was thinking, 'What's the point in me doing anything? He's kind of done it all already.'

So is it masochism or ambition that sends you back to your own writing?

Well, I suppose it's what I do now. I don't know. There were some books that I felt I really wanted to write and my primary focus was to write these books, and I feel like I've done that. I've written the books that I wanted to write, and now what I'm trying to do is write the books that people want to read. I'm very lucky that I got to write the books I wanted. A lot of people don't.

Has that liberated you in terms of creativity?

I'm not sure. I think on a pragmatic level it's given me

some of the technical tools that I need to be able to move on. At the outset, I don't know that I was in a position where I would have thought that I could have written a commercial thriller. It wasn't an option. When I was writing initially I was never thinking of an audience at all; I was just thinking of me. I was never thinking of getting published. The first two books I just wrote like I'd written the three before which never got published.

Do you see them ever getting published?

Oh no, they're terrible. I think it's very different if you're just writing for yourself and you're not aware of the industry, which I wasn't. I worked in a bookstore but I had no real idea of how publishing worked. The other thing with *Two-Way Split* was that I actually wrote something that was quite ambitious and that I would never consider writing now because I would think it was too ambitious from what I know. But luckily I didn't know that at the time. Kind of in the same way that Celtic won the European cup... They didn't know that they shouldn't. They just went out and did it.

Yeah, so having won the European cup I'm moving on to trying to win a trophy next season. What a bizarre analogy. I don't know where that came from.

Do do you enjoy the minor cups, for instance short stories?

Yeah! I find them quite difficult. I mean, the novellas I've written are really short stories. They're only 15,000 words long. That seems to be the required length for these books ... coincidentally, because they were all commissioned – and by two different publishers. I love that length. I'd just keep writing them and nothing else if I could.

Short stories ... when you're talking four, five thousand words, that length is horrible. About 15,000 is great because you've got the time to do decent character development and all the rest of it.

How large is the demand from publishers and readers?

The market is tiny. Crime Express is an imprint of Five

Leaves Publications who are based in Nottingham, and they do these lovely little paperbacks – dinky little paperbacks with flaps. They're great. I love them. The first time I saw them I said, 'That's brilliant. I'd really like to write one of those!' I ended up talking to the publisher and he was very keen for me to write one so I wrote *Killing Mum*.

The other one is Barrington Stoke who do books for reluctant adult readers. Stuart's written one called *Sawbones* and I wrote one called *Kill Clock*, and the new one, *Bye Bye Baby*. They're for readers with a reading age of eight-plus but have adult content, and getting that across seems to be really difficult because people keep going, 'Oh, they're young adult books.' They're not. They're adult novels for people whose reading skills are those of an eight-year-old or above. It's quite simple, I would have thought. Apparently not.

Is the editing process very different?

They use a team of consultants who are reluctant readers themselves and who come from all walks of life. They have about a dozen of them working on each book and they read the manuscript and then feed back to an editor who collates all the notes, and then they get back to you and say, 'This is what our consultants found problematic. This is what we need to address.'

How do these novellas differ from your usual work?

Well, I don't know because I don't tend to use any big words, because I quite often write character-specific narratives and the characters don't necessarily have that wide a vocabulary. I mean, some of the stuff that came back from *Kill Clock* was like, 'They found this word that this woman happens to say here problematic.' And I went, 'Well, they're right. It is problematic. She would never say that.'

One interesting thing is that when I was doing the first one I thought it might be helpful to put in little interpretive bits which I would never ordinarily do. It was a really stupid idea. On the phone with the editor after about ten pages, it became transparent that all the bits that the consultants were having difficulties with were the bits that I'd added in to 'help' them: all the bloody interpretation. Didn't do that with the next one: no interpretation at all.

It's the same with writing for kids, you know. They don't want to be told that somebody is a princess. Or have it explained to them. They want to see somebody being a princess. There's no interpretation required.

You said earlier that you used to write intuitively and fast. Has that changed?

When I started out, yeah. These days? Incredibly slow. Stunningly, stunningly slow. Unbelievable, the difference and I'm not quite sure why that is but I have an idea …

You do?

Well … yeah. When I started – when I was writing *Two-Way Split* – I would just write whatever was in my head and let the story go where it wanted to go. So I could sit down and write a couple of thousand words and that was fine. I just can't do that now. I can't even get to the next line without contemplating how I should get to that next line and whether that next line is in fact the right next line, which obviously takes a lot longer than just writing it and worrying about it later. So yeah, it's a problem.

Do you edit as you write?

Yeah, oh yeah – horribly. At Christmas I had about 60,000 words of this new book, and I've written every single day since then with maybe one or two exceptions, and I now have about 35,000 words. Bizarrely, I'm actually closer to being finished than when I had 60,000.

So it's going to be a short book?

No. When I had 60,000 it was going to be ridiculously long.

Do you ever reread your books once they're published?

Not from start to finish, no. Obviously when I'm doing a reading, but then I edit it to read out loud, because it's shite so I have to edit it to bear reading it out loud.

Have any of your readers ever caught you?

Not that I'm aware of. *Hard Man* was designed to be read aloud, incidentally, so it's an exception. The final edit I did on it was a 'read aloud' edit. I made the edits according to how it sounded, and the reason I did that was primarily so I wouldn't have to edit everything when I had to do a reading. But that was the only time I did it, so consequently with all the other books I end up having to edit anything I have to read aloud; sometimes quite heavily. If something is not written to be read aloud it can be really difficult to get across. I mean really basic stuff like … if you imagine that you don't use many dialogue tags in a conversation then on the page you can tell who's speaking because the dialogue is on separate lines. You try reading it aloud and unless you use different voices for different characters it sounds like absolute nonsense.

How do you feel about adverbs? Should the verb do all the work?

Well, where feasible, I try to get the verb to do all the heavy lifting. It depends. There's a place for adverbs occasionally, maybe, but yeah, generally I don't use them much.

You don't seem to have much use for exclamation marks either.

The American version of *Savage Night* has quite a lot of exclamation marks. The copy editor added a whole pile of them and I couldn't be bothered to take them all out. Generally speaking the problem with exclamation marks is when you start using them it's like, 'Well, where do you stop?' So it's easier not to use them and then when you do use them occasionally they have the impact that you might want them to have. Less is more and all that.

Do you have any other writing rules?

Yeah, hundreds of them… It might have been helpful if you'd advised me of this in advance then I could have taken some notes with me, couldn't I? Ha! I mean, I've kind of assimilated them all now but I used to have a physical list written down and when I was learning to write I would go through the manuscript and verify that I was doing everything that I had on my checklist.

Since then it's been more in my head so I'm doing it as I'm going along and don't use a checklist. Although, it might be quite handy given how much I forget and go, 'Yeah, I know I shouldn't have done that,' and yet I've gone and done it.

Can you name any clichés you consciously avoid?

I consciously avoid all clichés, but I've only done that since *Slammer*. There was a point where it crossed my mind – I'm not very quick on the uptake you know – that one of the biggest differences between crime fiction and so-called literary fiction, in terms of the prose, was that a lot of commercial fiction is built on clichés. You'll get entire sentences that are built on clichés, and after a while you forget that's what you're reading. In literary fiction that's a rarity. I hadn't been aware of that and the minute I did I decided that I was going to try to do something about it.

Occasionally in speech it's fine. You could argue that if you're writing from a character-specific point of view then surely they should be able to have clichés in the narrative too because that's their voice, to which my answer is: maybe, but it's much more appealing if they don't. I write characters who have their own clichés: speech tics or whatever that become clichés throughout the book. Own your clichés, folks!

How about an example?

The lone woman hearing a noise in the cellar and getting a torch and going downstairs to investigate. Oh, read Donna Moore's *Go To Helena Handbasket*. She parodies the clichés we should all avoid. It's far easier to write in clichés, though. That's another reason why I write much more slowly because I won't allow myself to write: 'He was as cool as a cucumber.' I have to find an original way of saying the same thing, and so it takes longer. For me it's become an important thing. It isn't necessarily for anybody else. It probably makes sod-all

195

difference to the general reader.

Ah, but who is the general reader?

Well, there you go… It's a very good question.

Is it fair to say you don't much care about the answer?

My sales would reflect that. But that's my mistake. Or indulgence.

So why do you write and why would you like people to read your work?

To entertain themselves, hopefully. If there's more there to be got out of it then great but, you know, primarily I would like to write books to entertain as many people as possible.

Any chance you might find an original way of saying what almost every crime writer has said – 'I write to entertain'?

Ah, well, I suppose I mean I want to intrigue, initially, and then hold the attention of the reader – provide surprise and suspense, which are the Holy Grail to me. They're very difficult bedfellows. They're almost incompatible. You can do it but it's very difficult. The aim is to do that, rather than tell stories that appear to repel people and disturb them. 'Hello! What do you want to do today?' – 'Oh, I want to be repelled and disturbed.' – 'Right, read an Allan Guthrie novel.' – 'Cool. Thanks. Well done, Al!'

Moving on from your plaudits, Ray Banks said of your praise for his work: 'Allan Guthrie is a very kind man. And while it's a lovely blurb, I think it's a million miles away from the truth.' Were you overly generous when you called him the 'UK Heavyweight champ of literary Noir'?

Absolutely not. My three favourite crime writers in the UK are Stuart MacBride, Ray Banks and Charlie Williams, who's not Scottish but he does have a Scottish grandmother and I've known him since before either of us were published. I commissioned Ray's debut novel when I was an editor for a small American publishing company called Point Blank Press. I think what happened was that he submitted the opening chapter to my website Noir Originals which I'd set up to showcase for new writers and soon after that I got the commissioning editor opportunity and Ray was a really obvious decision. Yeah, he's a very talented guy, and *Beast of Burden* is just fantastic … phenomenal achievement. He's a very brave writer, Ray, he really is. Lovely bloke too. Fine kisser.

I thought he might be. Why do you think the sales figures don't always correspond to the daring originality of such work?

I suppose because 'daring' and 'original' aren't necessarily what people are looking for. Like you mentioned before, people like the comfort of a series, for instance. They do not want something daring and original; they want what they're accustomed to, if you look at what sells. I'm not saying that there aren't readers who are more adventurous – there are – but the vast majority of readers are not. They know what they like and they want more of it. I think the same is probably true of film, isn't it? Art house stuff – which might be daring and original – doesn't do so well. Of course it might be shite too.

You know, crime fiction sells well as a genre, but when you break it down into sub-genres then you become more restricted. A lot of people prefer detective fiction to crime fiction, for instance, and a lot of people don't want to read about criminals; they want to read about the detectives catching the criminals, which is a very different thing.

Also, a lot of Noirish, transgressive fiction is quite a male domain. There was a survey done by Orange a few years ago, which was fascinating because it was all about reading habits of men and women, and the books that had most influenced men. If you looked at the top ten, seven or eight of them were transgressive works … *Lolita*, *The Heart of Darkness*, *Trainspotting* and the like. Transgressive fiction tends not to work so well on the wider market because men read far less fiction than women. The ratio's four or five to one in favour of women, and so the market reflects that. Publishers' buying habits reflect that. In terms of writing it seems to me that there are as many male as female writers. I don't see any imbalance there at all; it's purely in terms of reading.

Do you advise your clients to make changes according to these demographics?

It would be on a case-by-case basis. There's a manuscript I just finished reading that has three lead detectives and they're all male. I suggested that it might be interesting from the point of view of the dynamics between them if one of them was a woman. There would be, perhaps, a greater commercial appeal as a result. I don't know, but just in terms of the actual story I thought it could use a strong woman in there anyway. So it's hard to say what the artistic and what the commercial decision is, sometimes.

I think a lot of men write fiction thinking that their main audience is going to be male. If it is it's going to be a pretty small audience … kind of like mine. Male fiction has become a really difficult thing for agents to sell. I don't mean crime fiction. Male fiction's just really hard in general to sell. In the same way that it's hard to shift hardcovers now. The thing is, the whole of publishing is shrinking. You get certain books that do incredibly well, and that impacts on average sales figures because they sell much better than they've ever done in the past. But what you'll find is that once upon a time not that long ago – only a few years back – quite a few books were selling 10,000 copies. These days very few books will do that. Publishers are much more risk-averse as a result and they're looking for things where the demographic is such that they can position it in the marketplace much easier.

Is Stendhal still right, then? 'Politics in the middle of things of the imagination is like a pistol shot in the middle of a concert.'

I don't know what he means because I don't know what his opinion of a pistol being shot at a concert is, whether that's a good or a bad thing, and I'm not making any assumptions.

There are instances where that might be quite good, you know. We were talking about what 'entertaining' means before. That would be one form of entertainment. It would also be quite intense, wouldn't it? And it would be intriguing because you would want to know what would happen next, and there would be suspense and the shock and surprise of the pistol shot, so in many ways that's a good thing.

How about the metaphorical meaning of his quote?

I don't like any kind of didactic fiction at all. Like I said before, I try to keep myself out of what I write as much as possible. The characters I write about all have their own political views so it really boils down to them and how much they are affected, overtly or not, by politics. But for me writing fiction is not about that. If you want to do that – that's fine. Or you could just write a tract. Have a pamphlet that you can hand out ... at concerts. Before you fire your gun.

And after you anchor your story in its cultural context?

Why would you want to date something? That's generally thought of as being a bad thing.

Well, according to Chris Brookmyre 'there's a split whereby readers will always want escapism and yet want to read something that will relate to them directly.' Don't you provide such a frame of reference in your writing?

No, I don't think I do. I mean, much of *Slammer* is set in 1992 so there are elements – bits of music playing or whatever – that are there to help create the illusion that it is 1992. So it depends, I suppose, on the book and what you're trying to do. The book I'm writing at the moment, I don't want to give it a date. I want to make it appear as if it could be happening now so I'm very conscious of not putting in anything that would date it because then the reader is going to go, 'Well, that's already happened. This can't be the case and that can't be the case.' So I'm chucking in a few things that don't exist that they're not going to know about. For instance, there's a scene that takes place in a mortuary that's just been built by

Edinburgh city council around the Holyrood area – because I thought it would fit in really nicely with everything else around there like the government and the Abbeyhill flats. As far as I know, there are no plans to build a new mortuary.

Is Edinburgh as a setting important to your work?

Depends on the book, again. Hugely important in *Two-Way Split*. I don't think I could have written that book and set it anywhere else. The book is all about divides and polarisation, and Edinburgh fits very nicely into that. The Old Town/New Town split being the obvious geographical one. But other books could have been written and set anywhere. If you do choose to set something somewhere it becomes important simply in conveying a proper sense of place.

Why is a 'proper sense of place' important to you?

It's important in terms of grounding the reader in the world of the book, creating the illusion that they are in the real world. I think you need to do that wherever the book happens to be set but it doesn't necessarily matter *where* it's set. You could take *Hard Man* and set it in Flint, Michigan. You would obviously have to change certain things (like using samurai swords as weapons of choice) but I think it would still work.

You have to talk about relocating things when you talk about film, as well. There's some interest in *Slammer* at the moment and that would be a case of relocating it to America. No question about that.

And yet the source is quite specific. What's your verdict on the Jacobean revenge tragedy?

Good stuff, yeah! Bring it back. We want more of it. I came across it when I was at school and absolutely loved it. Read stacks of it as a teenager.

Do any stand out in your memory?

The Revenger's Tragedy, which when I was at school was by Cyril Tourneur but which is now by Thomas Middleton. It's funny how times change, but that one stands out in my memory because it was actually an A-Level text that I ended up studying. *Hamlet,* I suppose, is a Jacobean revenge tragedy of sorts even though it's Elizabethan, as well as *Titus Andronicus.* John Ford's *'Tis pity She's a Whore.* What else? *Women Beware Women* by Thomas Middleton ... Christopher Marlowe.

It was an interesting time in terms of writing. I mean just slight differences. There wasn't the same idea that one person would write a play. There's lots of collaboration, for example, which I think is fantastic; the more collaboration the better. I believe you're only as good as the people around you, and I'd like to see more of that these days – more collaborative fiction rather than this auteur approach that we have. Most writers aren't as good as they think they are. Especially the ones who think they don't need editors.

Do you deliberately write in this visceral tradition?

Not to begin with, certainly, but when I wrote *Savage Night* that to me was very Jacobean. It's a blood feud between two families; there are severed heads ... that was very deliberate. But that's the only time that it has been deliberate. There's a scene in *Savage Night* where somebody is made to kiss a severed head, which is from *The Revenger's Tragedy* specifically, where somebody is poisoned by being forced to kiss a skull that has lipstick on it and that has fooled him into thinking it is actually his lover. You could get away with things like that in those days and the masses believed it. Like CSI today.

The Jacobeans were obsessed with sex and death and weren't afraid to take things to what would be seen as extreme levels these days, and I like that. Have you read any Garth Ennis? He wrote *Preacher.* Absolute genius. It's just wonderful stuff and it's kind of like modern Jacobean drama in graphic novel form. So yeah, I've always been very fond of anything that takes things to the extreme. Also, I've always been very fond of absurdity, and I think absurdity and Noir are quite close bedfellows.

Does this blend of the extreme with the absurd suggest a comparison with the Saw *movies?*

I've always enjoyed that aspect of fiction. It's the revelatory aspect of it. How do you find out who a character is at his core? That's how you do it: by pushing that person to their extreme. As a writer I have to do that otherwise I don't know who the hell they are. I totally believe you are what you do. Character is action. There is nothing else. You can say what you like; I won't believe a word of it. It's what you do that matters – always – and that manifests itself in the books. Let's find out who these characters are by finding out what they do when they're in this particular situation. It's a primal thing. Know thyself: put thyself in extreme jeopardy. I suppose you could say that of *Saw* as well, though I don't know. I don't like those films.

Why?

I thought they were really badly put together. I felt like the first one was just a big cheat. There's a guy in it who's in the medical profession and who has a particular task that he's given, but the first time you see him he's really enjoying the situation where he's holding a knife against a woman's throat. He's been tasked with it. Why is he enjoying it? That's cheating. The motivation is all screwed up. The plot's driving the character. You can't do that.

Is your objection a purely technical one?

Yeah, it's the only way that I ever really object to anything … from a technical point of view. I quite like the idea.

How does the movie's violence compare to your Jacobean revenge tragedy?

From what I recall the violence in *Saw* is choreographed. It's much more elaborate and contrived than the violence in *Savage Night,* which is quite mundane. Even the chopping up of the body at the start … there's no great design behind that. They have to get rid of the body.

Saw seems to be a very different kind of thing to my

mind because it's all built on artifice and testing people for a particular reason whereas mine tends, I think, to be more situational. These are situations that people have found themselves in and which all arise from very little if you look at what's actually happened in the first place, but I like that idea of saying, 'What spark could have ignited this monstrous fireball of violence?'

And yet there are critics who refer to such fiction as 'pornography of violence'.

But couldn't you say that about Cormac McCarthy's *Blood Meridian*, for instance, which is one of the most violent books I've ever read? Nobody would ever say, 'Oh, pornography of violence!' What they would say is 'poetic violence' but what is the difference? The difference is one of language, perhaps. Is that it? If I could write like Cormac McCarthy I would, and then I could be a poet of violence too, but I can't, so I'm just a pornographer. You hear that a lot – 'pornography of violence', 'torture porn' … what does it mean?

What did you make of the claim that Hard Man *strays dangerously close to a literary equivalent of 'torture porn'?*

I didn't see it then and I still don't. If the idea of porn is to titillate then I don't understand how anybody can be titillated by any of the violence in *Hard Man* because it's really excruciatingly painful and unpleasant. If you're a masochist, fair enough, but I don't think that everybody who's reading the book is a masochist, although that's clearly the case, by definition, with the people who think it's porn. Isn't it?

So tell me: how would you describe your approach to violence?

It depends on the book because it's depicted differently in *Hard Man*, for instance, from *Slammer*, and again, that is very different from how it's depicted in *Two-Way Split*. The violence in *Two-Way Split* is entirely reportorial whereas in *Hard Man* it's deliberately written from the point of view of the victims, and part of the reason that I wanted to do that was that hardly any writers do because it's actually very difficult to write about pain in a convincing way. That was part of the challenge for me. I actually thought that by doing it that way it would never be considered to be what it was then accused of being, which was 'torture porn'. How can it be pornographic if it makes you feel uncomfortable? That's hardly going to make you reach for the Kleenex.

All the stories are different so by definition they have a different approach to violence, the way violence is presented, and the effect it has on the perpetrators and victims. I don't really have some overarching, unifying approach, and indeed I would envisage it as changing considerably with each book.

Is there anything you're still uncomfortable with as a writer?

Yeah: the comedy paedophilia novel. That's one I thought I'd best avoid. But seriously, the only restriction for me is whether or not I'm good enough to deal with the subject matter. I remember being asked a similar question once and answering 'rape', that's a really difficult one, wouldn't want to go anywhere near that. And then somebody pointed out that I did in *Kiss Her Goodbye* and I thought, 'So I did. I'd forgotten.' It was done retrospectively from the perspective of the rape victim in the form of diary, which I thought worked quite well.

So I don't know that there would be anything that was off-limits. It's just about whether or not I feel as if I'm able to deal with it in the context of the story and do it justice. There are some things that maybe I wouldn't want to write about because they don't really interest me, but not in a controversial sense. I wouldn't be put off by controversy. On the other hand, I'm not looking for it. I actually get surprised sometimes at what shocks people. It's like nobody's ever read a splatterpunk novel. A lot of readers seem to be much more squeamish than I would ever have imagined, but I know that now and I'm taking the 'squeam' out of the next book. Maybe.

How would you review your own work?

'Needs to try harder... Shows promise... Give him a few years. He might come up with something.' I don't know. I can't even review other people's books. I've tried reviewing and I find it very difficult so I would find it particularly difficult to do my own. But I would definitely see the flaws in it and I would pinpoint all the technical inadequacies. It's all about the execution and a lot of reviews don't even come close to discussing the execution. It's some gut reaction as to whether or not they liked the content and then some kind of justification of their own opinion which has nothing to do whatsoever with the book and how well it's done as a piece of work.

So I'd probably do it that way and as a result would almost certainly not be terribly flattering... It might be interesting. I don't understand the idea of something being finished other than the fact that I have a deadline. To me that's when I stop, but other than that I've never encountered a situation where I couldn't see how to improve something that I've written. I would never finish anything. I'd just keep rewriting it – hopefully improving it – so if I don't have a deadline I'm kind of screwed, which is why I've been writing this current book for nearly two years.

Are you still with Polygon?

No. When nobody else would come anywhere near me Polygon took a massive gamble. They gave me a very nice advance and have published five novels. At the time other publishers could have picked up *Two-Way Split* and they didn't, so I've nothing but good things to say about Polygon. They tried really hard to sell as many books as possible and I'm pleased I've earned out and given them a nice return on their investment and hopefully will continue to sell more of the books they already publish. But the new novel is a change of direction and circumstances are such that we'll be looking for a new home for it.

So when are you and Stuart getting your collaboration underway?

When there's time. Possibly towards the end of the year. We don't know what it's going to be yet. Don't even know whether it's going to be a novel. Maybe a novella. But I don't know. It's up in the air – deliberately so. We decided not to discuss it in any detail at all until we have the time to focus on it.

You said earlier that with this current book you're plotting more consciously. Do you mind using it as an example to clarify your writing routine?

The current one is mapped out. There is a fifteen-page single-lined synopsis for it so I know exactly what's going to happen at any point in time and I don't have to write it chronologically. I just choose a particular scene that I fancy writing today and go ahead and write it. I did that once before and haven't done it since.

Most books, like *Hard Man*, are totally different. All I had was an opening idea and I just ran with it. I never knew what was coming beyond the next chapter.

How do you go about scripting a scene?

Slowly and painstakingly. What I try to figure out first of all is the point of the scene. I have to know what I'm trying to do in the scene so I have to know what the point-of-view characters' objective is and what's stopping them achieving that objective. That's fundamental. Then I immerse myself as much as possible in the point-of-view character's head: what does he see? What does he hear? What does he smell? ... All that kind of sensory stuff. Not necessarily to write it down but just so as I know where he's coming from. If you're doing multiple points of view you also have to get yourself into their current mindset: where they've just been, what's just happened to them, what the emotions are, and what they think of the people around them. If you're me, you'll most likely have forgotten that.

Then I pretty much start writing the scene from there and

see where it goes. Then I go back and cross it all out and start again.

As you're editing, do you come across scenes that make sense but fail to advance the story?

Well, there were, funnily enough, in the novel that I've just been writing. I had an awful lot of them because I was getting a bit carried away and being unusually elliptical. I went back through it and asked, too many times, 'What's this scene doing? What happens if I remove it? Does it make any difference?' Horribly enough, several of them made no difference whatsoever. You know those rules I was talking about before, that I used to write down? That was one of them and I don't write it down any more, and that's why I should.

What's the rule?

It's to do with redundancies: if a scene doesn't move the story forward, if – when you remove it – it makes no difference to the story, then it should certainly not be there in the same way that a word that makes no difference shouldn't be there or a sentence that makes no difference shouldn't be there. For some reason, that reminds me of the question about adverbs. The thing with adverbs is that they're telling words and I prefer to show things rather than tell them. If someone does something annoyingly I like to know what that means, I like to see what the annoyance is and how it manifests itself physically: facial tic or thumping fist or whatever. Adverbs are kind of a shorthand method of dramatising things, which isn't dramatic, and I prefer dramatic to non-dramatic.

Does that explain the trend resistance of Noir?

Noir has never been trendy. It's always been a sub-genre. It was probably at its most successful with James Cain in the 30s and that was really before the term was applied. David Goodis in the 50s did okay with one or two books but even then people thought of him and certainly think of him now as something of a failure, even though *Cassidy's Girl* sold 1.5 million copies. I don't think he was a failure in the least but that's how he's presented, as somebody who had a very sad life and never lived up to his initial promise.

Do you have any such misgivings?

No, absolutely not. If I hadn't written what I've written then I wouldn't be where I am, and I'd rather be where I am than not be published at all. I don't know what else I could have done that I was capable of writing back then. I need to be where I am now to be able to write the books I'm capable of writing now. So no, I've no misgivings whatsoever.

Are you where you want to be as a writer?

I don't think any writer is ever where they want to be, because if you were you'd stop writing. Obviously, I would like to have a bigger readership but I think that's probably true of almost every writer I know. It's very unusual that you will find writers who celebrate what they have because you're always looking at what's next, and you don't stop and go, 'Right, I've published five novels, been translated into ten languages, won the Theakstons Old Peculier Crime Novel of the Year, and I never thought any of that would happen.'

When I started out writing I just wanted to write novels and see if anybody might possibly one day be interested in buying one. But I was still writing them for me without actually thinking I'd get published and I did receive somewhere in the region of four hundred rejections so I was right to think that. The evidence was certainly that I wasn't going to get anything published. That was before *Two-Way Split*. There were two novels before that. So you know, I had no expectations and I've actually ended up having some bits of writing that I can be quite proud of and there's potential for some more.

Can you name a few of those 'bits' that you're proud of?

The scene in the café in *Savage Night* – I like that one a lot. I've never seen it before and the mood that it creates is absolutely perfect in the sense of what I was trying to do. There's this guy with an appointment with Mr Smith, somebody he's never seen before. Mr Smith's blackmailing him and the guy's wondering how he's going to recognise him. Then this guy walks into this restaurant in the middle of the day wearing a balaclava ... 'Ah, that'll be Mr Smith then.'

The way that the balaclava-clad diner impacts on other people is a bizarre thing, and I'd never seen it. That's what I liked about it, the originality of it and the fact that it created exactly what I wanted. It's pictorial and it says so much about the character of Smith/Park, scary and absurd and lunatic, so that's a scene I wouldn't change very much or at all if I was rewriting it. I'm quite proud of that.

I like the structure of *Hard Man*, especially the second two-thirds of it. I would cut out a hell of a lot of the subjunctive stuff. There's far too much of that so I would probably make it fifty pages shorter if I was to go back and trim its considerable flab. *Slammer*, over all, works pretty well. It's probably my favourite. I like the melancholy of it. It's different from the others in the way the violence works, and I think it worked out quite well given what I started out trying to do. Largely thanks to my editor, Stacia Decker, and my first reader – poor bastard – Mr Ray Banks. The final result, I think, is not bad. A lot of people disagree ... It's polarised opinion, but then quite a few of my books seem to do that.

The main difference, I suppose, is the comic element in them. *Hard Man* is a farce. *Savage Night* is a tragicomedy with lots of black humour. *Slammer* is depressing, with the occasional laugh ...

Between writing, reading for pleasure, and working as a literary agent, how do you manage your time?

As with a lot of people who have quite a lot going on, you end up giving your time to what is most urgent. For instance, I'm in the middle of a university course at the moment so I have to prioritise doing some feedback for some of my colleagues as soon as possible and then I have to weigh that stuff up with what I have to read from clients. I've been closed to submissions (i.e. new clients) on that front since October so the only material I'm getting through now comes from existing clients, of which I have seventeen. So that workload has come down immensely as a result. I'm on top of that for once. I'm able to get back to my clients much quicker, which is great and frees up a lot of time. Which is where I want to be.

So there's no set routine. All I try and do is make sure that every day I write for two hours. That sometimes means I don't get to bed until pretty late but I'm fairly self-disciplined that way and sleep's overrated.

Would you like to teach writing?

I would love to. I do a lot of workshops with Stuart MacBride and we have a lot of fun doing them. I've always enjoyed talking to writers and being in that environment, so yeah, I would really like to teach. That's one reason I'm doing this postgraduate Creative Writing degree at Lancaster University. The other reason is so that I can learn how to be a better writer.

Can writing be taught?

If you think that I can write then the answer is self-evidently yes because I have no innate talent or flair for writing. I am entirely and utterly self-taught. I learned how to do it.

How?

I wrote a couple of novels without bothering to learn the craft. They had certain things that weren't, I suppose, too bad but overall they weren't that good, and I thought at one point: 'If I was a musician I would learn how to play and I wouldn't even think twice about it. What makes me think I know how to write? Why do I just sit down and write a novel when I don't have the first clue about how to write? It's insane.' I'd spent two or three years prior to that scribbling away thinking that if I just kept writing I would get better and all the rest of it, and it may be feasible to do that, but that wasn't what happened to me. I just kept making the same mistakes over and over again because I didn't know that I was making them. So I started reading everything I could on the art of writing from other writers, from editors, from anybody who was prepared to talk about it. Taking all the stuff from it that I thought made sense and clarified what I was thinking. I then gave myself building blocks on which to write, and so I would say – from doing that for maybe three months – I improved without writing a word ... overnight, in three months.

When I started writing again, all of a sudden I was writing stuff that I felt was in a different league from what I'd been writing before. Whether that's true or not I don't know – it's all subjective – but that's how I felt. I was much more confident about what I was doing and I felt like there might be a chance that I could end up getting something published. So do I believe that you can learn how to write? Absolutely. You can certainly learn how to improve. Whether you can get to a publishable standard, I don't know. But I don't see why not.

How do you see the role of the writer today?

Writers are supposed to be talented marketers and publicists as well, and they're supposed to be stand-up comics. I think the market is very difficult and it would be very helpful if, and some publishers do, they actually had some kind of collaborative approaches with writers to come up with the kind of books that they felt they would be able to sell. What happens a lot is that a writer will write a book in the hope that some publisher's going to want to sell it, and increasingly the case is that nobody does ... It just seems like such an utter waste of time and it's hugely demoralising for the writer.

I'm not talking about people that haven't published before. I'm talking about published novelists. The collaborative approach of working with editors and publishing houses would pre-empt that, as would publishers who are prepared to buy fiction as if it was nonfiction, by which I mean looking at a synopsis rather than an entire novel. Generally speaking, if it's fiction they want to see the whole thing, which strikes me as a phenomenal waste of everybody's time. Even that level of collaboration would be useful.

211

I think that if I was a smart entrepreneurial person I would probably start up the equivalent of paperback originals but with e-books and do some heavily targeted… I think that's maybe what the future is in: specific branding of particular sub-genres. The whole e-book boom enables you to take risks that you can't take otherwise as a publisher because the production costs are so much lower for e-books. There's an opportunity to do that and I think it will happen.

Where do you see your own future?

I haven't the foggiest. At the moment I'd just be happy to find an enthusiastic publisher for my new book and take things from there.

Any other thoughts you'd like to share?

Yeah, Stuart MacBride is a very sexy man, despite his increasing portliness, and he'll be happy to be acknowledged as something of a sex-god. He clearly is … a bearded sex-god.

You'll be happy to know that he said something very similar about you.

Did he? Well, I don't understand that. I don't have a beard.

Louise Welsh
Darkness in the Beyond

L ouise Welsh was born an artist. Had she known that at the
time, she wouldn't be an artist. That or she wouldn't have
waited until 2007 to be included in the Waterstone's list of
'Twenty-five Authors for the Future', and Glasgow might have
long laid claim to the title of Scotland's literary capital. Then
again, you might just have to be Glaswegian to understand
how she could know all along and still decide to fortify her
creative urge by suppressing it. An honours degree in History
later, Louise decided to look deeper into the world of fiction by
first selling and then studying the books she would soon write.

By 2000 she had run her own secondhand book shop and
graduated with an MLitt (Distinction) in Creative Writing
from the Universities of Glasgow and Strathclyde. By 2002
Louise had made it impossible to write her a profile, unless
of course one enjoys award lists. Having written a single
novel, *The Cutting Room*, she was nominated for the Orange
Prize for Fiction, jointly awarded the Saltire Society Scottish
First Book of the Year Award, and won a CWA John Creasey
Memorial Dagger along with a Robert Louis Stevenson Award.
She has since been named writer in residence at the University
of Glasgow, and has received numerous honours, including a
Hawthornden Fellowship, a Scotland on Sunday/Glenfiddich
Spirit of Scotland Award and a City of Glasgow Lord Provost's
Award for Literature. Her work has been translated into
twenty languages.

Better still, it has earned her the respect of her peers, and
Val McDermid knows why: 'It's not magic that takes us to
another world – it's storytelling. And Louise Welsh is mistress

213

of that dark art.' In her novella, *Tamburlaine Must Die* (2004), we enter Christopher Marlowe's sixteenth-century England. In her mystery, *The Bullet Trick* (2006), we travel with William Wilson from Gothic Glasgow to a Berlin and London that Edgar Allen Poe would trade for the comfort of his coffin. And in her latest crime novel, *Naming the Bones* (2010), we follow Murray Watson from urban universities to the remote island of Lismore, from the safety of satire to dark obsession. The vehicle of these journeys to 'another world' is the intensity of the way Louise sees things, the way she knows how and when to occupy entirely a state of mind, body or feeling.

With an imagination that is both expansive and generous, Louise has written in most literary forms and British broadsheets, and although different in kind and intention, both have shaped her artistic energy to great effect. With a few words, Louise can switch on a current in her audience's mind that will bring text and page to the same beautiful life as story and stage. *Memory Cells* (2009) marked her debut in the performing arts and *Remembrance Day* (2009), a libretto with music by Stuart MacRae, was included in Scottish Opera's Five:15 series. Having discovered a liking for such collaborative success in the arts, Louise decided to present radio features, most recently 'The Gorbals Vampire' for BBC Radio 4 (2010) and 'Tibet on the Banks of the Clyde' for BBC Radio 3 (2010).

What I expected her to be like in person is hard to say when we so often find our writers to be at their best when they write, i.e. professional loners, while we wish they were conférenciers, boulevardiers, raconteurs and all manner of self-styled ambassadors to the avant-garde. Thankfully, Louise makes it rather irrelevant to set the scene for any of those caricatures. Upon her invitation to Glasgow, and the publication of her latest novel, *Naming the Bones*, the following interview would prove to be in turn reassuring and surprising. Yes, there are authors who appreciate the label 'crime writer' and no, an introduction alone cannot do justice to Scotland's most versatile practitioner of the art. There is something to be said for firsthand observation of the artist at work, and with Louise that means to meet her in conversation.

~

Louise, your novels are those rare and celebrated hybrids: they're enjoyed by readers who wouldn't usually share a taste in literature. Can you say what brought you to crime fiction?

Yeah, it's an interesting one, isn't it? Because I never really know how well I sit within the genre. I'm really happy to be put in the genre; I think it's done me a lot of good. When I first started to write *The Cutting Room*, which was my first novel, I think I thought I was writing a Gothic book, and I was very conscious of the Gothic conventions and tropes in it. I didn't want to write a horror novel, but I did want to draw on that Gothic tradition which has always been allied to crime – the idea of exploring the victim, the way that we portray the victim, but also the urge to have a strong narrative and not to concentrate on these things but somehow have them as part of a strong story, which crime lends itself very much to.

At that point I was very conscious of the portrayal of women's bodies and I think it's something that crime fiction often does actually quite badly, does quite offensively – the use of the naked female form to turn the plot and often a lack of respect for victims, which is perhaps more to the fore in television adaptations where you see this prone naked female body. I think I wanted to explore things about that. Maybe it's quite naive in some ways but in that book there's use of photographs and this attempt to somehow distance us from the body and to ask the questions, 'Is somebody dead? How do we know that they're dead?'

I think the thing to remember about first novels is that you never know that anyone's going to read them. So you have this huge amount of freedom that you can go for it and should go for it. I guess I wanted this to be published – I actively pursued publication – but I wasn't ever sure that it would be published. There wasn't a commercial angle to it. I actually thought it wouldn't be sellable because of the location, because it's very firmly set in Glasgow and for a lot of people the city you live in, you can't really imagine that other people are that interested in it. Also the sexuality: having a strong gay character at the centre I could imagine gay men reading it, I could imagine some women reading it, but I couldn't really imagine straight men reading it. So it wouldn't actually be commercial for those reasons, I thought. I was really pleasantly surprised when it came out. I was astounded, actually.

Let me ask you about two related issues: one, your refusal to write body-in-the-drawing-room crime fiction; two, Ian Rankin's early resistance against the genre. He said he would walk into bookshops and move Knots and Crosses *to the general fiction section because he felt he was writing in a Scottish Gothic tradition.*

Ha! That's funny. When I started *The Cutting Room* I was reading Elaine Showalter, who has written some really interesting feminist history, and I was conscious that I didn't want to reproduce that kind of sexualised female body in my book. I thinks this connection between Eros and Thanatos is human nature: the attraction of the woman once she's quiet – you get it all the time in advertising, these passive women in perfume adds – and what could be more quiet than being dead?

I wanted people to see the body. I wanted them at points to be disgusted or to be worried or scared but I didn't want this sexualised form. Although I often write in a male voice I do consider myself a feminist and I think often the body is absent from the books. In *Tamburlaine Must Die* we do have a death, but really it's Marlowe's death that we're waiting for and we don't see that death. We know that it's going to happen but we don't actually see it. I was very interested in G.W. Pabst's movie *Pandora's Box* which is based on Frank Wedekind's plays *Erdgeist* and *Die Büchse der Pandora*. There's a very beautiful, lively dancer: she makes love to men, she makes love to women, and she seems completely amoral ... she lives for fun. She commits a murder by mistake and in the end she goes to London. It's very atmospheric and she's murdered by Jack the Ripper, because she has to be killed in the end.

Death in the name of poetic justice?

Yes, exactly! So in *The Bullet Trick* I wanted to play with that and have that supposed death, but there isn't a death. There's a resurrection and it's all part of some illusion. In this book, *Naming the Bones*, there is a death but we're not sure how that came about. There are several deaths but they're not conventional murders.

Have you always been intrigued by unconventional perspectives or why is your way with words as dark as it is intelligent?

That's a nice thing to say. I don't think this is peculiar to Scotland, but I do think we have a tradition of working-class intellectualism. You can have a good and inquiring conversation with somebody you met ten minutes ago in a pub who wouldn't necessarily have gone on to further education but will nevertheless be informed through their own reading. When I had a bookshop we couldn't keep philosophy books on the shelves, and it wasn't purely students we were selling them to – we were selling them to guys in overalls, to guys who were going to the pub looking for something to read. There's still a respect for learning. That is a strong part of a Scottish tradition that I respect, that I'm pleased by.

Alcohol, of course, is a big part of it. I myself am labouring under a slight hangover at the moment. Ha! There's this idea that we're often looked down on as a country because of how much we drink, and yet I think we should be compared to the Scandinavians because a lot of that has to do with the weather.

And they are also celebrating a literary renaissance thanks to their crime writers –

– Yeah! I was going to ask you about that, actually.

Interviewing 101: 'Enough about me, let's get back to me!' But isn't it interesting that the Irish have the same reaction to climate change? The worse the weather gets, the better writers seem to drink and drinkers seem to write.

Ha! I just wonder – we're natural allies in that way. The further north that you get, you get shared behaviour, a shared sense of humour as well. I find them a lot of fun, anyway.

As do a lot of publishers. Have you noticed the mileage they're getting out of the reverend Robert Louis Stevenson?

Yeah, the thing about the light and the dark, the Jekyll and Hyde ... I actually worry a little bit about that. Maybe it exists but maybe we talk about it too much.

And ignore anything besides his focus on duality? If so, might the actual commonality be your view from the margins – your sideways reflections on extremes?

Might well be, actually. I guess it's true and I guess we are drawn to extremes. This idea of extremes, I think, is a very good one. Obviously, as writers you don't get much say in how you're marketed or what goes on your jacket but I think that's a very nice plus point of somehow being identified as this genre of extremes. With this new book (*Naming the Bones*) I kept the tone quiet for quite a long way through. I wanted to experiment with that ... a little bit like the actor coming on stage and seeing how long they could hold the silence for. And part of what enables that is the idea that the reader has this foreknowledge that something is going to come, so it's an interesting thing for me to do.

It's not often that such opportunities for original story-telling are recognised as dispensations of the genre. Can you afford to spend time developing character and atmosphere because you draw us in with the genre's promise of a crime and our hope of justice?

Absolutely! I think we're on page 300 or somewhere pretty far in before we get a body. Yeah, that's fun and it's quite delicious to be able to do that.

How important is humour to you as a crime writer?

It's really necessary, I think.

What did you make of the cultural differences between the German and Scottish sense of humour when you set The Bullet Trick *in Berlin and Glasgow?*

Part of what I wanted was for William to go to a place that isn't actually so different from home, because I think we have a lot of shared culture between Germany and Scotland. And yet there are differences so there's just that light wrong-footedness that you get when you think you're on solid ground and then suddenly you realise, 'Oh, actually, I just got that wrong. I got that completely wrong.' Maybe humour is a part of that because it's also him as an individual. He's not a confident person and his lack of confidence makes him a bit unattractive to people at points.

Also, the cabaret scene is genuinely active in Berlin and it's not a frozen-in-aspic cabaret scene. There are actually some quite fun, quite interesting avant-garde things that go on there. So that place was where William could operate as a professional. There's a straightforwardness about things that is very attractive to us because we don't have it.

How much of this deeper structure is on your mind as you write, and how much of it do you add as you edit – is it even possible to say why and when you make changes?

Gosh! It's hard, isn't it? It all becomes the same, especially a few years on, because inevitably you're working on something else. I'm thinking about starting a new novel just now and I start very much with notebooks … trying not to recognise what a big task it is, you know. Just not to scare yourself and to take lots of little notes and to read around things… The Pabst thing (*The Bullet Trick*) was very conscious. I'd wanted to write about that really for quite a long time. The Gothic was very conscious in *The Cutting Room.*

How about the cultural context of Tamburlaine Must Die?

That's probably the most researched book just necessarily because it was about Marlowe.

Were you aware of the literary controversy that surrounds Marlowe and his death when you started out?

No, no, not at all. I didn't study English literature and this is going to sound really ridiculous: I wanted to write about Marlowe because I'd shared a flat with somebody who was doing theatre studies and they had been very interested in Marlowe. We talked a lot about Marlowe and then I went to see just about every version of *Doctor Faustus* that I could see in Glasgow ... really, really loved it. That was part of my life and I'd moved on, and when I came to think about writing about Marlowe I didn't realise how interested lots of other people were.

I didn't know that, for instance, there was a Marlowe Society, although I did know that there were people who said that Marlowe had written all of Shakespeare's plays, but I didn't realise they actually had the society and were so serious about it. If I had, who knows, it might have put me off, it might not have.

Instead, Tamburlaine Must Die *became a perfect example of how crime fiction can raise awareness of a cultural phenomenon that few know about and most would say is beyond the genre's reach. Were you politically motivated at all?*

Aw, that's a nice thing to say. You know, I was conscious of being political in that book. What is the point in writing something historical if it doesn't somehow pertain to our times? At that point I was interested in Dungavel prison, an asylum seekers' prison. There were children being locked up and all sorts of awful things going on. That was very much part of my consciousness when I was writing *Tamburlaine Must Die*. That and the Elizabethan period and its hatred, fear, distrust – whatever you want to call it – of outsiders, of immigrants. That was the idea but it's very much embedded. It's not at the front of the book but nevertheless that concern I think is there somehow.

Perhaps if I'd realised how brilliant he is I possibly wouldn't have written this book in his voice. I think I found out a lot as I was doing it and I still have a huge affection for Marlowe… I was very worried about writing a false history, because I studied history at university and I was a really bad student. I thought, 'No, if I add a bibliography it suggests that this is a learned book.' So I said, 'I got a lot of information from this book and this book.' I mentioned two or three books that had been good sources for me but I didn't put in a bibliography because I thought it would be showing off. Any interested reader, all we have to give them is three books. They'll find their own bibliography.

Speaking of Marlowe, how do you feel about the crime writer's reputation as a literary outsider?

In a way I quite like it, actually. Obviously I want to sell books and I've been really lucky. But if there's an outsider in literature I'd rather be with that outsider, I'd rather be with the person in the street, and I think maybe that's why there's a little snobbishness about crime fiction because it is what everybody hopefully feels empowered to pick up. It doesn't mean that it's not well written; it doesn't mean that it doesn't have intelligent points. But everybody seems empowered to lift those books off the shelf, and that's where I want to be; I'm much more comfortable there. I wouldn't want to put myself in opposition to literary fiction, but I don't want to write books where nothing happens.

What kind of books do you want to write?

I want to make people feel something. Yeah, I want to give my reader an experience. But I don't have a writing manifesto. I don't think there's a right way to do it and that I've found the right way.

*When you say you want to give your reader an 'experience',
does that include a sense of place?*

I think a strong sense of place is really, really important in
my fiction. I think it's important for me as the writer to get
there, to experience it and to feel it, and hopefully it enhances
the reader's experience as well. I live in Scotland and it's the
country that I know best. I do still think that I'll set things
elsewhere. *Tamburlaine Must Die* is set in London. In *The
Bullet Trick*, as we said, he goes to Berlin. The next book that
I'm thinking of writing, I'm not sure it'll be set in Scotland; I
might just turn my back on it for a book.

*Do you think you could turn your back on more than just
the place?*

I think as Scots we've always travelled widely. Maybe a
Scotsman abroad is more identifiable than a Scottish person
at home … So I'm not sure about that.

*Given the large community of Scottish crime writers, are
you comfortable in their company?*

Oh yeah. I'm really happy with that both in person and on
the shelf. I think people are actually pretty nice to each other.
Within Scotland and that crime community – if you can call
it that – it's not like you see people terribly often but when
you do it's really nice. I get a real feeling that people want to
pull somebody else up with them. If they can help someone
out, especially a new person, then they will. That's certainly
been my experience; people have always been very welcoming,
very nice. And fun. I don't know if other genres are like that
but I'm very happy to be included in all of that.

*Speaking of community spirit, do you read reviews of your
own work?*

I do read reviews, yeah. I tend to get them in a bundle, if I
can, and read them all in a bundle because the publisher sends
them to me that way, and also to get some kind of balance.

*Is it fair to say that you enjoy the critical feedback as part
of the editorial process?*

Yeah, I really like the editorial process. We usually have a long discussion and I like that ... I've never had an argument with an editor although we don't always agree on everything. I think in that discussion you should be able to say why you somehow don't agree.

Do you have any idea how your readership changes with every book?

I've no idea, absolutely no idea – it's just out there. I don't think about readers really, or some fantasy reader. Readers are hopefully pretty diverse ...

Until quite recently, writers would have seen very few of their readers but these days –

– You have to go out and about. You have to go to festivals.

Do you enjoy this new side of the writing life?

Yeah! The people that I seem to meet are different ages, different classes, different ethnicities, different genders, different sexualities ... It's actually quite nice. I didn't really think that would happen. I went to the Edinburgh Festival and I enjoyed it very much but I tend to go and see music or I go and see theatre or film. I think that the reading scene is kinda bizarre actually. I can't think why people want to go and hear somebody read a book that they could read quite well themselves.

Do you feel at home in both worlds – the solitary writing as well as the social networking?

That is good fun because I am a very sociable person. I work until it's time to stop. That Jekyll and Hyde thing, you know. I like to be on my own for hours and hours and hours, and then right about six o'clock I think, 'I wonder where I'm going tonight?' I like to be out. I've got lots of friends, and I like to mix it up a bit. So I went to the Larne Festival this weekend which is where Dylan Thomas used to live. It's just a complete booze-up from the moment you step off the train. There was lots of great music going on. I didn't get to hear anybody read. I just went to lots of music things and hung out.

Yeah, it was a really nice party. I lost my mobile phone … So I enjoy that part. I don't like it when it goes on for too long because then you're away from your work and you're away from your friends and family.

Do you have a writing routine?

I write nine to five. It's rather boring … like bankers' hours. You're not always inspired but a lot of what you're doing is quite technical stuff, as well. I'm writing a libretto at the moment and it's going slowly, but you just have to chip, chip, chip, chip, chip, chip … keep on going and then there will be these breakthrough moments. Yesterday I had this thing where I didn't actually write very much in terms of a novel but in terms of a libretto a lot and I was really happy. See, you might say that was the product of two hours, but actually it was the product of about two weeks of just trying to keep on going and doing a lot of reading and trying to get voices right. So you're not inspired every day but you're quite often setting things up to be inspired by doing a lot of work on structure or going back and editing, and editing it again … and editing it again.

How long does it take you to get a book from the note-books to the printers?

With the first book it took a year. The second book, which is half the length, took roughly the same time. The third book took two years, and this one took three years. So it's getting slower.

Isn't this one also a lot longer than your previous three?

Yeah, I think it was about 20,000 words longer even before I edited it. It could have been massive. I stripped it back a bit, which was good. It was necessary because I rewrite a lot as I go along. Also, when you talk about time and writing a book, of course you're not doing it continuously because there're times when you walk away. I wrote a play, a short libretto, and some short stories in the time I was writing this. But I probably spent a year on and off editing and I'd do it from beginning to end. I'd do it in order, which is quite methodical in a lot of ways, quite slow.

I think J.G. Ballard said that if you don't write 1,000 words a day then it's just not worth it. I don't write 1,000 words a day. I write 500 or so. You know, it's quite a slow process. They're closely worked but there's still a lot of shit in there ... always, always. It just needs to really be worked out.

After spending all that time on your writing, do you read your own novels once published?

Never, no. I'd have to kill myself.

Why is that – would it feel like going back to a part of your life that you've left behind?

Yeah, I think it's that. I think you've left that bit behind. You will have to go back to them sometimes – at readings and things like that – but you want to get onto the next thing. There are great books out there! You would never sit down and read your own book when you could be reading Elizabeth Taylor or something.

To all those who haven't yet read your books, which one would you recommend as a starting point?

Oh, gosh! It would depend on the person really. I think *The Cutting Room* still seems to go down the best, and I don't know if it's got a particular energy or something about it. Of course, I think that *Naming the Bones* is the best – partly because of technical things.

Would you say that your writing has changed?

You hope that you get better at it, you know, just that you get better at your craft. I think it's better for reasons, hopefully, that the casual reader wouldn't notice – things like structure and unity. Of course the next one that I do is just going to be so perfect...

Is there anything you'd like to say about that next one?

I'm hoping that will have a female heroine. I'm hoping it'll be edging more towards horror – not supernatural horror – but I'm hoping it'll be pushing those boundaries a little bit further and working with tension, maybe going back to the Gothic.

Speaking of 'going back', do you ever consider going back to previous characters or did their lives end with the books?

Oh no, they live on. They march on through the fictional ... If I were to go back it probably would be to the first character, Rilke. I'm very dubious about whether I'd ever do that now because it's ten years on and I've changed a lot in that time, as you should, and I don't know that I could do that actually. I'd kinda hate to let him down because I do have a conscious-ness of him and I'd hate to write a shit book after doing one where it worked quite well. But if I wanted to then I'd just go back and do it and I think the fact that I haven't done it is indicative that I don't really want to.

Do you keep an open file on your characters?

No. No, I don't do any of that stuff which is possibly a good idea and if you were doing a series it might be a really good idea ... I do kind of believe in them. When I'm writing them I can see them, and I care about them as well. I think this is something that I'd like to explore a bit more if I manage to do another book. To have somebody who is a bit more of an unreliable narrator, which I think is the hardest thing to do and yet so satisfying as a reader. Patrick McGrath does it so well. There'll suddenly be a point where you think, 'Oh shit, I don't know if I believe what you're telling me now.' I think as a reader that's a lovely moment. So I would quite like to do something like that.

I went to a festival in China recently, in the Forbidden City. It's just amazing the way you go through these gates and then you go through other gates and through other gates as you get closer and closer to the centre of this place. It would be so interesting to structure a book like that somehow, that you're getting closer and closer and think, 'Is there a truth there? Actually, there are many truths, aren't there?' I thought I might start with that – the idea of somebody telling somebody else what's happened. It's that classic Gothic thing. Anne Rice does it in *Interview with the Vampire*. You come into this room. I follow you along the corridor. I follow you into this room. You sit down and you're talking to this person and suddenly this is the story that we're with, which has its own appeal. So we'll see how that works out.

You seem full of ideas and yet you said it all depended on whether you managed another book. How many more have you signed on to do?

None. I'm free as a bird. I've signed to do a libretto which I'll deliver, all being well, in about three months. I'll do a play for the autumn, a short play, and then I'm going to America for a residency for a month, and I'm hoping that when I go to America I'll have notebooks that I'll take with me and just see what happens.

Do you write in longhand?

No. I often take notes in longhand but I write on a computer – a word processor, basically. No internet, no bells, no whistles … nothing to distract me.

Do you listen to music as you write?

If I'm writing in the evening. Sometimes in the afternoon I'll put music on. I think it's more a way of marking time but I tend to prefer silence. But yeah, sometimes for company late at night… I don't write a lot late at night but some scenes I think are nighttime scenes and it's good to write them in the evening.

Music and poetry have both been important themes in your writing, but has their shared sense of rhythm also affected the way you write?

Maybe, gosh! I do write very rhythmically. In *The Cutting Room* I used all these poems … I think I was saying to people, 'God, these poems are great. You should read these poems; they're brilliant!'

They had a similar effect on the protagonist of Ken Bruen's Rilke on Black. *Do you share his appreciation of Rilke and his belief in the ineffable?*

I haven't read any of Ken Bruen's books, though I feel like I should go and get them now... I remember when I was at university I shared a flat with an engineer and she had engineering friends who just thought that the arts were a waste of time. And I guess we need engineering, of course we do, but art is what makes life worthwhile. Yeah, it's pretty straight forward: Art is necessary.

Somebody said that children need stories as much as they need food. When you're with children it's all they want – a story and then that story again. It's really necessary. It's how we understand the world.

Is it fair to say that there might be a healing quality in storytelling?

You know, I think it's a really lovely idea. I think it probably could happen in that when you're feeling really ill sometimes nice music can actually make you feel better physically, but then I also remember that scene in *A Clockwork Orange*: the perversion therapy. I don't know that it always has the power to redeem ... but I do believe in art. We all want to be transported, don't we?

What does that say about the criticism that crime fiction is escapism and therefore a lesser art?

I think it's such a silly criticism because often we're writing about a world that people recognise. We're not writing about a rarefied world.

Speaking of the real world, how do you feel about the charge of cultural tourism?

I think it's interesting when Scottish writers are criticised for not portraying the country well. Periodically somebody will say, 'Oh these writers, they could be writing...' I think that's funny. As if your book would somehow cast a pall across a whole nation. Also, the idea that literature should serve a tourist industry in that way is silly, isn't it? Just ridiculous.

Do you enjoy the sense of shared appreciation when you

discover your home town along with your readers who might even travel to the settings of your novels?

Yeah, that's nice. I think in a way those things are incidental to you as a writer, and if it does happen then that's great. Actually what you're hoping for is to give some kind of integrity to the book. The location is adding to the book as a whole rather than being an ingredient. Often when you're doing any teaching of writing then you break things down into these ingredients which are there. It's not a false division and yet it is because it's much more part of something else, isn't it? – So yes, I like this city, I like being here, I like walking about and looking at it and thinking about it.

Does it inspire your writing?

Yeah, I think it inspires aspects of it. Sometimes you see things and you think, 'Ah, gosh! I'm going to file that away for later.' Yeah, the weather, the sky … but I like being able to write about other places as well. I'm not sure why that is. I think partly because you don't want to repeat yourself. I think there's a great skill in being able to keep a character going in a series of books.

Would you ever be interested in writing a series?

Not at this moment, but in the future, who knows? I'm much more interested in seeing the character walk off… I really wouldn't want to write about a policeman or a lawyer or a forensic scientist. I wouldn't like doing the research. You'd have to hang out with policemen. Can you imagine? That would be awful. Ha! That sounded really snobby. I didn't mean it to sound snobby, although all the right-wing nonsense you'd have to listen to wouldn't be natural for me.

But isn't the genre, which is politically rather left wing, very popular with police officers?

Yeah! They do love it. In fact, about six months ago there was some really high scaffolding out opposite us and the workmen hadn't secured it. Some little kinds, who were about eight or nine years old, were running about on this high scaffolding and going in and out of the building, and I thought, 'Fuck! There might not be floors or anything. They could have an accident.' So I phoned up the police station to say, 'Could you send somebody around?' People in the street were trying to get the kids down but the kids were high up there. They weren't having any of it. And I gave the policeman my name and he said, 'I've just finished your book. Oh, it was marvellous!' And we talked for about twenty minutes because I was so pleased.

No, that sounded really snobby of me. I just don't want to hang around because it doesn't interest me enough that environment and I think there are people who do it really well. Maybe these books are more what-if situations – they're certainly some kind of quest. Although, I love Val McDermid's books. I just finished her new one (*Fever of the Bone*) recently. I really get a kick out of reading them but I don't want to write them. I have the wrong kind of brain for it and maybe that has something to do with why I couldn't be an academic. Although I like the idea and I like studying and I like learning, but that long focus that you need to be a good and effective academic – I don't have. I would possibly make an okay journalist because I can get stuck into something for a reasonable length of time and then I need to move on.

Not unlike your characters, wouldn't you say?

Certainly Rilke does a job that wasn't so different from mine. I was a secondhand bookseller. He's an auctioneer. It's not worlds apart. He'd earn a wee bit more money, probably, than I did. The world of the university, which is the world of *Naming the Bones*, is a world I'm familiar with in various guises. Often the shared sense of humour, that's probably where I appear most, I guess. But you're trying to get away from yourself. Whether I manage to do it or not I don't know.

Yeah, the autobiographical thing: Most writers' lives are pretty dull. It wouldn't make much of a story... I've been reading a bit of Patricia Highsmith and I'm so pleased she made Ripley into a series.

Have you considered following her example by bringing Rilke back once every ten years?

Yeah, that's quite a nice thought. He'd be very old by the end. There's a sadness there if the author gets older and the character stays the same age.

Assuming he'd age, would you enjoy writing about a changing Glasgow from his point of view?

It's quite an attractive idea when you think of it, and I do have a vague story for him but it's very, very vague.

You just mentioned Val McDermid who has compared fiction writing to night driving: You can only see what's illuminated by your headlights but you know your destination and take direction from the road you've travelled. Is that an experience you're familiar with?

Yeah! It is… It's kinda horrible.

She also said there was at least one point in every book where she hated it –

– At least one.

Let me ask you then: What's your ambition for the future?

I would like to become a better plotter. I'd like to have more laid out in advance; this is my ambition. Certainly doing collaborative work on all this musical stuff we have a lot more laid out, and that is very interesting. It seems to save a lot of time, you know. It saves a lot of agony and going down wrong roads – all those lanes that somehow don't go anywhere.

And yet! It seems impossible to do. You know, I draw graphs, I write lists, mind maps … and at the end there will always be bits that you know you need to get to, but you don't know how you're going to get there… Actually, that's really exciting!

Much like the joy of interviewing?

Yeah! It was a pleasure … actually really good fun. We don't always know where we're going but we know when we get there in the end.

Afterword
by Louise Welsh

Can you trust the words of people who make up stories for a living? Writers are not fantasists. For the most part we know the difference between the fictions we invent and the real world and, with a few obvious exceptions, have at least as good an acquaintance with concepts of right and wrong as the rest of the population. But are we to be depended on in a discussion about our own work?

In the last twenty years or so a riot of literary festivals has stormed Britain. Little towns, which might in the past have tolerated an arty eccentric or two, are engulfed for weeks at a time by authors and poets who (and this is amazing) are given a hearty welcome and paid to talk, talk, talk, about themselves and their work. For many writers, especially those new to the circuit, it's a humbling, sometimes bewildering experience. Ours is a sedentary profession not known for its good looks, and writers are rarely as at ease in the world as our fictional protagonists. Yet intelligent people line the corridors of city libraries and town halls, tickets clutched in their hands, waiting for the doors to the auditorium to open, and for us to speak.

The phenomenon isn't confined to Britain. Lucky authors tour Europe, North America, Australia, Asia and beyond, taking to the stage each night and jumping into their act, like clockwork monkeys banging tiny silver cymbals together; clang, clang, clang.

Don't get me wrong. Festivals can be a joy. Who wouldn't want to tour the world staying in nice hotels and meeting people who think your work is great? But writing is not theatre and the performance, the talking about the book, cannot be truer than the book itself.

There are dangers in coaxing writers into the light. We are poor fleshy creatures, and though some praise is vital for us to flourish, too much can inflate our low-self-esteem-big-egos to the detriment of the prose we have less and less time to write. As the tour goes on we slip into slick routines, repeating what we said the last time and the time before that. Laughter means the audience is interested and so we go for the laugh, and laugh along like drunken uncles at a wedding before the fight kicks off. Afterwards we sit in our hotel rooms wondering what variety of fool we made of ourselves tonight – or maybe that's just me.

Most writers are more at home at their desk than on the stage. Our daily progress isn't forged in the blinding furnace of creativity portrayed in biopics of artists' lives, though inspiration is one of our guiding forces. A large part of what we do is technical, and rather boring. It's no wonder that when we talk we tend to make the process sound easy. Who wants to relive the bloody tedium of the daily grind?

So is there any point in asking authors about their work? Can you trust the words of people who make up stories for a living? Personally I'd trust the authors interviewed here with a substantial loan, I'd let them stay in my house and I know that if they dented my car, they'd send it to a panel-beater tout de suite. But do I trust them when they talk about their writing?

I trust them as much as I trust myself. We are crime writers. Our professional life is all about interrogation and so we're quick with the answers. And we are sincere. I can look you in the eye and tell you the truth, no word of a lie. But there's a shape-shifting quality to our psyche. This is a profession of the imagination and we know the trick of inhabiting other people's minds. We can mentally switch gender, nationalities, political allegiance, our entire personality in the service of fiction. Sometimes when you meet a writer, it's like meeting a ghost (or do I mean vampire?) there's so little of their essential self left.

So is this collection of interviews with Scottish crime writers a waste of your time? Not at all, good answers rely on interesting questions and Len Wanner has put the writers he's encountered through their paces.

But like any work of crime fiction *Dead Sharp* invites you the reader to turn detective. So look not only at what we writers say, but what we don't say. Remember it is possible for contradictory beliefs to be held by an individual at the same time, but notice when we contradict ourselves. Be aware of our vanities, our need to please and posture, but please be kind. Take what you will from our discussions; we hope they'll add another dimension to our texts, but don't let us tell you what to think about our novels. After all, authors do not write for critics, academics or even themselves, they write for you, mystery reader, and it's up to you to decide your verdict, sometimes in spite of what we intend.

Appendix 1
The Interviewer's Ten Commandments

So how does interviewing work? What's the trick? – Good questions...

Whether you have come to this book as a fan or a friend, chances are you have read enough of it to answer at least one question: Am I good enough an interviewer to tell you how to become a better one? If you have come to this book as a student, you have read the introduction. Welcome back. Having no way of knowing why you are reading this, I do know one thing for certain: I have had the pleasure of sharing all three perspectives at one time or another, most recently at the reading, writing, and rethinking stages of this book. I now have the pleasure of sharing my experience. That means:

- No bleeding heart liberalism ... 'It's not your fault: There are no stupid questions.'
- No false commandments ...'There is only one rule: Rules are there to be broken.'
- No esoteric exit clauses ... 'The first rule of interviewing is: Do not talk about interviewing.'

Alas, if you believed that kind of nonsense, you wouldn't be reading this. You'd most likely be giving your time and savings to Scientology. At any rate, you'd have given up on interviews a long time ago. But since you are reading this, you might already know the difficulty of finding inspiration in platitudes. You might even know the difficulty of finding legal representation after telling the last in a long line of busybodies that their question, ever so thoughtfully introduced with an anecdote about their pet dog, surely deserves more than the interviewee's eloquent 'hmm'.

Please, take a moment to remember all those times your head exploded with canned chatter at what seemed like endless re-runs of low-budget sitcoms – all those times when all those pointless questions left the most obvious one unanswered: 'Why bother?' The sad truth is that over decades and airwaves, vacuous anchormen and pompous talk-show hosts have lowered our expectations of interviews almost as far as their general standard. Unfortunately, while their strategy may not be lifted from the pages of A Confederacy of Dunces, the result of all this collaborating with demographic profilers is much the same: a conversational anaesthetic. It is generally accepted that droves of interviewers showcase the sheer magnificence of their personality in place of any sincere dedication to the person of interest. The result is that what may once have been the cardinal sin of interviewing seems to have become its driving force: 'Enough about me. Let's get back to me!'

If you object to such intellectual swagger because it squanders the opportunity of an interview, then we are agreed: posturing is a waste of everybody's time, and it does not make you a better interviewer. What does make you a better interviewer is a sense of humour. That, and dispatches from the front:

1. Get in the door. Before you get to ask any questions, you need to get your interviewee's attention. There are various ways of doing that, whether or not you know your subject, and your success will largely depend on your social skills. To get an interview with a personal friend, use your own judgment. To get an interview with a friend of a friend, use your mutual acquaintance as a character reference. If all you have is the

name of your interviewee or the need of suitable sources for a research project, use telephone directories, online search engines and third parties to find contact details for anyone you know by name or association. Contrary to popular belief, it's not all about the people you know. It's all about the people you can get to know. Somewhere, someone has what you need: access. Your task is to find out where relevant information is held and by whom it is controlled. You might want to search the internet for clubs, conferences and conventions which keep records of members, attendees and staff. If your source is not in the habit of sharing contact details with the public, ask yourself who is or how to be the exception. In short, you will get in the door if you can persuade others to open doors for you. So if your target group or person is not listed, if they have no website, blog or social network profile, contact their professional representation: find an official spokesperson, personal assistant, legal advisor, agent, editor or publisher. Given their financial interest in public relations, lead with what you can do for their client's publicity.

Remember: whoever you talk to, observe the rules of etiquette and do not make demands. Make offers. It is in your best interest to set yourself apart as the interviewer of their choice. Consider what they are asking themselves: what are you interested in? Which audience will be interested in your interview? Why should you get this interview? – Your hook, the angle that makes you the ideal person for the job, can take many forms: it might be your expertise, your inclusion of aspects not appreciated by other interviewers, or your slant towards a different audience. The key is to make your interview both different and better. Ask yourself: what kind of interviewer does this job require? – Act the part.

2. Plan for the best, prepare for the worst. Consider time and place when scheduling an interview. Take note of your interviewees' preferences, and make reservations to guarantee

the availability of the most suitable setting. When you are conducting interviews in private, make sure the context is no cause of confusion: you probably deserve that bubble bath, but is this really the best time? When you are conducting interviews in writing or over the phone, make sure to avoid closed questions as well as lengthy monologues, and to be intelligible as well as personable despite the lack of immediacy: although short answers like 'yes' or 'no' can lead to amicable banter when you are in the same room as the monosyllabist, they usually lead to awkward silence when you are not.

Finally, when you are conducting interviews in public, make sure to make a difference between a voluntary and an involuntary audience: encouraging and channelling crowd participation is part of your job only when that crowd is assembled to see you. If it is not, your valiant efforts may result in a restraining order. Remember: the one thing all live audiences and public places have in common is that they can suddenly become too busy and noisy for comfortable conversations and useable recordings. Be sure to choose or create an environment rich in atmosphere and poor in distraction, and, at the risk of stating the obvious, try not to be the distraction. You do not want to worry about missing your interview because of unexpected delays, nor do you want to worry about the state of your nerves and hygiene once you're in the hot seat. In short, whenever and wherever you do interviews, always know the location, get there early, and extend your interviewee and audience the courtesy of having a contingency plan and a change of clothes.

Also, to avoid legal conflicts and injury to your reputation, make sure your interviewee agrees to being recorded and signs a release form clarifying editorial rights to the transcript. Above all, respect your interviewee's privacy: do not invade anyone's personal space or private life. If you are told anything 'off the record', your professional integrity, if not future, depends on your confidentiality. If you have inadvertently given offence, be quick to make a full apology and repair any damage caused. In any event, foster relations and return favours: pay back when you must. Pay forward when you can.

3. Pay attention. A good interviewer finds questions in answers, so-called follow-up questions that hide between the lines of every answer, even a one-liner. Pay attention to what you are being told by not being told. Once you get your interviewees talking, do more than just wait for your turn to ask another question. If you have learned how to listen, do it whenever you can; not only when your interviewees are answering but when they are not. That might tell you if your question was ill-considered, how to give it more motive power, and what to ask next.

Most importantly, pay attention to other interviewers. Ask yourself this: are they getting the answers either of you were hoping for? How could certain questions be phrased more effectively in light of the interviewee's confusion? If they lose control of the interview or their interviewee's attention, how can you benefit from their mistakes? To answer those questions, pay attention to the way people around you speak, and learn how much they tell you about themselves when you do and do not ask them to. Pay attention to people's reasons for opening up, and you will develop your talent for helping them do so. When you are conducting your interview in front of a live audience, pay attention to how their attention shifts and how they signal curiosity. At the same time, pay attention to how comfortable interviewees are with crowd interaction. Before you take initiative against interruptions, pay attention to how other politicians, such as stand-up comedians and court marshals, handle hecklers. Before you involve the audience, pay attention to how other interviewers, such as priests and exotic dancers, work the room. Every signpost you recognise gives you a sense of direction as you navigate the capricious flow of conversation with professional authority.

In short, pay attention all the time. By recognising false notes, you can acquire an absolute pitch for questions.

4. Pay your dues. As an interviewer, you represent your audience with every question you ask. Make sure you deserve that mandate whenever you lay claim to it. If you expect your interviewees to pay close attention to questions and answers, match the courtesy. Every conversation is an opportunity to learn how and why people react to the devil's advocate, insistent probing, cavalier innuendo, reverse psychology, meaningful gestures, leading questions, a pregnant silence, and all your other tools of diplomacy. Because your medium is language – verbal as well as physical – experience and imagination are your best guides to probity of terms. Generally speaking, you are limited only by your modesty and honesty: accept that everybody has something to teach you about the paths to knowing others, and that you will only encourage disclosures if you know where to look for them.

If your communication skills are not always a guarantee of success, the reason is unlikely to be either blindness or deafness to words. Being obtuse is not a trait of character but a failure of craftsmanship. Study your use of language and improve it according to the principles of those who have reached your goals. Remember: talking to you should be rewarding for all parties concerned, and while you owe every interviewee a modicum of respect, it takes more to be the interviewer of somebody's choice. What it takes is experience, so get some of your own. Ask yourself when your agenda is best worn on your sleeve or deliberately concealed. Learn why and when either approach offends, talk to as many people as you can, and be courteous towards them lest they rightly consider you a manipulative ... sophist. Remember two truths: one, everybody has their bag of hammers. Two, if all you have is a hammer, everything becomes a nail. – Direct as well as indirect lines of questioning can have their advantages, and every chat over coffee that offers an insight-generating change-up is as valuable a learning experience as the interviewee who walks out on you because you failed to intrigue.

5. Be different. Whatever way you choose to set yourself apart from all the other interviewers who could be doing your job, there is only one lastingly successful way of doing so: do your job better than anybody else. Be known for your competency, not your complacency. That means: learn from every mistake you and others make. Make sure you are always better than yesterday, and never too good to admit that you are worse than tomorrow. And never forget: your interviewee may or may not be a 'born storyteller'. What is a given is that, because of or in spite of the reasons for your interest, he or she contends with the same personal and interpersonal challenges as you and me. With that in mind, do your audience a favour and accept three responsibilities few interviewers even acknowledge: one, convincing familiarity with the topic of conversation is as rare as it is likely to engage even the most reluctant interviewee, so give yourself enough time for adequate research. Two, whatever you do not know about your subject on the day of your interview, make sure you do know how to cover any gaps in your knowledge. Three, have a plan B in case plan A fails to overcome the obstacles of attitude and inattention.

Remember: it helps to know the body and context of your interviewee's work. To bolster your confidence in a charged exchange, to avoid insult and embarrassment, and to minimise the odds of touching a nerve, run a background check on your interviewee. As a matter of fact, interviews thrive on changes of direction and dynamic. As a matter of experience, you are far better equipped to deal with either if you share a frame of reference. The trick is to find a common denominator that leaves your critical integrity intact. For what it's worth, common sense suggests you also avoid standard protocol with regard to ingratiation, because most interviewees do not appreciate false adulation, and most audiences consider gossip an insult. Then again, even the afore-mentioned 'born storyteller' will be unlikely to give you more than rehearsed material unless you set yourself apart. How? Just ask yourself: who does not enjoy discovery, especially that of shared interest?

6. Make lists. Annotated bibliographies of primary and secondary reading material help you research and revise your subject before you draft your list of interview questions. Structure your preparation: write down what you know about your subject in form of a bibliographical or biographical sketch. Next, write down what you would like to know as a result of lacking sources or recent events. Finally, write down what you do not believe on grounds of unsubstantiated statements or inconclusive evidence. Now, cross-reference these lists with a list of similar questions your interviewee has already answered.

To balance investigative integrity with professional probity, be ambitious in your first draft and sensitive when you edit your final list. Bear in mind: ambiguity, like insult, is a matter of perspective, and both can be suffered in silence. You do not want to pay for either with your interviewee's attention or sympathy, so do everybody a favour: read your lists of questions out loud to yourself. If you have access to outside help, run them by a test person. Each time you rehearse you will find ways of clarifying your questions and identifying opportunities for follow-ups. Remember: the reality of interviewing lies somewhere between your idea of a worst-case scenario and a wet dream – that is less dramatic, less balletic, and, most surprisingly, quicker. Whatever your timeframe, you do not want to let pressure stifle creativity. That means: do not stick to a set list of questions once the interview is underway. When your interviewee suddenly veers off topic, asks you to rephrase a question, or has nothing to say, you

242

will appreciate having several lists with branching systems that allow you to accommodate changes of direction. If you feel more comfortable with a prop, bring a copy of your list and use it to punctuate the flow of conversation or prompt your memory. The best list is the one you keep editing, all the way through the interview.

7. Talk straight. Know your words and specify your terms. How can you mean what you say if you do not say what you mean? When a clearer synonym is available, avoid the use of jargon, technical language, and fancy wording. Their benefit rarely outweighs the risk of ambiguity. Think of it this way: a complex question can only lead to complex understanding if it is easily understood. It is your job to be critical, especially of your own curiosity and clarity. Phrase your questions in simple and direct language to allow others to concentrate on the answers. Rephrase a question and your interview loses momentum, which you may regret in front of a live audience. Remember: the mind tends to run along the groove of intention and is easily derailed by expression.

Remember this also when transcribing and editing interviews. Skill in 'writing up' consists in improving an interview's fitness in print. That means: unless interviewees speak in prose, do not quote verbatim. Unless you are conducting the interview for legal purposes, enjoy the liberties that lie beyond the reach of court stenographers. Direct speech performs several tasks that reported speech is spared, and vice versa. You do not have to quote every colloquial use of 'like', 'you know', 'I think', and other conversational props whenever interviewees halt for an idea. Unless the habit carries a significant load of information and implication, allow us to ignore it. This same generalisation holds true for tangential comments and sub-clauses that chop up utterance in disregard of a more commendable habit, the habit of the interview to go straight from the question to the answer. Edit your

243

questions with this same efficiency of communication. As a result you may even be able to give interviewees the credit of answering the question you asked. The notable fact is that to paraphrase does not mean to pull phrases about. It means to reword a statement, not to distort it. Remember: distortions require repeated reading, and that soon leads to irritation at your smartness. But worse still, they change the meaning of what was said in the interview, and that constitutes a breach of confidence. That means: only see a choice where there is one, but then make it. Avoid all affectation, poetic euphemism, and the childish desire to express your interest in scientific phraseology. Questions and ideas will best slide into the listener's mind when the word noise is least.

8. Hit first and hit hard. Your first question is your best chance to hook interviewee and audience. Remember: if you do not have anything interesting to say in the beginning, there might not be much you can do to make anybody pay attention to your subsequent questions. If you cannot hit the ground running, you have three options to stay on your feet: one, get warmed up before you start the interview by running through a few opening gambits. Two, get an early open question in that lets the interviewee talk about a favourite topic until you find your feet. Three, get another job. First impressions count. Everybody wants your first question to tell them that you will make it worth their time and effort. That means: take it easy, but take it. Know your own strength and rely on it. Whatever happens next, do not be afraid. The best answer you can hope for is the one that makes you forget your next question. If you do your job, this will happen. If you do your job well, you are already two questions ahead, so you have nothing to worry about.

Be sure to have your priorities in order, always. Know your main questions and get them in early. If you do not, you might not get to ask them at all. Remember: No matter how accommodating your interviewees are, they will get sidetracked, forget your questions, and sooner or later run out of steam. They might also be having a bad day, be in need of toilet breaks, or be called away unexpectedly. None of this has to be your problem: break the ice and ask your big questions. If you have selected and framed them well, your interest should be met with enthusiasm and energy. If you are charming in your refusal to ask obvious questions and accept obvious answers, chances are you won't have to do either. If you do, ask why: clichés are inherited propositions and like all unexamined ideas they will yield new meaning when reconsidered in the light of curiosity.

9. Educate and entertain. Whatever you may wish to accomplish with your interview, do not be boring. Even interviewees who love talking about themselves, and are loved by their audience for doing so, have more to say if you can ask questions that invite new answers. Consider your options before you start the interview or you might have to settle for a chat. Contrary to popular belief, if you lose or even neglect your sense of direction, most new paths only lead to old places. Clarity of conception benefits your questions so make sure you always know what you want to know. When you first notice the monotony of routine, do not be afraid to assert yourself by challenging received opinion with your own theory. Yet rather than rushing to the lectern with an encyclopaedic monograph, or taking the stage with your own stand-up show, aim for a different angle by turning the tables. However glib or final an answer may appear to be, use the element of surprise – the short interjection: What? Why? When? Where? Who? How? Each of these questions asks your interviewee to reconsider, and none of them is long or novel enough to shift attention from the question to you.

Remember: spontaneity can lead to revealing banter and unexpected insights, and whether you have to signal curiosity,

245

scepticism or disagreement to get there, do not be afraid to up the ante if it means that the next exchange might educate or entertain. The caveat is that good interviewers are known for trying neither on their own, if only because attention dwindles when the interviewee fails to shine. No matter how many laughs you might be getting on any given day, do not neglect other ways of stirring up the shared imagination. Polite witnesses might spare you the embarrassment of admitting as much, but there is nothing that goes from funny to sad as fast as a clown. So whether you are delivering the interview on the page or stage, see what interviewee and audience have to offer each other, and how you can expedite the exchange. Whether you are asking or editing, leave out everything that your intended audience is sure to ignore, see to it that answers are as arresting and amusing as can be, and that you are not the only one to say so.

10. Know your place. An interview is not about you but it is nothing without you. When you do it right, interviewing is not a performance art. That side of success finds those too busy looking for it. Your job is to make your interviewees look good, not to win any popularity contests, and that will require all your concentration even without the search for approval. Just think: if they do not like you, make them like your questions instead. If they like your questions, they will talk, and that is the only lasting way of engaging your audience. With that in mind, keep your ego in check. You do not do your job to get angry. You do your job to get paid. That means: Be polite from first contact to final edits. Remember: no one cares about your personal issues and value judgments. Be smart and persuade your interviewees to give us something of value – a new way of looking at their work. To make that happen, you should sense when to give your interviewee enough space to ramble and when to interrupt with a follow-up or a change of topic. Do not constrict freedom of expression by pressing for

preconceived answers if you want them to be original as well as sincere. Remember: good interviewing is a collaborative effort. In other words, you take account of the interest your audience has in your interviewees. You take care to put everybody at ease by being confident and professional. You take initiative whenever something unexpected is revealed. You take charge of an environment in which everybody is motivated and comfortable enough to speak freely, and you take responsibility for other people's feelings. You do not take command of the audience's attention. Your reason for taking note of all this is simple: you do not want to break the spell. Having created an atmosphere of rapt attention you want to avoid every distraction. Set the scene and step back. Develop a sense for what your interviewees want to tell you, and encourage them to develop their thoughts in front of you. Instead of hearing buzzwords, they will listen to your questions. They will look at you ... reflective, very still. The answers you get will be new to everybody.

Appendix 2
Recommended Reading: The ABC of Scottish Crime Fiction

A

Lin Anderson: *Driftnet*
Louise Anderson: *Death's Sister*
Campbell Armstrong: *Butcher*
David Ashton: *The Shadow of the Serpent*
Kate Atkinson: *When Will There be Good News?*

B

Iain Banks: *Complicity*
Ray Banks: *Beast of Burden*
MC Beaton: *Agatha Raisin and the Busy Body*
Margot Bennett: *Someone from the Past*
Sean Black: *Lockdown*
Tony Black: *Gutted*
Daniel Boyle: *Illusion*
Jimmy Boyle: *A Sense of Freedom*
Christopher Brookmyre: *Be My Enemy*
George Douglas Brown: *The House with the Green Shutters*
Gordon Brown: *Falling*
John Buchan: *The Blanket of the Dark*

C

Karen Campbell: *The Twilight Time*
Glenn Chandler: *Savage Tide*
Marten Claridge: *Nobody's Fool*
Julie Corbin: *Tell Me No Secrets*
Charles Cumming: *The Hidden Man*

D

Toni Davidson: *Scar Culture*
Carol Anne Davis: *Noise Abatement*
Margaret Thomson Davis: *Double Danger*
John Dodds: *Bone Machines*
Arthur Conan Doyle: *A Study in Scarlet*
Caroline Dunford: *A Death in the Family*
Bruce Durie: *The Murder of Young Tom Morris*

E

Chris Ewan: *The Good Thief's Guide to Vegas*

F

Michel Faber: *Under The Skin*
Helen FitzGerald: *Bloody Women*
Neil Forsyth: *Other People's Money*

G

Colin Galbraith: *Hunting Jack*
Gillian Galbraith: *Blood in the Water*
Alex Gray: *Shadows of Sounds*
Clio Gray: *The Brotherhood of Five*
Allan Guthrie: *Slammer*

H

Gerald Hammond: *A Shocking Affair*
James Hogg: *The Private Memoirs and Confessions of a
Justified Sinner*
Joyce Holms: *Missing Link*

I

C David Ingram: *The Stone Gallows*

J

Quintin Jardine: *Poisoned Cherries*
Paul Johnston: *Body Politic*
Doug Johnstone: *Smokeheads*
Morag Joss: *Half-Broken Things*

K

James Kennaway: *Tunes of Glory*
Philip Kerr: *Berlin Noir*
Bill Kirton: *Material Evidence*
Alanna Knight: *Legend of the Loch*
Bill Knox: *To Kill a Witch*

L

Iain Levison: *Dog Eats Dog*
Douglas Lindsay: *The Long Midnight of Barney Thomson*
Frederic Lindsay: *Brond*
Bill Liversidge: *A Half-Life of One*
Frances Lloyd: *Nemesis of the Dead*
Chris Longmuir: *Dead Wood*

M

Stuart MacBride: *Blind Eye*
Alistair MacLean: *Where Eagles Dare*
Charles Maclean: *Home Before Dark*
Shona MacLean: *A Game of Sorrows*
Angus MacVicar: *The Killings on Kersivay*
Michael Malone: *Handling Sin*
Peter May: *The Firemaker*
Alexander McArthur: *No Mean City*
Ken McClure: *Hypocrites' Isle*
Val McDermid: *The Mermaids Singing*
Iain McDowall: *Making a Killing*
Alexander McGregor: *Lawless*
Liam McIlvanney: *All the Colours of the Town*
William McIlvanney: *Laidlaw*
Pat McIntosh: *The Stolen Voice*
Reg McKay: *The Ferris Conspiracy*
Shirley McKay: *Fate & Fortune*
Grant McKenzie: *Switch*
Russel D McLean: *The Lost Sister*
James McLevy: *McLevy, The Edinburgh Detective*
Catriona McPherson: *Bury Her Deep*
William Meikle: *The Midnight Eye Files*
Denise Mina: *Still Midnight*
GJ Moffat: *Daisychain*
Aly Monroe: *Washington Shadow*
Grace Monroe: *Blood Lines*
Donna Moore: *Old Dogs*
Nicola Morgan: *Deathwatch*
Tom Morton: *Serpentine*
H&M Mulgray: *No Suspicious Circumstances*
Neil Munro: *The New Road*

P

Ian Pattison: *Sweet and Tender Hooligan*
Gillian Philip: *Crossing the Line*
Tony Pollard: *The Secrets of the Lazarus Club*

R

Hugh C Rae: *The Shooting Gallery*
Ian Rankin: *Resurrection Men*
Caro Ramsay: *Singing to the Dead*
Craig Robertson: *Random*
Dirk Robertson: *Deep Powder*
James Robertson: *The Fanatic*
Ross Robertson: *A Yearning for Jacob's Son*
Craig Russell: *The Long Glasgow Kiss*

S

MC Scott: *Boudica, Dreaming the Eagle*
Walter Scott: *Rob Roy*
Alastair Sim: *The Unbelievers*
Alexander McCall Smith: *44 Scotland Street*
Muriel Spark: *The Ballad of Peckham Rye*
Robert Louis Stevenson: *The Ebb-Tide*
Zoe Strachan: *Negative Space*

T

Aline Templeton: *Dead in the Water*
Josephine Tey: *The Daughter of Time*
Alice Thompson: *The Existential Detective*
Jeff Torrington: *Swing Hammer Swing!*
Nigel Tranter: *The Night Riders*
Alexander Trocchi: *Young Adam*
Peter Turnbull: *The Killing Floor*

W

Sue Walker: *The Reunion*
Alan Warner: *Morvern Callar*
Irvine Welsh: *Filth*
Louise Welsh: *The Cutting Room*
Campbell White: *White Rage*
Gordon M Williams: *The Siege of Trencher's Farm*
David Wishart: *Illegally Dead*

STE. MADELEINE
COMMUNITY WITHOUT A TOWN
METIS ELDERS IN INTERVIEW